Railway Track Diagrams

Book 4
Midlands & North West

Managing Editor
Mike Bridge

Railway Track Diagrams

Book 4: Midlands & North West

Contents

1st Edition 1990
Reprinted 1996
2nd Edition 2005
3rd Edition 2013

ISBN 978-0-9549866-7-4

Published by Trackmaps, Little Court, Upper South Wraxall, Bradford on Avon BA15 2SE
Web: www.trackmaps.co.uk

Produced by Trackmaps, Bradford on Avon BA15 2SE
Managing Editor: Mike Bridge
Digital Cartography: David Padgett and John Szwenk
Developed from the original cartography of John Yonge
Printed by Brightsea Press, Exeter EX5 2UL

Cover design by The Art and Web Co. Ltd, Swindon SN6 8TZ
Cover Photography

1	5
2	6
3	7
4	8

1, 2 & 8 © Geoffrey Dingle
4 & 7 © Doug Birmingham
3, 5 & 6 © Railimages, Leigh-on-Sea SS9 4AL

Publisher's Note

Every effort has been made by the editor to ensure the accuracy of the information in the book is as correct as possible at the time of going to press. Notwithstanding, the Publishers welcome corrections, updates or suggestions for application to future editions. Contributions are preferred through the Contact Us page on the website (we'll always respond within a couple of days) or by mail to the address above.

Railway Track Diagrams
Book 4: Midlands & North West, 3rd Edition

Preface to the Track Diagram Series

Quail Track Diagrams have been published since 1988 and provide a reference to Enthusiasts and Industry alike. They contain information which may exist elsewhere and in other forms but are unique in making it all available in one easily portable volume.

Originally published by the Quail Map Co, edited by Gerald Jacobs with cartography by John Yonge, the series covers the entire UK mainland network and includes freight lines, light rail, heritage railways and private railways. The information included is a combination of historical sources collected by Gerald Jacobs during his 40 years with British Railways, subsequently kept up to date with reference to Network Rail and its predecessors and supplemented by other data, by the kind assistance of other persons and by field observation. Since 2004, the volumes have been produced by Trackmaps and have been edited by Mike Bridge from 2010.

Railway Track Diagrams have become a popular work for railway enthusiasts and a de-facto standard in the rail industry and the editors have tried to provide good quality information. The Rail Network has been built up over more than 180 years, managed by individual companies, as a nationalised industry and now as individual train operating companies with a single infrastructure owner. Over that time, it has grown, stagnated, declined and grown again more than once. Many persons have produced records and maps at different times for different parts, both within the industry and outside and while many record systems complement each other, others conflict. Track Diagrams attempt to collate these diverse sources into one publication but, even so, space precludes the inclusion of much detail including, for example, signals.

The Editors have also tried to put down a standard where discrepancies occur; the case of mileages is typical. Mileages often vary slightly between different official records but, in general, those given in Sectional Appendix have been used. Station mileages are usually taken from the mid-point of the platforms or, in the case of a terminus, the buffer stops. The Railway is continually changing and, because of its diverse nature and varied history, discrepancies often arise between seeming accurate sources. In such circumstances, the Editor's judgment is applied.

Trackmaps, August 2013

Introduction to this edition

The Track Diagrams in this book cover the lines forming the London North West Route of Network Rail, together with parts of LNE and Wales Routes and a number of private railways and industrial layouts. They are, in general, up to date as at August 2013. Eight years have passed since the previous edition was published and over four thousand individual changes have been recorded. Some works commenced but not finished have been included in their final form and details of the NW Electrification project have been outlined to 2016. One major feature throughout the region has been the steady closure of signal boxes and re-control to major signalling centres. This will continue for some years

This 3rd Edition has a number of other changes to its predecessor. The Index has been extended to include as many individual locations as possible, now totaling some 3,500, an increase of 44%. The ELR index has been retained and an LOR Index added.

There has been some re-configuration of the maps including separate pages for Manchester Metrolink and a consolidation of leisure and miniature railways. Other publications cover these minor railways which now number around five hundred. As a consequence, Track Diagrams is reducing the inclusion of non-public service railways to standard gauge heritage lines, either attached to or previously part of the national network, or narrow gauge lines with a heritage of their own.

Acknowledgements

A tremendous amount of work goes into the Railway Track Diagram Series. Although much information is available from official sources, it still has to be assessed, varied in some cases and prepared before the cartographer can do his job. Many details off the beaten path and on private lines have to be teased out from elsewhere. For this edition, the Managing Editor has been extremely grateful for the significant input of Myles Munsey, Gerald Jacobs, Martyn Brailsford and Nigel Farebrother, together with contributions from Kev Adlam, Mike Ashton, Nick Bartlett, Rupert Brennan Brown, Wayne Brown, Steve Cheetham, Mike Christelow, Andrew Cotton, Peter Cousins, Dave Coxon, Steve Cramp, Mark Curran, Mick Donovan, Frank Duckworth, Iain Ellis, Andrew Emerson, Mark Fowler, Jack Gainford, Jerry Gold, Simon Gott, Anthony Gough, Shaun Hodges, Geoff Holt, Mike Honeyman, Norman Howlett, John D Jacobs, Andrew A Johnson, Simon Kemp, Matthew Lovelock, Andy Lynch, George Maund, Robin Morel, Alan Munday, Graham Peacock, John Poulton, Alistair Raisbeck, Paul Robertson, Martin Rose, Peter Rowland, Bob Sandlands, Dave Scotson, Greg Scott, Ryan Scott, Steve Sharpe, Ian Smith, Roger A. Smith, D L Southgate, Mike Stone, Richard Thackray, Kevin Thurlow, Darren A Towler, and Kevin Vince. Acknowledgements are also due to Phil Deaves whose website on railway codes has been an effective reference to sorting out ELR discrepancies (see the URL in the ELR index header). Branch Line News is another source of reference. The Managing Editor would like to give his thanks to the cartographers, Dave Padgett and John Szwenk, for their efforts; particularly Dave on whom the myriad of changes to layouts and final assembly activities have fallen. To every one of the helpers, with significant input or with small, your efforts are greatly appreciated.

Mike Bridge, Managing Editor, August 2013

KEY

Symbol	Description
	Running Line
	Siding
	Electrified overhead (25kV AC unless stated)
	Electrified 3rd rail (750V DC)
	Electrified 4th rail (LUL) (630V DC)
	Electrified, overhead & Conductor rail
	Proposed or under construction.
	Line obstructed
	Line 'in situ' but out of use, partly dismantled, buried, or overgrown
	Change of Signalling mandate
WR LNW	Network Rail Territory boundary
Preston (PN) | Carlisle (CE)	Signal Box / centre area limits (Within an area, plates on automatic signals may reflect actual line description)
	Diamond Crossing / Switch Diamond
	Tunnel
	Bridge under Rail or Viaduct
	Selected Motorway / Trunk Road bridges over rail
	Network Rail operated level crossing
	User-worked crossing with Telephone
	Track signalled in both directions (a double arrow indicates normal direction of travel)
	Private siding boundary, or gate
	Sand Drag / Trap Point
	Turntable / Ramp
	Gantry Rails (Freightliner Terminal)
	Fence
	Wall / Bank / Cliff
	Hot Axle Box Detector (HABD), Wheel Impact Load Detector (WILD) or Wheelchex Device

Symbol	Description
PBJ	ELR-Engineer's Line Reference (Prefix and suffix numbers indicate sub-divisions and their boundaries)
[MD 320]	Line of Route Code
93	Whole mileposts, shown on the appropriate side of the line
32	Whole kilometre posts
81.3	End of mileage run
113.76 / *105.70* **COM**	Lineside mileage change
3	Platform with number (May be supplemented by sub-divisions. e.g. (a), (b), (c), 'N' or North etc)
⑦	Indicates number of carriages per platform (approx 20m lengths)
	Provisional proposed platform
	Former Royal Mail platform
	Platform out of use
	Other feature (labelled)
	Loading bank / dock
Uttoxeter *(UR)*	ASC, IECC, SB, SC or SCC, with code (underlined text relates)
	Control Panel
	Gate Box
	Ground Frame GF / Ground Switch Panel GSP or Shunting Frame SF. Ⓢ Indicates 'Shut in' facility
	Radio electronic token block / Token exchange point
¶	Proposed closure
O	Water tower
Λ	Summit, height in feet
(Buxworth)	Indicates a former Jn, Station or Signal Box
86.34 *(Not italic if Station mileage)*	Distance in Miles and chains from specified zero 1 Mile = 1760 yards / 1.6km 80 chains = 1 Mile 1 chain = 22 yards / 20.11m
57.600	Distance in Kilometres

Guide references are given to pre-nationalisation, pre-grouping and sometimes pioneer railways e.g. LMS : L&Y

Traditional Line Descriptions may be quoted, e.g. **BIRMINGHAM WEST SUBURBAN LINE**

GENERAL ABBREVIATIONS

AA	Acid Application
ABP	Associated British Ports
AC	Alternating Current
ARR	Arrival
ASC	Area Signalling Centre i/c IECC, Power Box
bdy	boundary
BCH	Branch
BR	British Rail
CET	Controlled Emission Toilet Discharge
CL	Crossing Loop on Single Line
COM	Change of Mileage
CR	Cripple Siding
CW	Carriage Washer
C&W	Carriage & Wagon
D	Connections Disconnected
DA	Down Avoiding
DBS	D B Schenker Rail (UK) Ltd
DC	Direct Current
DE	Down Electric
DED	Diesel Electric Depot
DEP	Departure
DF	Down Fast
DG	Down Goods
DGL	Down Goods Loop
DL	Down Loop
DM	Down Main
DMD	Diesel Maintenance Depot
DMUD	Diesel Multiple Unit Depot
DN	Down
DPL	Down Passenger Loop
DR	Down Relief
DRS	Down Refuge Sidings
DS	Down Slow
DSB	Down Surburban
DT	Down Through
E	East
EB	Eastbound
EGF	Emergency Ground Frame
EMD	Electric Maintenance Depot
EMUD	Electric Multiple Unit Depot
Engrs	Engineers' Sidings
eol	End of Line
ERTMS	European Rail Traffic Management System
ESP	Emergency Signalling Panel
ETCS	European Train Control System
FA	Flushing Apron
FP	Fuelling Point or Footpath
ft	Feet
GC	Gantry Crane
GDS	Goods
GL	Goods Loop
GS	Goods Shed
H	Headshunt
HABD	Hot Axle Box Detector
HH	Hopper House
HST	High Speed Train
IECC	Intergrated Electronic Control Centre
Jn	Junction
Jt	Joint
km	kilometres
L	Wheel Lathe
LC	Level Crossing (locally operated)
LHS	Locomotive Holding Siding
loe	limit of electrification
LP	Loop
LPG	Liquified petroleum gas
LS	Locomotive Shed
LW	Locomotive Washer
M	Middle
M ch	Miles and Chains
M&EE	Mechanical & Electrical Engineer
MGR	'Merry-go-round'
MN	Main
MOD	Ministry of Defence
MU	Maintenance Unit
N	North
NB	Northbound
NIRU	Not in regular use
NR	Network Rail
OHC	Overhead Crane
OHLE	Overhead Line Equipment
OOU	Out of Use
ONS	Overhead Neutral Section
OTM	On-track Maintenance
P	Points padlocked
PAD	Prefabricated Assembly Depot
PL	Passenger Loop
PS	Private Siding
PSB	Power Signal Box
PW	Permanent Way
Qy	Query concerning distances etc, unresolved
REC	Reception
RETB	Radio Electronic Token Block
REV	Reversing or Reversible line
RR	Run-Round
S	South
S & T	Signal & Telegraph
SB	Signal Box or Southbound
SC	Signalling Centre
SCC	Signalling Control Centre
Sdg(s)	Siding(s)
SD	Sand Drag
SIMBIDS	Simplified Bi-Directional Signalling
SN	Shunt Neck
SP	Switch Panel
SS	Shunt Spur
TA	Tamper siding
TB	Turnback Siding
TEP	Token Exchange Point
TL	Traffic Lights
TMD	Traction Maintenance Depot
T&RSMD	Traction & Rolling Stock Maintenance Depot
U&D	Up & Down
UA	Up Avoiding
UE	Up Electric
UF	Up Fast
UFN	Until Further Notice
UG	Up Goods
UGL	Up Goods Loop
UH	Unloading Hopper
UL	Up Loop
UM	Up Main
UPL	Up Passenger Loop
UR	Up Relief
URS	Up Refuge Siding
US	Up Slow
USB	Up Suburban
UT	Up Through
V or Vdct	Viaduct
W	West or Wash Point
WB	Westbound or Weighbridge
WD	War Department or Wheelchex Device
WILD	Wheel Impact Load Detector
WL	Wheel Lathe
yds	yards

SUPPLEMENTARY ABBREVIATIONS FOR THIS BOOK

AR	Network Rail Anglia Route
Cal	former Caledonian Railway
CTRL	Channel Tunnel Rail Link
CLC	former Cheshire Lines Committee
EM	Network Rail East Midlands Route
GC	former Great Central Railway
GE	former Great Eastern Railway
GN	former Great Northern Railway
GSW	former Glasgow & South Western Railway
GW	former Great Western Railway
KT	Network Rail Kent Route
LBSC	former London, Brighton and South Coast Railway
LCD	former London, Chatham and Dover Railway
LMS	former London Midland and Scottish Railway
LNE	former London and North Eastern Railway
LNE	Network Rail London North East Route
LNW	former London and North Western Railway
LNW	Network Rail London North West Route
LPTB	former London Passenger Transport Board
LSW	former London and South Western Railway
L&Y	former Lancashire and Yorkshire Railway
LUL	London Underground Limited
MD&HC	Mersey Docks & Harbour Co.
M&C	former Maryport and Carlisle Railway
MSC	Manchester Ship Canal
MSJ&A	former Manchester South Jn & Altrincham Railway
Met	former Metropolitan Railway
Mid	former Midland Railway
NB	former North British Railway
NE	former North Eastern Railway
NS	former North Staffordshire Railway
N&SWJn	former North and South Western Jn Railway
S	former Southern Railway
SC	Network Rail Scotland Route
SE	former South Eastern Railway
SX	Network Rail Sussex Route
Wales	Network Rail Wales Route
WL	former West London Joint Railway
WLE	former West London Extension Joint Railway
WR	Network Rail Western Route
WX	Network Rail Wessex Route

LEVEL CROSSING ABBREVIATIONS

Abbreviation	Description
(ABCL) *	Automatic Barrier Crossing, Locally monitored
(AHBC) *	Automatic Half-Barrier Crossing
(AOCL) *	Automatic Open Crossing, Locally monitored
(AOCR)	Automatic Open Crossing, Remotely monitored
(BW)	Bridle Way (only shown if telephone provided)
(CCTV)	Full barrier crossing with Closed Circuit Television monitored by Signaller
(FP)	Footpath crossing (only shown if telephone provided)
(MCB)	Manually controlled Crossing with Barriers
(MCB-OD)	MCB with Obstruction Detection
(MCG)	Manually controlled Crossing with Gates
(MGH)	Manned Gates, Hand worked
(MGW)	Manned Gates with Wickets
(MSL(B)(F)(G))	Crossing with Miniature Stop Lights and (B) Barriers, (F) Footpath or (G) Gates
(MWL)	Crossing with Miniature Warning Lights
(MWL(F)(G)(O))	Miniature Warning Lights at Footpath, with Gates or at Open crossing
(OC) or (OPEN)	Open Crossing (non-automatic), without barriers or gates
(RC)	Remotely Controlled crossing with barriers
(R/G)*	UWC with Red and Green warning lights operated by approaching trains
(TMO)	Traincrew Operated crossing
(TMOB)	Traincrew Operated Barrier
(TMOG)	Traincrew Operated Gates
(UWC)	User-Worked accommodation or occupation crossing, with telephone
(UW(B)(G)(K)(W))	User-Worked crossing with (B) Barriers, (G) Gates Barriers, (K) Kissing gates or (W) Wickets
(WL)	Barrow or Foot Crossing with White Light indicators

* (-X) shown after these abbreviations (e.g. AHBC-X) indicates that the crossing works automatically for movements in the wrong direction.

In some cases, the code of the controlling signal box may be shown, e.g. Cresswell (AHBC-X).

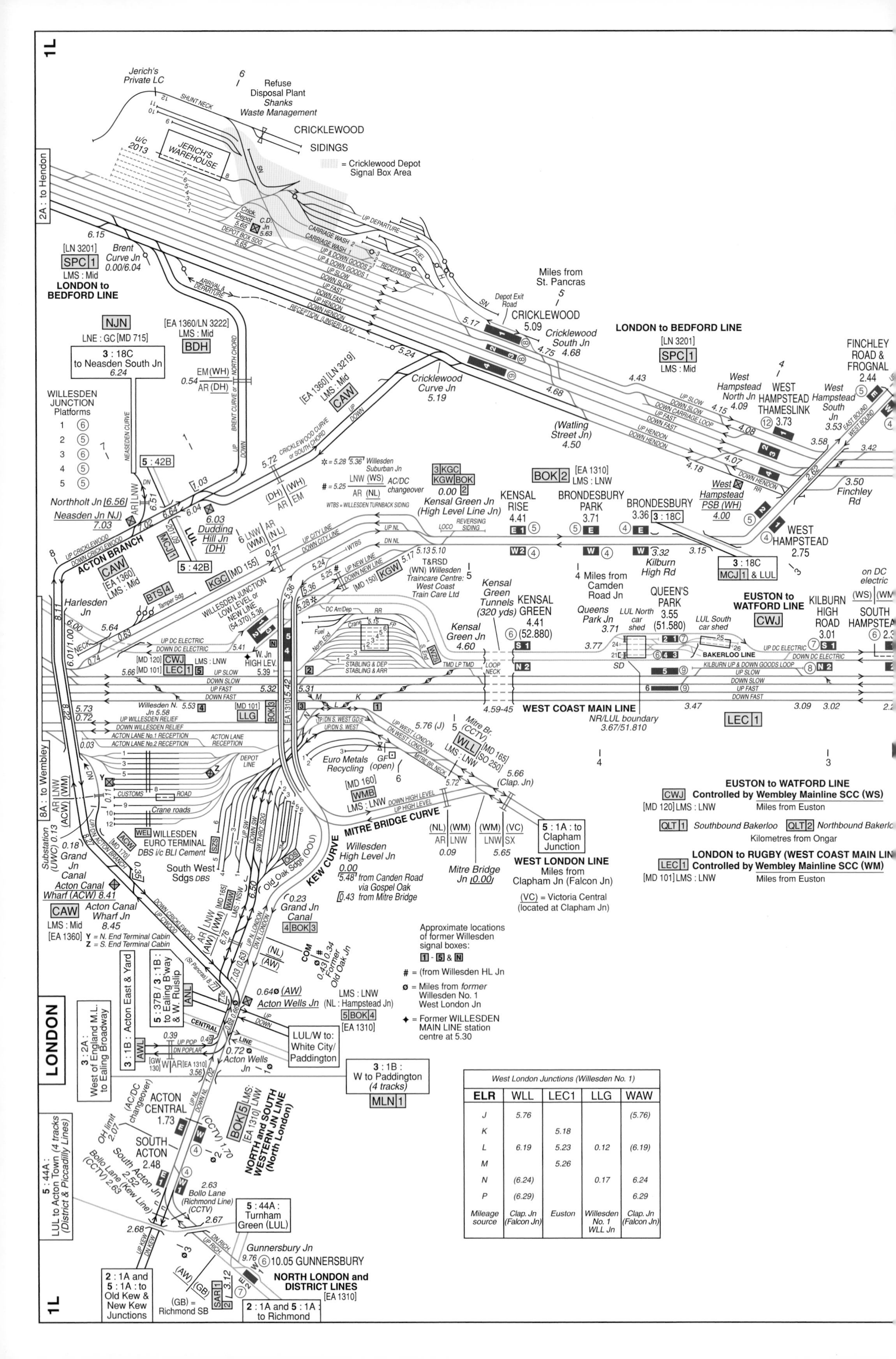

West London Junctions (Willesden No. 1)

ELR	WLL	LEC1	LLG	WAW
J	5.76			(5.76)
K		5.18		
L	6.19	5.23	0.12	(6.19)
M		5.26		
N	(6.24)		0.17	6.24
P	(6.29)			6.29
Mileage source	Clap. Jn (Falcon Jn)	Euston	Willesden No. 1 WLL Jn	Clap. Jn (Falcon Jn)

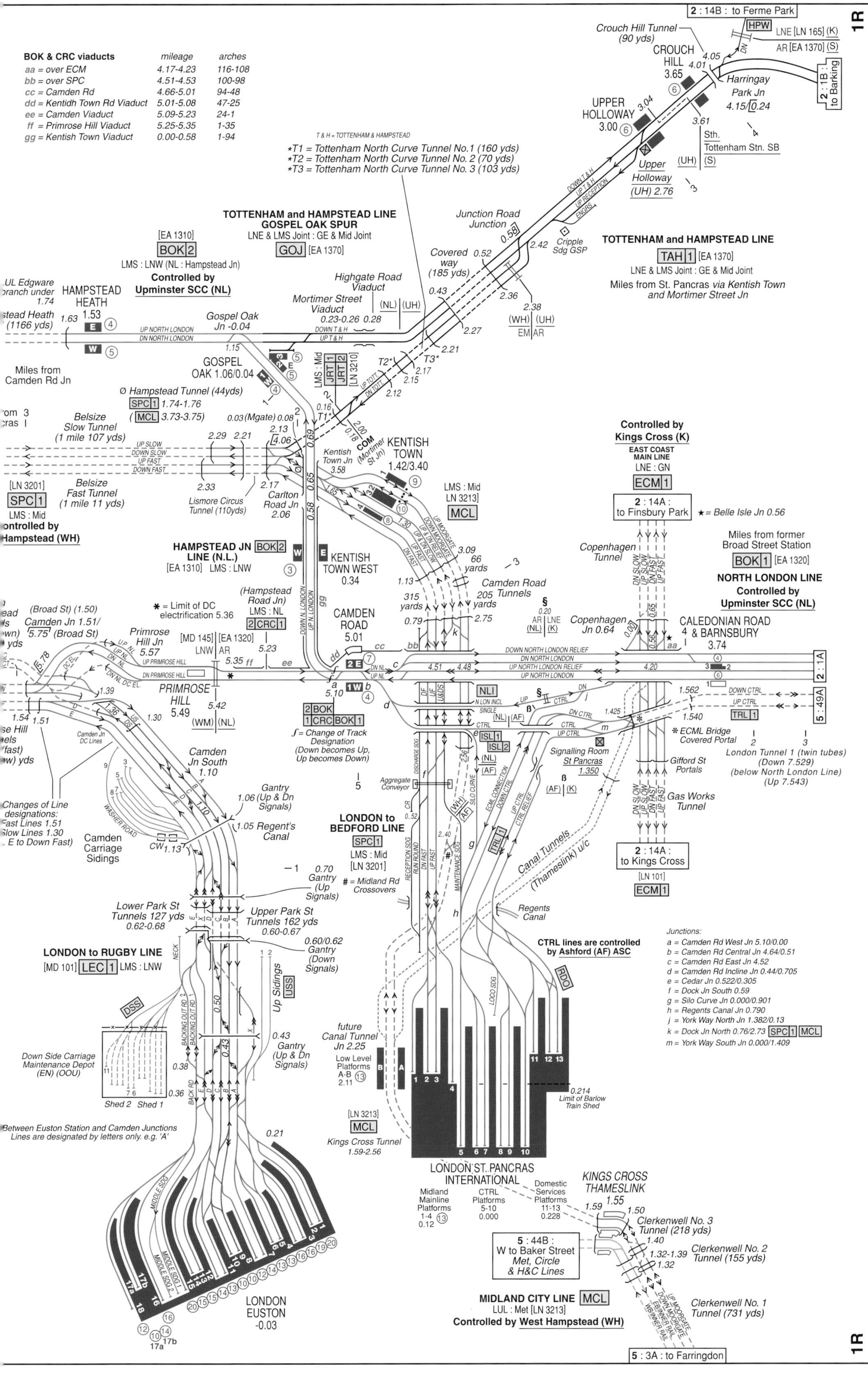

BOK & CRC viaducts

	mileage	arches
aa = over ECM	4.17-4.23	116-108
bb = over SPC	4.51-4.53	100-98
cc = Camden Rd	4.66-5.01	94-48
dd = Kentidh Town Rd Viaduct	5.01-5.08	47-25
ee = Camden Viaduct	5.09-5.23	24-1
ff = Primrose Hill Viaduct	5.25-5.35	1-35
gg = Kentish Town Viaduct	0.00-0.58	1-94

T & H = TOTTENHAM & HAMPSTEAD

*T1 = Tottenham North Curve Tunnel No.1 (160 yds)
*T2 = Tottenham North Curve Tunnel No.2 (70 yds)
*T3 = Tottenham North Curve Tunnel No. 3 (103 yds)

2 : 14B : to Ferme Park

HPW

LNE [LN 165] (K)
AR [EA 1370] (S)

Crouch Hill Tunnel (90 yds)

CROUCH HILL 3.65 (6)

4.05
4.01

2 : 1B : to Barking

Harringay Park Jn 4.15/0.24

UPPER HOLLOWAY 3.00 (6)

3.04
3.61

Sth. Tottenham Stn. SB (S)

Upper Holloway (UH) 2.76

(UH)

DOWN T & H
UP T & H
UP RECEPTION
ENGRS

Junction Road Junction 0.58

2.42

Cripple Sdg GSP

TOTTENHAM and HAMPSTEAD LINE
GOSPEL OAK SPUR
LNE & LMS Joint : GE & Mid Joint
GOJ [EA 1370]

[EA 1310]
BOK 2
LMS : LNW (NL : Hampstead Jn)
Controlled by Upminster SCC (NL)

TOTTENHAM and HAMPSTEAD LINE
TAH 1 [EA 1370]
LNE & LMS Joint : GE & Mid Joint
Miles from St. Pancras *via Kentish Town and Mortimer Street Jn*

Covered way (185 yds)
0.52
0.43
2.36
2.38
(WH) (UH)
EM AR
2.27
2.21

Highgate Road Viaduct
Mortimer Street Viaduct 0.23-0.26 0.28
(NL) (UH)

UL Edgware branch under 1.74

HAMPSTEAD HEATH 1.53 (4)

Hampstead Heath Tunnel 1.63 (1166 yds)

Gospel Oak Jn -0.04

UP NORTH LONDON
DN NORTH LONDON
DOWN T & H
UP T & H

1.15

GOSPEL OAK 1.06/0.04 (4) (5)

Miles from Camden Rd Jn

Ø Hampstead Tunnel (44yds)
SPC 1 1.74-1.76
(MCL 3.73-3.75)

LMS : Mid
JRT 1
JRT 2
[LN 3210]

T2*
T3*
2.17
2.15
2.12
UP TOTT
DN TOTT

0.16
T1*
2.00
0.18

0.03 (Mgate) 0.08
2.13
4.06

COM (Mortimer St Jn)

Kentish Town Jn 3.58

KENTISH TOWN 1.42/3.40 (9)

Belsize Slow Tunnel (1 mile 107 yds)
2.29 2.21
UP SLOW
DOWN SLOW
UP FAST
DOWN FAST
2.33
2.17

Belsize Fast Tunnel (1 mile 11 yds)

Lismore Circus Tunnel (110yds)

Carlton Road Jn 2.06

0.69
0.65
0.58

[LN 3201]
SPC 1
LMS : Mid
Controlled by West Hampstead (WH)

LMS : Mid
LN 3213]
MCL

DN MOORGATE
UP MOORGATE
DN & UP SLOW
UP & DN RELIEF
DN FAST
UP FAST

3.09
66 yards

HAMPSTEAD JN BOK 2 LINE (N.L.)
[EA 1310] LMS : LNW

KENTISH TOWN WEST 0.34 (3)

DOWN N. LONDON
UP N. LONDON
gg

Camden Road Tunnels
315 yards
205 yards
1.13
0.79
2.75

Controlled by Kings Cross (K)

EAST COAST MAIN LINE
LNE : GN
ECM 1

2 : 14A : to Finsbury Park

★= Belle Isle Jn 0.56

Copenhagen Tunnel

DN SLOW
UP SLOW
DN FAST
UP FAST

Miles from former Broad Street Station
BOK 1 [EA 1320]
NORTH LONDON LINE
Controlled by Upminster SCC (NL)

§ 0.20
AR LNE
(NL) (K)

Copenhagen Jn 0.64

CALEDONIAN ROAD & BARNSBURY 3.74

(Broad St) (1.50)
Camden Jn 1.51/ 5.75 (Broad St)

* = Limit of DC electrification 5.36

(Hampstead Road Jn)
LMS : NL
2 CRC 1

CAMDEN ROAD 5.01 (7)

Primrose Hill Jn 5.57

[MD 145] [EA 1320]
LNW AR
5.23
5.35 ff
ee

UP PRIMROSE HILL
DN PRIMROSE HILL
UP NL
DN NL
DN NL DC EL.
DC EL.

PRIMROSE HILL 5.49
5.42
(WM) (NL)

1.39
1.36
1.30
1.54 1.51

Camden Jn DC Lines

Camden Jn South 1.10

2 BOK
1 CRC BOK 1

∫ = Change of Track Designation (Down becomes Up, Up becomes Down)

a 5.10
b
c
d
1W
2E

DN NL
UP NL
DOWN NORTH LONDON RELIEF
DN NORTH LONDON
UP NORTH LONDON RELIEF
UP NORTH LONDON
4.51 4.48
4.20

2 : 1A
5 : 49A

NLI
N LON INCL
SINGLE
(NL) (AF)
CTRL
UP CTRL
DN CTRL
ISL 1
ISL 2
(NL)
(AF)

DOWN CTRL
UP CTRL
TRL 1
1.562
1.540
1.425

* ECML Bridge Covered Portal

London Tunnel 1 (twin tubes) (Down 7.529) (below North London Line) (Up 7.543)

Signalling Room St Pancras 1.350

β
(AF) (K)

Gifford St Portals

Gas Works Tunnel

2 : 14A : to Kings Cross
[LN 101]
ECM 1

Changes of Line designations:
Fast Lines 1.51
Slow Lines 1.30
, E to Down Fast)

Camden Carriage Sidings

WASHER ROAD

Gantry 1.06 (Up & Dn Signals)
1.05 Regent's Canal
CW 1.13

0.70 Gantry (Up Signals)

LONDON to BEDFORD LINE
SPC 1
LMS : Mid
[LN 3201]

= Midland Rd Crossovers

Aggregate Conveyor
DISCHARGE SDG
DF UF U&DS
SILO CURVE
ECML CONNECTION
DOWN CTRL
UP CTRL
CTRL RELIEF
(WH) (AF)
RECEPTION SDG
RUN ROUND
DN FAST
UP FAST
MAINTENANCE SDG
CR
0.52
2.40
2.56

Canal Tunnels (Thameslink) u/c

Regents Canal

Lower Park St Tunnels 127 yds 0.62-0.68

Upper Park St Tunnels 162 yds 0.60-0.67

0.60/0.62 Gantry (Down Signals)

LONDON to RUGBY LINE
[MD 101] LEC 1 LMS : LNW

NECK
Up Sidings USS

DSS

BACKING OUT RD 2
BACKING OUT RD 1
0.50
0.43
0.43 Gantry (Up & Dn Signals)
0.38
0.36
BACK RD

Down Side Carriage Maintenance Depot (EN) (OOU)

Shed 2 Shed 1

Between Euston Station and Camden Junctions Lines are designated by letters only. e.g. 'A'

0.21

MIDDLE SDG
MIDDLE SDG 1
MIDDLE SDG 2

LONDON EUSTON -0.03

CTRL lines are controlled by Ashford (AF) ASC

RDO
LOCO SDG

future Canal Tunnel Jn 2.25

Low Level Platforms A-B (13) 2.11

[LN 3213]
MCL
Kings Cross Tunnel 1.59-2.56

0.214 Limit of Barlow Train Shed

LONDON ST. PANCRAS INTERNATIONAL

Midland Mainline Platforms 1-4 0.12 (13)

CTRL Platforms 5-10 0.000

Domestic Services Platforms 11-13 0.228

KINGS CROSS THAMESLINK 1.55
1.59 1.50

Clerkenwell No. 3 Tunnel (218 yds)
1.40
1.32-1.39
1.32
Clerkenwell No. 2 Tunnel (155 yds)
Clerkenwell No. 1 Tunnel (731 yds)

5 : 44B : W to Baker Street Met, Circle & H&C Lines

MIDLAND CITY LINE MCL
LUL : Met [LN 3213]
Controlled by West Hampstead (WH)

UP MOORGATE
DOWN MOORGATE
EB INNER RAIL
WB INNER RAIL

5 : 3A : to Farringdon

Junctions:
- a = Camden Rd West Jn 5.10/0.00
- b = Camden Rd Central Jn 4.64/0.51
- c = Camden Rd East Jn 4.52
- d = Camden Rd Incline Jn 0.44/0.705
- e = Cedar Jn 0.522/0.305
- f = Dock Jn South 0.59
- g = Silo Curve Jn 0.000/0.901
- h = Regents Canal Jn 0.790
- j = York Way North Jn 1.382/0.13
- k = Dock Jn North 0.76/2.73 SPC 1 MCL
- m = York Way South Jn 0.000/1.409

LONDON

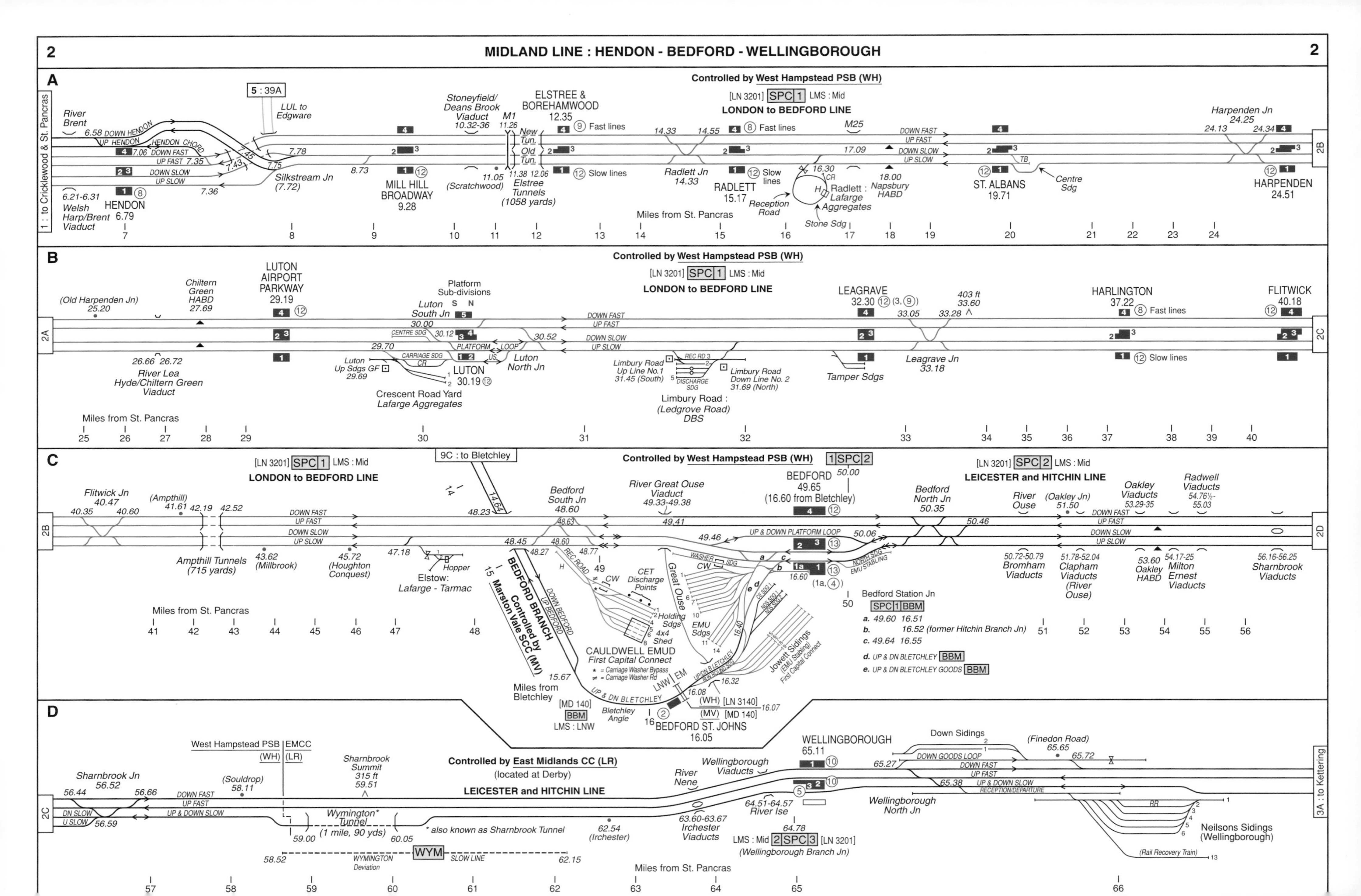

A
Controlled by West Hampstead PSB (WH)
[LN 3201] SPC 1 LMS : Mid
LONDON to BEDFORD LINE
1 : to Cricklewood & St. Pancras
5 : 39A
LUL to Edgware
River Brent
6.58 DOWN HENDON
UP HENDON
HENDON CHORD
7.06 DOWN FAST
UP FAST 7.35
DOWN SLOW
UP SLOW
7.45
7.43
7.75
7.78
7.36
Silkstream Jn (7.72)
6.21-6.31 Welsh Harp/Brent Viaduct
HENDON 6.79
8.73
MILL HILL BROADWAY 9.28
Stoneyfield/ Deans Brook Viaduct 10.32-36
M1 11.26
11.05 (Scratchwood)
New Tun.
Old Tun.
11.38 12.06 Elstree Tunnels (1058 yards)
ELSTREE & BOREHAMWOOD 12.35
9 Fast lines
12 Slow lines
14.33
14.55
8 Fast lines
12 Slow lines
Radlett Jn 14.33
RADLETT 15.17
16.30
CR
H
Radlett : Lafarge Aggregates
Reception Road
Stone Sdg
M25
17.09
18.00 Napsbury HABD
DOWN FAST
UP FAST
DOWN SLOW
UP SLOW
ST. ALBANS 19.71
TB
Centre Sdg
Harpenden Jn 24.25
24.13
24.34
HARPENDEN 24.51
2B
Miles from St. Pancras
B
Controlled by West Hampstead PSB (WH)
[LN 3201] SPC 1 LMS : Mid
LONDON to BEDFORD LINE
2A
(Old Harpenden Jn) 25.20
Chiltern Green HABD 27.69
26.66 26.72 River Lea Hyde/Chiltern Green Viaduct
LUTON AIRPORT PARKWAY 29.19
Platform Sub-divisions
Luton South Jn 30.00
CENTRE SDG
30.12
29.70
PLATFORM
LOOP
CARRIAGE SDG
CR
Luton Up Sdgs GF 29.69
LUTON 30.19
Crescent Road Yard Lafarge Aggregates
30.52
Luton North Jn
DOWN FAST
UP FAST
DOWN SLOW
UP SLOW
Limbury Road Up Line No.1 31.45 (South)
REC RD 3
DISCHARGE SDG
Limbury Road Down Line No. 2 31.69 (North)
Limbury Road : (Ledgrove Road) DBS
LEAGRAVE 32.30 12 (3, 9)
Tamper Sdgs
33.05
403 ft 33.60
33.28
Leagrave Jn 33.18
HARLINGTON 37.22
8 Fast lines
12 Slow lines
FLITWICK 40.18
2C
Miles from St. Pancras
C
[LN 3201] SPC 1 LMS : Mid
LONDON to BEDFORD LINE
9C : to Bletchley
Controlled by West Hampstead PSB (WH) 1 SPC 2
2B
Flitwick Jn 40.47
40.35
40.60
(Ampthill) 41.61
42.19
42.52
Ampthill Tunnels (715 yards)
43.62 (Millbrook)
45.72 (Houghton Conquest)
47.18
Elstow: Lafarge - Tarmac
Hopper
DOWN FAST
UP FAST
DOWN SLOW
UP SLOW
14.64
48.23
Bedford South Jn 48.60
48.63
48.45
48.60
48.27
48.77
REC ROAD
49
CW
BEDFORD BRANCH
DOWN BEDFORD
UP BEDFORD
Controlled by Marston Vale SCC (MV)
15.67
Miles from Bletchley
[MD 140] BBM LMS : LNW
River Great Ouse Viaduct 49.33-49.38
49.41
49.46
Great Ouse
CET Discharge Points
Holding Sdgs
4x4 Shed
EMU Sdgs
WASHER SDG
CAULDWELL EMUD
First Capital Connect
* = Carriage Washer Bypass
≠ = Carriage Washer Rd
LNW EM
UP & DN BLETCHLEY
Bletchley Angle
BEDFORD ST. JOHNS 16.05
16.08
(WH) [LN 3140]
(MV) [MD 140]
16.07
16.32
16.40
Jowett Sidings (EMU Stabling) First Capital Connect
BEDFORD 49.65 (16.60 from Bletchley)
50.00
UP & DOWN PLATFORM LOOP
50.06
16.60
(1a, 4)
NORTH SDG
EMU STABLING
Bedford Station Jn
SPC 1 BBM
a. 49.60 16.51
b. 16.52 (former Hitchin Branch Jn)
c. 49.64 16.55
d. UP & DN BLETCHLEY BBM
e. UP & DN BLETCHLEY GOODS BBM
[LN 3201] SPC 2 LMS : Mid
LEICESTER and HITCHIN LINE
Bedford North Jn 50.35
50.46
River Ouse
(Oakley Jn) 51.50
50.72-50.79 Bromham Viaducts
51.78-52.04 Clapham Viaducts (River Ouse)
Oakley Viaducts 53.29-35
53.60 Oakley HABD
54.17-25 Milton Ernest Viaducts
Radwell Viaducts 54.76½-55.03
56.16-56.25 Sharnbrook Viaducts
2D
Miles from St. Pancras
D
West Hampstead PSB (WH) | EMCC (LR)
Controlled by East Midlands CC (LR)
(located at Derby)
LEICESTER and HITCHIN LINE
2C
Sharnbrook Jn 56.52
56.44
56.66
56.59
DN SLOW
U SLOW
DOWN FAST
UP FAST
UP & DOWN SLOW
(Souldrop) 58.11
Sharnbrook Summit 315 ft 59.51
Wymington* Tunnel (1 mile, 90 yds)
59.00
60.05
* also known as Sharnbrook Tunnel
58.52
WYMINGTON Deviation
WYM
SLOW LINE
62.15
62.54 (Irchester)
63.60-63.67 Irchester Viaducts
River Nene
Wellingborough Viaducts
64.51-64.57 River Ise
64.78
LMS : Mid 2 SPC 3 [LN 3201]
(Wellingborough Branch Jn)
WELLINGBOROUGH 65.11
65.27
65.38
Wellingborough North Jn
Down Sidings
DOWN GOODS LOOP
DOWN FAST
UP FAST
UP & DOWN SLOW
RECEPTION/DEPARTURE
(Finedon Road) 65.65
65.72
RR
Neilsons Sidings (Wellingborough)
(Rail Recovery Train)
3A : to Kettering
Miles from St. Pancras

A

LEICESTER and HITCHIN LINE
SPC 3 [LN 3201]
LMS : Mid
Controlled by East Midlands CC (LR)
(located at Derby)
LMS : Mid SPC 3 [LN 3201]
LEICESTER and HITCHIN LINE

2D : to Wellingborough
Harrowden Jn HABD 67.36
Harrowden Jn 67.00
66.69
68.18 (Finedon)
69.27 (Isham & Burton Latimer)
Kettering South Jn 70.60
70.51
70.60
KETTERING 72.01 4 (9)
2 3
1
Engrs/Hot Box Siding (OOU)
72.20 Kettering Station Jn
Kettering North Jn 74.00
74.02
73.73
(Glendon North Jn) 74.77
Glendon Viaduct (R. Ouse) 75.22-75.26
78.39
Desborough Summit 436 ft
Baybrooke (UWC) 80.34
Little Bowden (R/G) (FP) 82.33
Market Harborough Jn 82.47
MARKET HARBOROUGH 82.74 1 (10)
2 (6) NIRU
H
86.20 East Langton HABD
DOWN FAST / UP FAST / UP & DOWN SLOW
DN FAST / UP FAST / UP & DOWN SLOW
DOWN FAST / UP FAST / DOWN SLOW / UP SLOW
UP & DN SLOW / UP
DOWN MAIN / UP MAIN
3B

67 68 69 70 71 72 73 74 75 76 77 78 79 80 81 82 83 84 85 86 87 88

KETTERING and MANTON LINE
LMS : Mid GSM 1 [LN 3601]
Geddington HABD 77.08
Geddington/ Harpers Brook Viaduct 77.38-50
East Midlands CC (LR)
Manton Jn (MJ)
UP
UP & DOWN CORBY
357 ft 78.65
CORBY 79.40
Corby North Jn 79.32/0.00
NR Bdy 0.16
BSC
3C
Controlled by Manton Jn (MJ)
79.49 79.58 RECEPTION RR
80.74
Corby Tunnel (1mile, 160yds)
82.01
Gretton Viaduct 83.05 - 83.08
DN CORBY / UP CORBY
85.00 (Harringworth)
Harringworth/ Welland Valley Vdct 82 arches max height 70 ft
85.18-76
Seaton Tunnel (206 yds) 86.24 - 86.33
87.30
Seaton Vdct 86.62
88.33
Glaston Tunnel (1mile, 82yds)
3B

79 80 81 82 83 84 85 86 87 88

C

3A
[LN 3610] CORBY AUTOMOTIVE BRANCH
Controlled by Manton Jn (MJ)
CORBY CORUS BRANCH [LN 3605]
BSC
A6086
1.10
Water Works LC 1.40
A427
Corus Tubes (Tata Steel)
Scrap
Exchange & Oil Sdgs
Overhead Crane
G. E. F. Co. Sdgs
2.05
Automotive Terminal
Ramps
Autologic Sdgs (OOU)
Ramps
Coil Unloading Pad

B

Controlled by East Midlands CC (LR)
3A
(Kibworth) 88.74
(Great Glen) 91.44
89.54 370 ft
LEICESTER and HITCHIN LINE
Kilby Bridge Jn 93.40
Cooks Lane (UWW) 93.56
DOWN MAIN / UP MAIN
UP & DOWN SLOW / DOWN FAST / UP FAST
95.38
3 SPC 4 [LN 3201] LMS : Mid
Wigston South Jn 95.37
[LN 3231] WGP LMS : Mid
WIGSTON SOUTH CURVE
96
Glen Parva Jn
Glen Parva GSP 14.53
96.07
14.57
Brook's River Viaduct 13.58-55
(Blaby Jn) 13.40
(LR) (CT)
SOUTH WIGSTON 14.57 (5)
WNS [LN 3232]
WIGSTON NORTH CURVE LMS : LNW
15.21
AVOIDING LINE
95.76 15.31 Wigston North Jn
96.02 15.36
RUGBY and LEICESTER LINE
Hinds (UWB) 12.55
12.15
NARBOROUGH 11.67 (5) (CCTV)
12.75 (former GC Overbridge) (107.24)
M1
12.17 Narborough HABD
Miles from Nuneaton (South Jn)
Durhams (UWS) 11.05
11.30 River Soar
[LN 3232] WNS LMS : LNW
SOUTH LEICESTERSHIRE LINE
10.20
10.04
River Soar
9.44
Croft Quarry : Bardon Aggregates
Loading Hopper
Holts (UWC) 8.76
M69 7.46
DOWN NUNEATON / UP NUNEATON
(5) HINCKLEY 4.00
Jericho (UWC) 3.31
Padge Hall Farm (UWC) 2.24
2.62
EM LNW
EMCC (CT) (WN) Rugby SCC
DN H. / UP H.
H. = HINCKLEY
11B : to Nuneaton

14 13 12 11 10 9 8 7 6 5 4 3 2

89 90 91 92 93 94 95

KETTERING and MANTON LINE
Wing Tunnel (353 yds)
Wing Viaduct 89.65-89.68 (River Chater)
88.33 89.22 89.39
89.73
DN CORBY / UP CORBY
90.16
Manton South
Engrs' Sdgs
LMS : Mid [LN 3601] 1 GSM 2 [LN 3615]
Manton Jn 0.00/90.23
Manton Jn (MJ) 90.18
Manton Jn GF 0.14
90.26
90.61
Manton Tunnel (749 yards)
(Manton North Jn) 91.05
Gunthorpe (UWC) 91.24
Goodridges (UWC) 91.61
Pattersons (UWC) 92.00
Egleton (UWB) 92.27
Rutland Water
0.50 River Chater
Wing (UWC) 1.03
LMS : Mid PMJ [LN 3615]
LMS : Mid (Syston & Peterborough)
DOWN MAIN / UP MAIN
Brooke Road (CCTV) 93.22
Oakham 93.56 (5)
(MCB) OAKHAM 93.61 (6)
DN GOODS / DN MAIN / UP MAIN / UP GOODS
Cemetery Sdg
= former Ashwell Branch Jn 97.22 with ASB to Cottesmore (see 51, Rutland Railway Museum)
Langham Jn (MCB) 95.06
Miles from St Pancras via Corby
SYSTON and PETERBOROUGH LINE
Ashwell Gate House (MCBR) 96.47
Ashwell (MCB) 96.67
(Ashwell) 99.69 #
Teigh (FPG) 98.00
Luffenham (CCTV)
4.11
Naylors (UWC) 5.46
Loading Silos
Hanson Cement (Heidelberg)
Meadows Exchange Sdgs
Ketton Cement Works
7.60
Ketton (K) 6.60
(MCB)
Wards Sdgs GF
Wards (UWC) 7.66
Tinwell (UWC) 8.36
STAMFORD 10.11
10.20-36
UP STAMFORD / DN STAMFORD
(4) 2 Stamford Tunnel (341yds)
Hoods Mill (UWB) 11.08
Uffington (UN) 12.75
(MCG)
13.09 Brassey (UWC)
13.57 Aldwinkle (UWC)
EM LNE 13.60
2 : 24D
Peterborough (UN) (P)
Miles from Manton Jn

8 9 10 11 12 13

99.01 River Eye
Whissendine 99.15
(MCB) Wymondham (MCG) 99.67
DN MAIN / UP MAIN
Brets (UWC) 102.02
Freeby (UWW) 102.15
Rippings (UWC) 102.73
Wyfordby (MGH) 102.38
Brentingby (UWW) 103.22
Speckles (UWC) 103.05
Hubbards (UWC) 103.41
104.19
103.75 River Eye
MELTON MOWBRAY (4) 105.22
DGL / DN MAIN / UP MAIN / UGL
105.17
Crane
PPF No 2
MIDDLE CRANE
Melton Stn 105.27
105.31
DALBY NK
Melton Jn
DN P. / UP P.
ASFORDBY BRANCH
4C : to Old Dalby Test Centre
LMS : Mid 2 GSM 3 [LN 3615]
(Leics) 113.36 mileage meet
(Corby) 105.70
Miles from St Pancras via Leicester
Greens (UWC) 112.19
Asfordby (AHBC) 111.40
Mill Deeping (UWW) 110.41
(FY)
Woods (UWC) 110.47
110.17 Frisby (MCB)
Washstones (R/G) (UWCM) 109.51
Rippins Main (UWW) 109.00
Brooksby (AHBC) 108.31
Hives Farm (UWC) 107.55
Rearsby (AHBC) 107.05
Poachins (UWC) 107.25
Mucky La (UWC) 106.47
Broome Lane (AHBC) 106.00
105.11-105.09
Flood spans
P. = PETERBOROUGH
(FY) SB (LR) EMCC

99 100 101 102 103 104 105

SPC 4 [LN 3201]
97.30 97.34 Knighton Vdct
SHUNT LINE
DOWN MAIN / UP MAIN / UP & DN GOODS
97.45 Knighton Jn (ex Knighton South Jn)
98.02 Knighton Tunnel (104 yds)
LMS : Mid KSL [LN 3525]
LEICESTER and BURTON LINE
UP & DOWN BURTON
7B : to Coalville & Burton
Knighton Old Sdgs-Engrs (OOU)
¥ All Platforms subdivided (a) south (b) north
Platforms 1 (13) 2-4 (14)
ø former London Rd Jn
ø LEICESTER 4 SPC 5 99.07
98.74
98.07 98.36
DN FAST / UP FAST / UP/DN SLOW
99.18
Leicester South Jn
Carriage Sidings
Leicester North Jn
Loco Sidings (LR) EWS
99.30
Bell Lane 99.59
No. 5 TOP SDG / REC No. 1 / UP/DN GOODS / DOWN FAST / UP FAST
Humberstone Road
SHUNT NECK 100.20
UP AND DOWN SLOW
100.31
Humberstone Road Jn (100.20)

Leicester Sidings
A Under the Box
B Accident Van Road
C Old Shed Side
D Coal Road 1
E Coal Road 2
F Coal Road 3
G Slip Road
H Pass Pit Road
J Goods Pit Road
K Fuel Road 1
L Fuel Road 2
M Shop Road
N Long Coal Road

Controlled by East Midlands CC (LR)
[LN 3201] SPC 5 LMS : Mid
Thurmaston Wheelchex 101.78
DOWN FAST / UP FAST / UP & DOWN SLOW
Syston South Jn 103.72
103.62
SYSTON 103.63 (3)
[LN 3201] SPC 5 Syston North Jn 104.25
GSM 5 [LN 3615]
DOWN FAST / UP FAST / DOWN SLOW / UP SLOW / UP & DN PETERBORO
103.75
0.00
DN / UP N. CURVE
SEN [LN 3234] 0.17 0.29
104.22 Syston East Jn
DOWN P. / UP P.
LMS : Mid GSM 3 [LN 3615]
4A : to Loughborough

100 101 102 → 103
113 112 111 110 109 ← 108 107 104 106 105

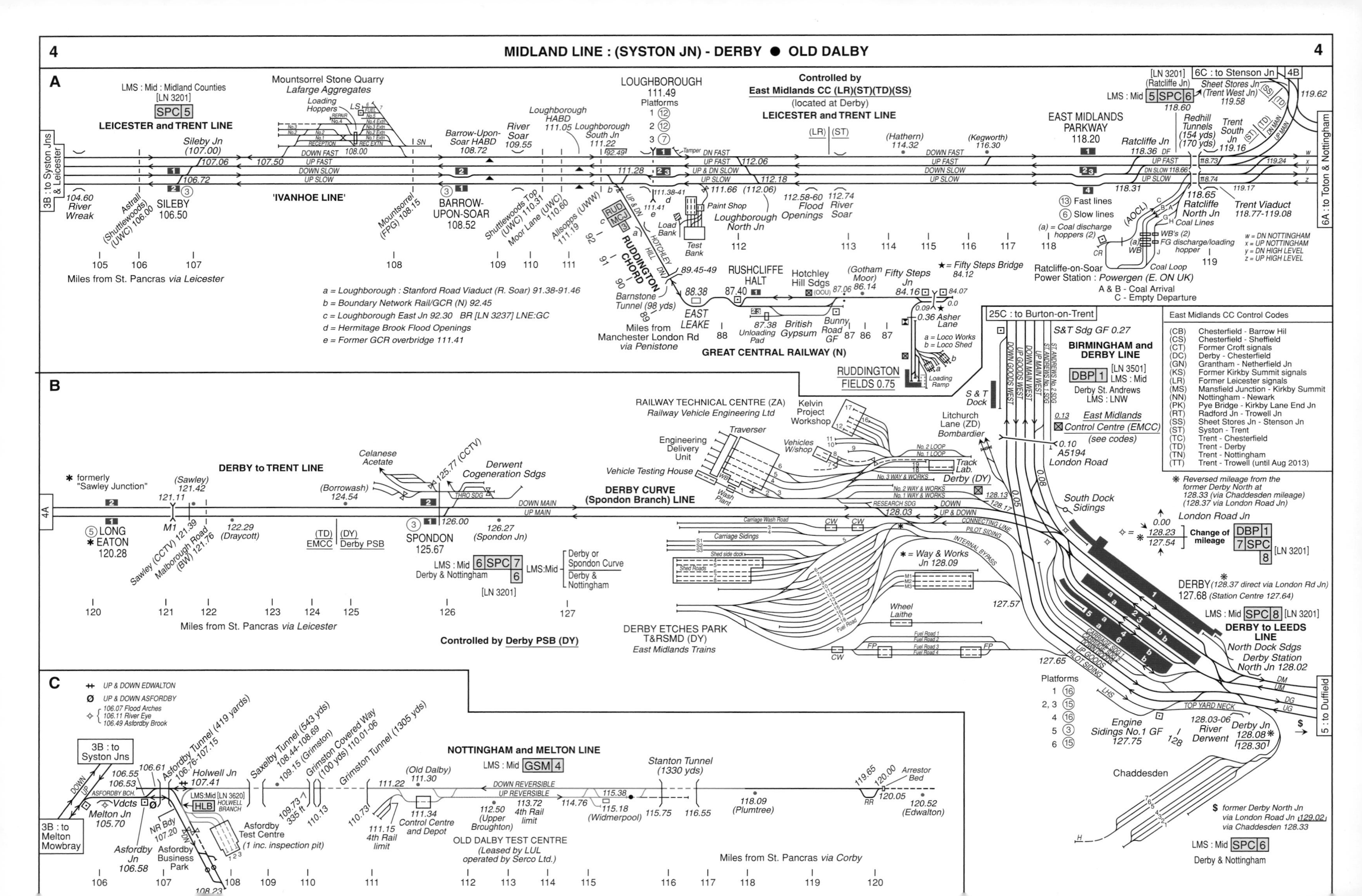

A
LMS : Mid : Midland Counties
[LN 3201]
SPC 5
LEICESTER and TRENT LINE
3B : to Syston Jns & Leicester
104.60 River Wreak
Sileby Jn (107.00)
107.06
106.72
SILEBY 106.50
Astrall (Shuttlewoods) (UWC) 106.00
Mountsorrel Stone Quarry
Lafarge Aggregates
Loading Hoppers
107.50
108.00
DOWN FAST
UP FAST
DOWN SLOW
UP SLOW
'IVANHOE LINE'
Mountsorrel (FPG) 108.15
Barrow-Upon-Soar HABD 108.72
BARROW-UPON-SOAR 108.52
River Soar 109.55
Loughborough HABD 111.05
Loughborough South Jn 111.22
Shuttlewoods Top (UWC) 110.31
Moor Lane (UWC) 110.60
Allsopps (UWW) 111.19
LOUGHBOROUGH 111.49
Platforms
1 (12)
2 (12)
3 (7)
111.28
111.38-41
111.41
Paint Shop
Load Bank
Test Bank
111.66 (112.06)
112.06
112.18
Loughborough North Jn
112.58-60 Flood Openings
112.74 River Soar
Controlled by
East Midlands CC (LR)(ST)(TD)(SS)
(located at Derby)
LEICESTER and TRENT LINE
(LR) (ST)
(Hathern) 114.32
(Kegworth) 116.30
EAST MIDLANDS PARKWAY 118.20
(13) Fast lines
(6) Slow lines
(a) = Coal discharge hoppers (2)
Ratcliffe Jn 118.36
118.31
118.65 Ratcliffe North Jn
Redhill Tunnels (154 yds) (170 yds)
Trent South Jn 119.16
Trent Viaduct 118.77-119.08
Coal Lines
WB's (2)
FG discharge/loading hopper
Coal Loop
Ratcliffe-on-Soar Power Station : Powergen (E. ON UK)
A & B - Coal Arrival
C - Empty Departure
w = DN NOTTINGHAM
x = UP NOTTINGHAM
y = DN HIGH LEVEL
z = UP HIGH LEVEL
[LN 3201] (Ratcliffe Jn)
LMS : Mid 5 SPC 6
6C : to Stenson Jn 4B
Sheet Stores Jn (Trent West Jn) 119.58
118.60
119.62
6A : to Toton & Nottingham
Miles from St. Pancras via Leicester
a = Loughborough : Stanford Road Viaduct (R. Soar) 91.38-91.46
b = Boundary Network Rail/GCR (N) 92.45
c = Loughborough East Jn 92.30 BR [LN 3237] LNE:GC
d = Hermitage Brook Flood Openings
e = Former GCR overbridge 111.41
RUDDINGTON CHORD
HOTCHLEY HILL
89.45-49
Barnstone Tunnel (98 yds)
88.38
EAST LEAKE
RUSHCLIFFE HALT 87.40
Hotchley Hill Sdgs
87.38 Unloading Pad
British Gypsum
Bunny Road GF
(Gotham Moor) 86.14
Fifty Steps Jn 84.16
★= Fifty Steps Bridge 84.12
84.07
0.36 Asher Lane
a = Loco Works
b = Loco Shed
Loading Ramp
Miles from Manchester London Rd via Penistone
GREAT CENTRAL RAILWAY (N)
RUDDINGTON FIELDS 0.75
B
25C : to Burton-on-Trent
S&T Sdg GF 0.27
BIRMINGHAM and DERBY LINE
DBP 1 [LN 3501] LMS : Mid
Derby St. Andrews LMS : LNW
East Midlands Control Centre (EMCC) (see codes)
0.10 A5194 London Road
S & T Dock
East Midlands CC Control Codes
(CB) Chesterfield - Barrow Hil
(CS) Chesterfield - Sheffield
(CT) Former Croft signals
(DC) Derby - Chesterfield
(GN) Grantham - Netherfield Jn
(KS) Former Kirkby Summit signals
(LR) Former Leicester signals
(MS) Mansfield Junction - Kirkby Summit
(NN) Nottingham - Newark
(PK) Pye Bridge - Kirkby Lane End Jn
(RT) Radford Jn - Trowell Jn
(SS) Sheet Stores Jn - Stenson Jn
(ST) Syston - Trent
(TC) Trent - Chesterfield
(TD) Trent - Derby
(TN) Trent - Nottingham
(TT) Trent - Trowell (until Aug 2013)
* Reversed mileage from the former Derby North at 128.33 (via Chaddesden mileage) (128.37 via London Road Jn)
London Road Jn
Change of mileage
DBP 1
7 SPC 8
[LN 3201]
DERBY (128.37 direct via London Rd Jn) 127.68 (Station Centre 127.64)
LMS : Mid SPC 8 [LN 3201]
DERBY to LEEDS LINE
North Dock Sdgs
Derby Station North Jn 128.02
South Dock Sidings
Litchurch Lane (ZD) Bombardier
Track Lab.
Derby (DY)
RAILWAY TECHNICAL CENTRE (ZA)
Railway Vehicle Engineering Ltd
Kelvin Project Workshop
Traverser
Engineering Delivery Unit
Vehicles W/shop
Vehicle Testing House
Wash Plant
* formerly "Sawley Junction"
DERBY to TRENT LINE
(Sawley) 121.42
121.11
M1
LONG EATON 120.28
Sawley (CCTV) 121.39
Malborough Road (BW) 121.76
122.29 (Draycott)
(Borrowash) 124.54
(TD) EMCC
(DY) Derby PSB
Celanese Acetate
125.77 (CCTV)
Derwent Cogeneration Sdgs
SPONDON 125.67
126.00
126.27 (Spondon Jn)
LMS : Mid 6 SPC 7 6
Derby & Nottingham
[LN 3201]
LMS:Mid Derby or Spondon Curve / Derby & Nottingham
DERBY CURVE (Spondon Branch) LINE
4A
Miles from St. Pancras via Leicester
Controlled by Derby PSB (DY)
DERBY ETCHES PARK T&RSMD (DY)
East Midlands Trains
Carriage Wash Road
Carriage Sidings
Shed side dock
Shed Roads
* = Way & Works Jn 128.09
Wheel Laithe
Fuel Road
128.03
128.13
128.17
127.57
127.65
Platforms
1 (16)
2, 3 (15)
4 (16)
5 (3)
6 (15)
Engine Sidings No.1 GF 127.75
128.03-06 River Derwent
Derby Jn 128.08*
128.30
5 : to Duffield
Chaddesden
$ former Derby North Jn via London Road Jn 129.02 via Chaddesden 128.33
LMS : Mid SPC 6
Derby & Nottingham
C
UP & DOWN EDWALTON
UP & DOWN ASFORDBY
106.07 Flood Arches
106.11 River Eye
106.49 Asfordby Brook
3B : to Syston Jns
3B : to Melton Mowbray
106.55
106.53
106.61
Vdcts
Melton Jn 105.70
Asfordby Jn 106.58
NR Bdy 107.20
Asfordby Business Park
Asfordby Tunnel (419 yards) 106.76-107.15
Holwell Jn 107.41
LMS:Mid [LN 3620] HLB HOLWELL BRANCH
Asfordby Test Centre (1 inc. inspection pit)
108.23
Saxelby Tunnel (543 yds) 108.44-108.69
109.15 (Grimston)
109.73 335 ft
Grimston Covered Way (100 yds) 110.01-06
110.13
Grimston Tunnel (1305 yds)
110.73
111.15 4th Rail limit
111.22
(Old Dalby) 111.30
111.34 Control Centre and Depot
NOTTINGHAM and MELTON LINE
LMS : Mid GSM 4
DOWN REVERSIBLE
UP REVERSIBLE
112.50 (Upper Broughton)
113.72 4th Rail limit
114.76
115.38
115.18 (Widmerpool)
Stanton Tunnel (1330 yds)
115.75
116.55
118.09 (Plumtree)
119.65
120.00
Arrestor Bed
120.05
120.52 (Edwalton)
OLD DALBY TEST CENTRE
(Leased by LUL operated by Serco Ltd.)
Miles from St. Pancras via Corby

WIRKSWORTH BRANCH Ecclesbourne Valley Railway (Wyvern Rail plc)

[LN 3243] DJW

(Hazelwood) 134.77
SHOTTLE 136.43
IDRIDGEHAY 138.05
Engrs
LC 138.08
Gorsey Bank 140.79
WIRKSWORTH 141.34
GF 141.28
141.39
pit
Incline
RAVENSTOR 142.04
∞ = Derailer
✱ = Dust Dock

a = North GF
b = South GF
Duffield Tunnel (52 yds)
133.20-22
133.03 Branch Platform
DOWN
UP DN

DEX
former Derby Friargate Line overbridge 129.22

Controlled by Derby PSB (DY)
LMS : Mid : North Mid
SPC 8 [LN 3201]
DERBY and LEEDS LINE

Nottingham Road Viaduct 128.40-43
St Mary's South Jn 128.53
129.17
129.06
129.35
128.49 (Nottingham Road)
St Mary's North Jn 129.00
DOWN REC
DOWN MAIN
UP MAIN
DOWN GOODS
UP GOODS

Breadsall 130.58
Little Eaton Jn 131.06
DM
UM
UP DENBY GOODS
Burley Viaduct (River Derwent) 131.54-58
Duffield Jn 132.79
132.63 Duffield Jn HABD
133.08 DUFFIELD
Little Eaton Station (TMO) 131.35
Village (TMO) 131.51
DENBY GDS
UP (OOU) DOWN
133.01 (Coxbench)
133.03 Coxbench (TMO)
133.23 Holbrook (TMO)
A38 134.71
(Kilburn)
134.33-37
Kilburn (TMO) 134.75
Denby North Park Lane (TMO) 135.46
(Denby) 135.56
Denby Street Lane (TMO) 135.59
135.73
135.58 NR Boundary
former Denby Disposal Point

LED [LN 3240]
LMS : Mid : Ripley Branch
Gates fixed open on all crossings

Swainsley Viaduct (River Derwent) 134.57-61
[LN 3201] SPC 8
River Derwent / Broadholme Vdcts 136.11-18 136.41-47
DPL
Ambergate South Jn 137.61
133.67
134.25 Milford Tunnel (855 yards)
Belper GSP 134.61
Belper : Engrs
BELPER 135.55
Belper Rd
Broadholme 136.48
138.07-12 Toadmoor Tnl (129 yards)
Ambergate North Jn
River Derwent Viaducts 137.70-75/137.71-76
River Amber 138.23
AMBERGATE 138.18
138.35
DOWN MAIN
UP MAIN
UPL

WHATSTANDWELL (UWC) 140.13
140.06
140.51
140.19-26 Whatstandwell Tunnel (149 yds)
High Peak Bridge 141.33
RD*
141.42-56 Lea Wood Tunnel (315 yards)
Lea Wood Bridge 141.58
C*
CROMFORD 143.10
Willersley Tunnel (764 yards) 143.13-48
MATLOCK BATH 143.73
High Tor Tunnels
1* 1A* 2* H*
MATLOCK 145.00 (Platform 2 : Peak Rail)
145.03 Matlock GF
1 AJM
LMS : Mid [LN 3246]
cablecar line
144.60 Boathouse Bridge Road
AMBERGATE and ROWSLEY LINE

Miles from St Pancras via Leicester & Chaddesden (129 130 131 132 133 134 135 136 137 138 139 140 141)
Miles from St Pancras via Leicester & Chaddesden (142 143 144 145)

RD* = River Derwent Viaduct 140.51
C* = Cromford Viaduct 143.03-06
1* = High Tor No. 1 Tunnel (321 yards) 144.06-21
1A* = High Tor No. 1A Tunnel (58 yards) 144.21-24
2* = High Tor No. 2 Tunnel (378 yards) 144.24-41
H* = Holt Lane Tunnel (126 yards) 144.65-70

139.47
139.59
Wingfield Tunnel (261 yards)
140.40 River Amber
141.11 (Wingfield)
Derby PSB (DY)
EMCC (DC)
Miles from St Pancras via Leicester & Chaddesden (141 142 143 144 145 146 147)
[LN 3201] SPC 8 LMS : Mid : North Midland
DERBY and LEEDS LINE
145.31 (Stretton)
DN MAIN
UP MAIN
146.21
Clay Cross Tunnel (1 mile, 24 yards)
147.22
former Clay Cross South Jn
[147.69] 8
SPC 9 [LN 3201]
[LN 3207] TCC
142.10
DCCL = DOWN CLAY CROSS LOOP

Controlled by East Midlands CC (DC)(TC)
Main Lines (DC) - Erewash Lines (TC)

GOLDEN VALLEY LIGHT RAILWAY 2' 0" gauge
Newlands Inn 0.64
LC
0.19
Brands Crossing 0.10
Butterley Park 0.03 0.00
Brands Siding 0.17
LC's
H
Diesel Shed
Engrs
Matthew Kirtley Museum, with loco running & repair shop
Richard Levick Workshop
Butterley Works Branch
'West Shed'
Historic carriage & wagon repairs
Carriage Shed
LC's
135.05
*a
*b
*c
BUTTERLEY 135.57
HAMMERSMITH 136.04
S & T Depot
SOUTH LINE
NORTH LINE
RR
136.11
causeway (Butterley Reservoir) 135.63-74
134.76
0.00
0.22 Swanwick Branch
SWANWICK JN 134.78
MIDLAND RAILWAY-BUTTERLEY
Midland Railway Trust Ltd

*a former Kettering SB
*b former Ais Gill SB
*c former Kilby Bridge SB

LMS : Mid TCC [LN 3207]
EREWASH VALLEY LINE
LANGLEY MILL 129.68
DOWN EREWASH FAST
UP EREWASH FAST
UP & DN EREWASH SLOW
Langley Mill HABD 129.27
1 = CR
2 = RR
3 = Loading Line
Codnor Park Sdgs (OOU) (former Forge & Monument Open Cast)
(Codnor Park & Ironville) 132.46
Cromford Canal 132.67
Codnor Park Jn 132.76
LMS : Mid TCC APB CPC
APB APB CPC
Ironville Jn (old)
133.21
Ironville GF 133.20
133.04
CPC
Riddings 0.22
Ironville Jn (new) 133.18
133.38 (Pye Bridge)
133.67 (Pye Bridge Jn)
(TC) (PK) (Slow Line)
Miles from St Pancras via Leicester & Toton (130 131 132)

ALFRETON 136.07
135.11
135.50 Alfreton Tunnel (840 yards)
136.27 BLACKWELL SDG
Blackwell South Jn 136.67
(Westhouses & Blackwell) 137.09
137.16 (former Tibshelf & Blackwell Branch Jn)
(Doe Hill) 138.51
400 ft
DOWN EREWASH
UP EREWASH
UP & DN BLACKWELL SLOW
Morton Jn 139.09
LMS : Mid
[LN 3207] TCC **EREWASH VALLEY LINE**
Coney Green Jn 141.24
147.43
DCCL
147.69
142.64
143.12
(Clay Cross South Jn)
Clay Cross North Jn 142.77
144.15 (Hasland)
(Horns Bridge) 144.68
(former LMR/ER Regional Bdy)
DOWN MAIN
UP MAIN
DOWN EREWASH
UP EREWASH
DERBY and LEEDS LINE (North Midland)

Controlled by East Midlands CC (KS)(MS)(PK)(TC) (located at Derby)

LMS : Mid [LN 3273]
Pye Bridge & Kirkby PBS 1
PINXTON BRANCH
(Pinxton & Selston) 135.42
Sleights (CCTV) 134.76
Pinxton (CCTV) 135.46
UP KIRKBY
DOWN KIRKBY
M1 135.63
Lower Portland Farm (UWC) 136.29
Upper Portland Farm (UWC) 136.71
Upper Portland (AHBC) 136.71

"ROBIN HOOD LINE"
RAC [LN 3255] NR/LNE : GC/GN
134.20 NEWSTEAD
NEWSTD LP
DN & UP MANSFIELD
135.00
134.30 Newstead (AHBC)
134.68 Stockyard (UWC)
135.31 Warren House (MWL)
135.75
135.49-57 Kirkby Tunnel (198 yds)
(MS) (KS)
Grives Lane (AHBC)
Kirkby South Jn 138
DN MFLD
UP MFLD
136.04
136.66
KIRKBY-IN-ASHFIELD 138.38
136
UP KIRKBY
DN KIRKBY
Kirkby Lane End Jn 138.31
(PK) (KS)
137.67 Sowters (UWC)
SUTTON PARKWAY 137.60
Kirkby Summit Crossover COM
138.79 137.11
1 PBS 2 [LN 3273]
✱ former Kirkby Jn 138.50 via Pinxton, 136.55 via Newstead and former Midland Line
Sutton Jn (CCTV) 138.23
Sutton Forest (AHBC) 138.50
Kings Mill No. 1 (BW) 139.22
DN MANSFIELD
UP MANSFIELD
139.33-38 Break Hills Hermitage Mill Viaduct
MANSFIELD 140.44
Mansfield Viaduct 140.52-65
140.40
2 PBS 3
[LN 3273] South Mansfield Stn
(NOTTINGHAM and MANSFIELD) [LN 3273] 3 PBS PSE [LN 768] (MANSFIELD and WORKSOP)
LMS : Mid
MANSFIELD WOODHOUSE 142.17
142.05
142.13
Mansfield Woodhouse Jn
McKenzies (UWC) 142.79
EM LNE
143.40
143.43-47 Littlewood Viaduct
(KS) (SJ)
"ROBIN HOOD LINE"
SHIREBROOK 145.06
DRS
DOWN MAIN
UP MAIN
144.69
145.10
145.11
144.64-65 Sheepwash Viaduct
145.14 Shirebrook Jn (SJ)
W H Davis Wagon Works
Shirebrook East Jn 145.62
(SJ) (EC)
LANGWITH-WHALEY THORNS 147.14
Norwood (MCG) 147.71
Elmton & Creswell Jn SB (EC)149.37
CRESWELL 149.26
WHITWELL 150.56
150.03-28 Whitwell Tunnel (544 yds)
2 : 30A
Miles from St Pancras via Leicester & Toton (135 136 137 138 139 140 141 142 143 144 145)
Miles from St Pancras via Corby & Newstead and former Midland Line (135 136 138 139 140 141 142 143 144 145 146 147 148 149 150)

4B : to Derby
7A : to Toton
6D : to Hucknall & Nottingham
7D : to Rowsley South (Peak Rail)
2 : 28E : to Chesterfield
2 : 30A : to Worksop

August 2013

A

Controlled by East Midlands CC (located at Derby)

(SS) (ST) (TC) (TD) (TN)

EREWASH VALLEY LINE

7A : to Toton Yard & Trowell Jn

4B : to Derby

6C

4A : to Loughborough

Long Eaton Jn 120.64

Long Eaton Town (CCTV) 120.53

North Erewash (CCTV) 120.36

Trent East Jns 119.70

Sheet Stores Jn (Trent W. Jn) 119.58

[LN 3228] TES COM 0.30 0.00 119.56

SPC 6 [LN 3207]

TOC [LN 3207] THL [LN 3261]

THL [LN 3261]

TSN 1 [LN 3207]

THL [LN 3261]

119.16

119.17 Trent South Jn

120.06 119.75 120.20 120.01 (Trent PSB)

120.55

Meadow Lane Jn 0.00

[LN 3264] AML

Meadow Lane (CCTV) 120.31

0.62 Barton Lane (AHBC-X) 121.36

Attenborough (CCTV) 121.70

ATTENBOROUGH 121.76

121.02 Attenborough Jn

Nature Reserve (BW) 122.46

BEESTON 123.22

Beeston Down Sdgs

Beeston South Jn 123.62

J. McIntyre (Sims Metal Mgmnt)

N. = NOTTINGHAM
UAC = UP ATTENBOROUGH CURVE
DAC = DN ATTENBOROUGH CURVE

TSN 1 [LN 3204]

a = DN TRENT PASS. LOOP
b = DN NOTTINGHAM
c = DUPNOTTINGHAM

LMS : Mid

DERBY and NOTTINGHAM LINE

Controlled by East Midlands CC (TN)

Miles from St. Pancras *via Leicester and Trent*

Miles from St. Pancras *via Corby*

7A : to Trowell Sth Jn

Moor Farm 128.72

RADFORD and TROWELL LINE

UP TROWELL / DOWN TROWELL

6D

Radford Jn 125.55

[LN 3253] RAC

[LN 3252] 2 MJT 1

–125 124.66

Lenton North Jn 124.56

LMS : Mid

NOTTINGHAM and MANSFIELD LINE

[LN 3249] LSN

[LN 3252] MJT 1

0.27 0.00

Lenton South Jn 125.27

125.64 124.22 124.15

Mansfield Jn (mileage meet)

1 TSN 2 [LN 3204] LMS : Mid

* (from St. Pancras via Corby and Plumtree)

A LINE / B LINE / C LINE / D LINE

Nottingham West Jn 123.52

NOTTINGHAM 123.39 (TN) (NN)

COM 123.23 0.00

LMS : Mid [LN 3204] 2 TSN NOB 1 [LN 3625] LMS : Mid

DERBY and NOTTINGHAM LINE | NOTTINGHAM and LINCOLN LINE

Nottingham East Jn 123.27

EASTCROFT DOWN SDG 0.22

Sneinton FP (MCB) 0.35

Nottingham TMD (NM) East Midlands Trains

Eastcroft Depot : Engrs

Trent Lane FP (R/G) 0.56

6B

Gregory Boulevard

The Forest (*Park & Ride*)

High School

Nottingham Trent University

Royal Centre

Old Market Square

Lace Market

Broadmarsh (proposed)

Station St

NOTTINGHAM EXPRESS TRANSIT (NET) 750dc Line 1

NOTTINGHAM Platforms	
1	15
2	4
3	14
4	5
5	7
6	14
7	13

a = Carrington Street overbridge 123.48
b = NET overbridge (former GCR alignment) 123.43 (see 6E)

Controlled by East Midlands CC (NN) (located at Derby)

(Ø former London Road Jn 123.18)

B

LMS : Mid NOB 1 [LN 3625]

[LN 3625] NOB 1 LMS : Mid

NOTTINGHAM and LINCOLN LINE

Controlled by East Midlands CC (NN)

6A

Colwick (CCTV) 1.04

Netherfield (Mid) Jn 2.35

Netherfield HABD 2.26

CARLTON 2.78

BR 26 formerly DEX to Gedling Colliery

BR [LN 3635] 2 NOG 1 COM LNE : GN

2.54 125.25

NETHERFIELD 125.13

Netherfield Jn 125.08 (Colwick West Jn)

Stoke Lane (AHBC-X) 3.54

Zulus (UWC) 4.16

5.00 (AHBC-X) Trent Gardens (UWC) 5.38

Bulcote (AHBC-X) 6.10

BURTON JOYCE 4.77

Colwick Oil Depot (OOU) Total

DERBYSHIRE EXTENSION BRANCH (LNE : GN)

DEX

Branch Sdgs Rectory Jn 123.72

Radcliffe Viaduct 123.71-53

Up Sdg

123.66

Trent Fields Vdct 0.10 0.18

formerly CCB 1 to Cotgrave Colliery

LOWDHAM 7.31

Lowdham 7.27

Club Gardens (BW) 7.54

Gonalston (AHBC) 8.31

THURGARTON 9.43

Plot (UWC) 10.00

BLEASBY 10.55

Marriots (UWC) 10.47

Gorsey Lane (UWC) 11.36

Morton (MCG)

Fiskerton Jn 12.03

FISKERTON 12.46

Fiskerton Stn (MCG) 12.43

(MGH) 13.08

ROLLESTON 13.13

Rolleston Mill (UWC) 13.24

Brettles (UWC) 13.67

Arnolds Flood Bridge 14.49-51

Weightmans Viaduct 15.04-06

15.43-46

15.53-55 Flood openings

Old Trent Dyke Vdct 15.79-16.02

14.20 Staythorpe Crossing

15.21-35 Averham Weir Viaduct

Staythorpe Crossing

Newark Castle 16.02 EM | LNE

2 : 27D : to Newark Castle

2 : 25B : to Grantham & Sleaford

RADCLIFFE (Notts) 123.08

Bingham Road (UWC) 122.57

NOTTINGHAM BRANCH (GN)

[LN 3635] NOG 1 LNE : GN

Saxondale (UWC) 120.71

BINGHAM 119.39

Bingham (BM) 119.57

(GN) (BM) 121.15

Cogley Lane (UWC) 119.08

Scarrington Lane (19) (AHBC-X) 117.73

(17) (AHBC-X) 117.20

ASLOCKTON 117.22

ELTON & ORSTON 115.34

Orston Lane (11) (MCBR) 114.16

Normanton (10) (AHBC-X) 113.10

Bottesford (UWC) (9) 112.75

Taylors (UWC) 111.72

Bottesford West Jn (BW) 113.78

BOTTESFORD 112.68

111.60 Allington Jn

UP GRANTHAM / DOWN GRANTHAM

Miles from Kings Cross

C

Miles from St. Pancras *via Leicester*

25C : to Peartree & Derby

25C : to N. Stafford Jn & Burton-on-Trent

4.50 4.58 Stenson Jn

132.12

UP CHELLASTON / DOWN CHELLASTON

[LN 3520] 2 SSJ MJS 1 SSJ 1

127.70 127.27

(Chellaston W. Jn) LMS : Mid 'Stenson & Weston' | (Chellaston E. Jn) LMS : Mid 'Sawley & Weston'

LMS:Mid 'Derby and Melbourne'

(Weston on Trent) 126.19

Derby PSB (DY) | EMCC (SS) 125.00

Cottons (UWC) 125.28

Flood arches 124.66-62

R. Trent Vdct 124.57-50

Flood arches 124.49-47

Elliots (UWC) 124.44

Castle Donington 123.28

123.33

M1

121.70

Whites (UWC) 121.35

River Trent Viaduct

Flood arches

120.68-65

120.60-55

Grammers (UWC) 120.44

Lock Lane Crossing (CCTV) 120.29

4A

D

RAC [LN 3255]

LMS : Mid : Nottingham & Mansfield

"ROBIN HOOD LINE"

5 : to Kirkby-in-Ashfield

NEWSTEAD 134.20

former GC over 132.76

Linby Station (ABCL) 132.70

Linby Colliery (ABCL) 132.24

(Linby) 132.69

Moss & Plums (FP) 132.00

Hucknall (*Park & Ride*)

HUCKNALL 131.65

Brickyard & Lane (private) (ABCL) 131.21

Hucknall No. 3 (UWC) 131.11

Hucknall No. 4 (UWC) 131.04

Butler's Hill

Moor Bridge (*Park & Ride*)

DOWN & UP MANSFIELD

Bestwood Park Jn 130.20

Miles from St Pancras via Corby

Bulwell Forest

129.52

129.42 former GC Viaduct over

Bulwell Forest Crossing (CCTV) 129.35

NR Controlled by East Midlands CC (MS)

Phoenix Park (*Park & Ride*)

Cinderhill

Bulwell

Highbury Vale

BULWELL 128.76

Bulwell South Jn 128.65

128.23 (former GC branch to Derby over)

128.14 Basford Chemicals (UWC)

David Lane

Basford

Lincoln St (CCTV) 127.60

River Leen 127.07

127.36 (Basford)

Wilkinson St Overbridge 126.65

Wilkinson St (see inset) (*Park & Ride*) & Depot

Radford Jn 125.55

Radford Rd

Shipstone St

Hyson Grn Market

Beaconsfield St

Noel St

6A

[LN 3255] RAC

LMS : Mid : Nottingham & Mansfield

NOTTINGHAM EXPRESS TRANSIT (NET) 750dc Line 1

Alongside Network Rail 126.65-131.65

E

future NET Phase 2 at Nottingham Station for Lines 2 & 3 for, completion 2014

Broadmarsh (proposed)

(former Nottingham Station Street)

Lace Market

Carrington Street Bridge

Nottingham Station

Line 3 to Toton Lane Park & Ride

Line 2 to Clifton

WILKINSON STREET TRAM DEPOT AND CONTROL ROOM (NET)

CW

Sanding

Wheel Lathe

Car Park

LC

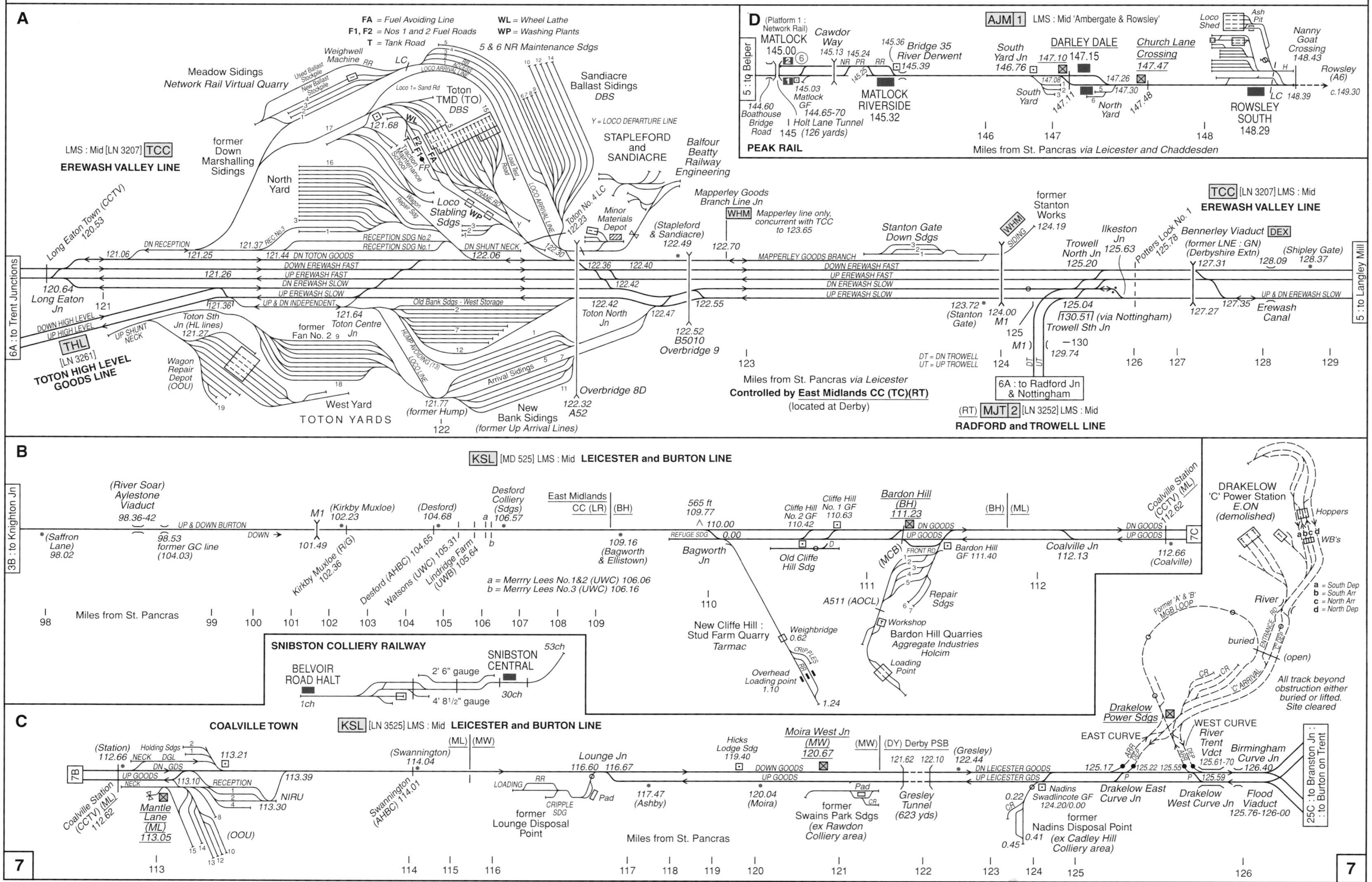

A

FA = Fuel Avoiding Line
F1, F2 = Nos 1 and 2 Fuel Roads
T = Tank Road
WL = Wheel Lathe
WP = Washing Plants
5 & 6 NR Maintenance Sdgs

LMS : Mid [LN 3207] TCC
EREWASH VALLEY LINE

Meadow Sidings
Network Rail Virtual Quarry
Used Ballast Stockpile
New Ballast Stockpile
Weighwell Machine RR
LC
LOCO ARRIVAL LINE
Loco 1= Sand Rd
Toton TMD (TO) DBS
121.68
Traction Maintenance School
Load Test Road
CRANE RD
Sandiacre Ballast Sidings DBS
Y = LOCO DEPARTURE LINE
STAPLEFORD and SANDIACRE
Balfour Beatty Railway Engineering
former Down Marshalling Sidings
North Yard
Wagon Repair Sdg
Loco Stabling Sdgs
Toton No. 4 LC 122.23
Minor Materials Depot
(Stapleford & Sandiacre) 122.49
Mapperley Goods Branch Line Jn
WHM Mapperley line only, concurrent with TCC to 123.65
122.70
Long Eaton Town (CCTV) 120.53
121.06 DN RECEPTION 121.25
121.37 REC No.3
121.44 DN TOTON GOODS
RECEPTION SDG No.2
RECEPTION SDG No.1
DN SHUNT NECK 122.06
122.30
DOWN EREWASH FAST
UP EREWASH FAST
DN EREWASH SLOW
UP EREWASH SLOW
UP & DN INDEPENDENT
121.26
121.36
120.64 Long Eaton Jn
121
6A : to Trent Junctions
DOWN HIGH LEVEL
UP HIGH LEVEL
UP SHUNT NECK
THL [LN 3261]
TOTON HIGH LEVEL GOODS LINE
Toton Sth Jn (HL lines) 121.27
Wagon Repair Depot (OOU)
former Fan No. 2
121.64 Toton Centre Jn
Old Bank Sdgs - West Storage
HUMP AVOIDING (13)
LOCO LINE
Arrival Sidings
West Yard
TOTON YARDS
121.77 (former Hump)
122
New Bank Sidings (former Up Arrival Lines)
122.32 A52
Overbridge 8D
122.36 122.40
122.42
122.42 Toton North Jn
122.47
122.52 B5010 Overbridge 9
122.55
123
MAPPERLEY GOODS BRANCH
Stanton Gate Down Sdgs
WHM SIDING
former Stanton Works 124.19
123.72 (Stanton Gate)
124.00 M1
124
125
M1
DT = DN TROWELL
UT = UP TROWELL
Trowell North Jn 125.20
Ilkeston Jn 125.63
125.04
130.51 (via Nottingham)
Trowell Sth Jn
—130
129.74
126
Potters Lock No. 1 125.78
TCC [LN 3207] LMS : Mid
EREWASH VALLEY LINE
Bennerley Viaduct DEX
(former LNE : GN) (Derbyshire Extn)
127.31
127.27
127
128.09
(Shipley Gate) 128.37
127.35
UP & DN EREWASH SLOW
Erewash Canal
128
129
5 : to Langley Mill
Miles from St. Pancras via Leicester
Controlled by East Midlands CC (TC)(RT)
(located at Derby)
6A : to Radford Jn & Nottingham
(RT) MJT 2 [LN 3252] LMS : Mid
RADFORD and TROWELL LINE

D

AJM 1 LMS : Mid 'Ambergate & Rowsley'
5 : to Belper
(Platform 1 : Network Rail)
MATLOCK 145.00 ⑥
144.60 Boathouse Bridge Road
145.03 Matlock GF
144.65-70 Holt Lane Tunnel 145 (126 yards)
Cawdor Way 145.13
145.24 NR PR
145.25
145.36 Bridge 35 River Derwent 145.39
RR
MATLOCK RIVERSIDE 145.32
South Yard Jn 146.76
South Yard
146
147.08
147.10 147.15
147.11
DARLEY DALE
147
147.26 147.30
North Yard
Church Lane Crossing 147.47
147.48
148
Loco Shed
Ash Pit
Nanny Goat Crossing 148.43
H
LC 148.39
ROWSLEY SOUTH 148.29
Rowsley (A6) c.149.30
PEAK RAIL
Miles from St. Pancras via Leicester and Chaddesden

B

KSL [MD 525] LMS : Mid **LEICESTER and BURTON LINE**

3B : to Knighton Jn
(Saffron Lane) 98.02
(River Soar) Aylestone Viaduct 98.36-42
UP & DOWN BURTON
98.53 former GC line (104.03)
DOWN →
M1 101.49
(Kirkby Muxloe) 102.23
Kirkby Muxloe (R/G) 102.36
(Desford) 104.68
Desford (AHBC) 104.65
Watsons (UWC) 105.31
Lindridge Farm (UWB) 105.64
Desford Colliery (Sdgs) 106.57
a b
a = Merrry Lees No.1&2 (UWC) 106.06
b = Merrry Lees No.3 (UWC) 106.16
East Midlands CC (LR) | (BH)
109.16 (Bagworth & Ellistown)
565 ft 109.77
^ 110.00
REFUGE SDG 0.00
Bagworth Jn
New Cliffe Hill : Stud Farm Quarry Tarmac
Weighbridge 0.62
CRIPPLES
RR
Overhead Loading point 1.10
1.24
Cliffe Hill No. 2 GF 110.42
Cliffe Hill No. 1 GF 110.63
D
Old Cliffe Hill Sdg
Bardon Hill (BH) 111.23
DN GOODS
UP GOODS
FRONT RD
(MCB)
Bardon Hill GF 111.40
A511 (AOCL)
Repair Sdgs
Workshop
Bardon Hill Quarries Aggregate Industries Holcim
Loading Point
(BH) | (ML)
Coalville Jn 112.13
Coalville Station (CCTV) (ML) 112.62
112.66 (Coalville)
7C
Miles from St. Pancras
98 99 100 101 102 103 104 105 106 107 108 109 110 111 112

DRAKELOW 'C' Power Station E.ON (demolished)
Hoppers
WB's
a = South Dep
b = South Arr
c = North Arr
d = North Dep
River
ENTRANCE RD
DEP
(open)
buried
Former 'A' & 'B' MGB LOOP
CR
'C' ARRIVAL
All track beyond obstruction either buried or lifted. Site cleared

SNIBSTON COLLIERY RAILWAY
BELVOIR ROAD HALT 1ch
2' 6" gauge
4' 8½" gauge
SNIBSTON CENTRAL 30ch
53ch

C

COALVILLE TOWN
KSL [LN 3525] LMS : Mid **LEICESTER and BURTON LINE**
7B
(Station) 112.66
Holding Sdgs NECK DGL
DN GDS
UP GOODS
NECK
113.21
113.10 RECEPTION
113.39
NIRU 113.30
Coalville Station (CCTV) (ML) 112.62
Mantle Lane (ML) 113.05
(OOU)
(Swannington) 114.04
Swannington (AHBC) 114.01
(ML) | (MW)
LOADING RR
CRIPPLE SDG
former Lounge Disposal Point
Lounge Jn 116.60 116.67
Pad
117.47 (Ashby)
Hicks Lodge Sdg 119.40
DOWN GOODS
UP GOODS
120.04 (Moira)
Moira West Jn (MW) 120.67
(MW) | (DY) Derby PSB
121.62 122.10
Pad
CR
former Swains Park Sdgs (ex Rawdon Colliery area)
Gresley Tunnel (623 yds)
(Gresley) 122.44
DN LEICESTER GOODS
UP LEICESTER GDS
0.22 CR
Nadins Swadlincote GF 124.20/0.00
0.45
0.41
former Nadins Disposal Point (ex Cadley Hill Colliery area)
EAST CURVE
Drakelow Power Sdgs
ARR DEP
125.17
P
125.22 125.55
Drakelow East Curve Jn
WEST CURVE
River Trent Vdct 125.61-70
DEP ARR
125.59
Drakelow West Curve Jn
Birmingham Curve Jn 126.40
Flood Viaduct 125.76-126.00
25C : to Branston Jn : to Burton on Trent
Miles from St. Pancras
113 114 115 116 117 118 119 120 121 122 123 124 125 126

August 2013

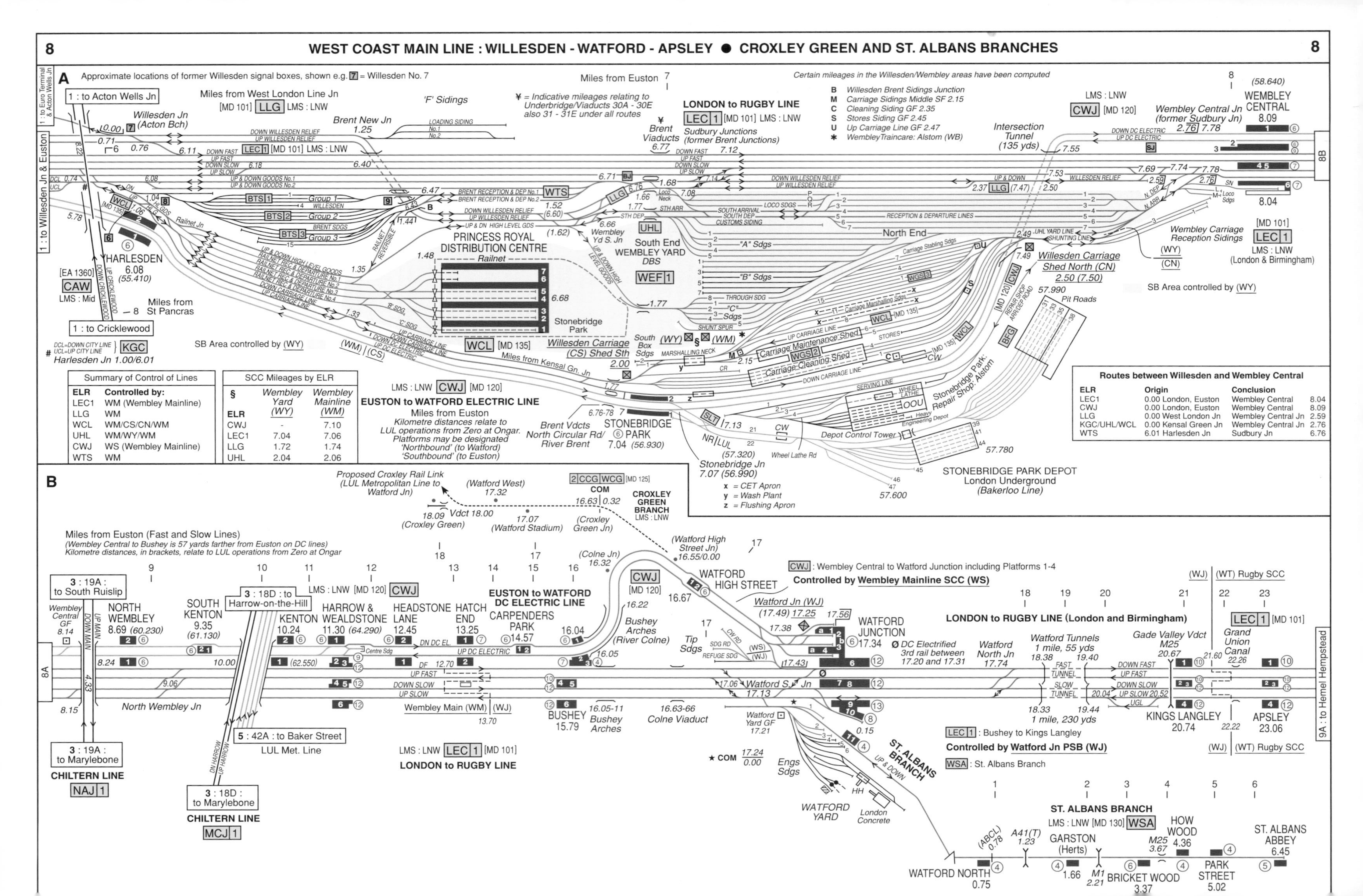

Summary of Control of Lines

ELR	Controlled by:
LEC1	WM (Wembley Mainline)
LLG	WM
WCL	WM/CS/CN/WM
UHL	WM/WY/WM
CWJ	WS (Wembley Mainline)
WTS	WM

SCC Mileages by ELR

§ ELR	Wembley Yard (WY)	Wembley Mainline (WM)
CWJ	-	7.10
LEC1	7.04	7.06
LLG	1.72	1.74
UHL	2.04	2.06

Routes between Willesden and Wembley Central

ELR	Origin	Conclusion	
LEC1	0.00 London, Euston	Wembley Central	8.04
CWJ	0.00 London, Euston	Wembley Central	8.09
LLG	0.00 West London Jn	Wembley Central Jn	2.59
KGC/UHL/WCL	0.00 Kensal Green Jn	Wembley Central Jn	2.76
WTS	6.01 Harlesden Jn	Sudbury Jn	6.76

WEST COAST MAIN LINE : HEMEL HEMPSTEAD - WOLVERTON ● BLETCHLEY - (BEDFORD)

A

Miles from Euston: 24, 25, 26, 27, 28, 29, 30, 31, 32, 33, 34, 35, 36, 37, 38, 39, 40, 41, 42, 43, 44

[MD 101] LEC 1 LMS : LNW **LONDON to RUGBY LINE (London & Birmingham)**

8B : to Watford Jn

HEMEL HEMPSTEAD (12) 24.39
24.14
BACK RD
Boxmoor Sdgs
Bourne End Jn 25.40
25.22
25.64
25.21 Grand Union Canal
BERKHAMSTED (12) 27.75
FAST LINES
28.76
DS
US
29.12
Northchurch Tunnels (349 yds)
30.07 Northchurch HABD
400 ft
Rugby SCC (WT) | (TK)
Tring South Jn
TRING 31.50
31.30
RELIEF
H
Tring Sdgs
Tring North Jn 32.00
Platforms: 1 (13); 2 (12); 3-5 (13)
DOWN FAST
UP FAST
DOWN SLOW
UP SLOW
Grand Union Canal 34.53
34.60 Cheddington Wheel Chex
CHEDDINGTON (12) 36.08
Ledburn Jn 37.35
37.15
37.58
LEIGHTON BUZZARD (12) 40.14
40.60
DF
40.73
MIDDLE
US
Linslade Tunnels (287 yards) (down fast 283 yds)
Stoke Hammond HABD's 42.68
9B

Controlled by Rugby SCC (WT)

Controlled by Rugby SCC (TK)

B

3 : 13A : to Oxford

1.31
Line closed from gate to 11.79 (future East/West link)
1.27
End of Line (Miles from Bletchley)
1.23
[MD 735] OXD
OXFORD BRANCH
LMS : LNW
Swanbourne Sidings
1
0.76
Bletchley Flyover Jn 0.66
OXD 0.64
COM
0.00 BFO
DOWN BLETCHLEY
UP BLETCHLEY
BR BFO [MD 735]
0.36

Platforms: 1 (12); 2 (12); 3 (12); 4 (13); 5 (13); 6 (6)

45, 46, 47, 48, 49, 50, 51, 52, 53, 54, 55

Drayton Road Jn 45.46
9A
DF
UF
DS
US
Water Eaton Road Jn 46.25
LEC 1 BBM 46.46 0.00 COM
0.53
BLETCHLEY 46.54/0.04
Bletchley South Jn 46.41
Bletchley North Jn 46.62
NECK
Hopper Sdgs
RMC Discharge Point
BLT 3
DN VALE
UP VALE
BLT 1
Bletchley East Jn 0.12
Carriage Sdgs
BCS
Up Yard
CW
Freight Sdgs
ARRIVAL LINE
DBS
Miles from Euston
LEC 1 [MD 101]
DOWN FAST
UP FAST
DOWN SLOW
UP SLOW
BLETCHLEY RELIEF 1
BLETCHLEY RELIEF 2
DOWN BLETCHLEY
UP BLETCHLEY
1.37
DHF [MD 735]
(MV) (TK)
1.00
0.23
Top Yard
BBM
S&T
Summit of Flyover Jn 0.68
BR BFO [MD 740]
0.66
DOWN BLETCHLEY CHORD
UP BLETCHLEY CHORD
VALE REFUGE SIDING
UP VALE
DOWN VALE
(TK) (MV)
0.40
Vale Sdgs
Civil Engrs'
Bletchley TMD (BY)
BLT 2
Refuelling Road
EMU Stabling
Bletchley Yard
1.23
Flyover Single Line Jn
0.49
9C
= Single Line Jn
✱ = Up & Dn Bletchley Chord
✱ = Up & Dn Vale

Controlled by Marston Vale SCC (MV)

A5(T) 47.72
Denbigh Hall North Jn (48.48)
48.31
48.53
Knowhill Jn 48.75
49.26
49.53
MILTON KEYNES CENTRAL 49.65
#MKRF
#MKRS
SBK
Milton Keynes South Jn 49.43
(TK) (KR)
Milton Keynes North Jn 50.10
Denbigh Hall South Jn 47.52/1.73
Bletchley Flyover North Jn 1.59/47.40
LONDON to RUGBY LINE (London & Birmingham)
LMS : LNW
Controlled by Rugby SCC (TK) (KR)

Platforms: 1 (12); 2 (15); 2a (6); 3 (15); 4 (15); 5 (15); 6 (15)

# Line names:
MKRF = Milton Keynes Reversible Fast
MKRS = Milton Keynes Reversible Slow

INCLINE SDG
51.60
51.66
Wolverton Deviation 51.40 - 52.72 (35 Yards Longer)
CENTRE SDGS
WOW 1
B = Back of the wall
"UNDER THE BOARDS"
Church Street (TMO)
WOLVERTON 52.33 (12)
52.18
52.40-52.42
Grand Union Canal
(Royal Train Shed)
52.72-53.01 Wolverton/Haversham Viaduct
Castlethorpe 54.60
10A : to Northampton

WOLVERTON WORKS (ZN)
Railcare Ltd
(Not Verified)
Wheel Shop
Lifting Shop
WKS 2
(OOU)
(OOU)
(OOU)
Haversham Sdgs
WKS 1

D

LEIGHTON BUZZARD RAILWAY
2' 0" gauge

PAGE'S PARK 0.00
Loco. & Carriage shed
Western Avenue
Stanbridge Road
Leedon Loop 1.10
Hockliffe Road
Appenine Way
Fifty Penny Curve
Vandyke Road
(VANDYKE ROAD HALT) 2.08
Shenley Hill Road
Redlands
Stonehenge
STONEHENGE WORKS
Works
Shed
Mundays Hill
3.00

C

Miles from Bletchley: 1, 2, 3, 4, 5, 6, 7, 8, 9, 10, 11, 12, 13

BEDFORD BRANCH "MARSTON VALE LINE" LMS : LNW BBM [MD 140]

Controlled by Marston Vale SCC (MV)

A = Grand Union Canal
B = A5(T)

9B
Fenny Stratford Jn
0.76
1.48
1.19
U&D VALE
1.36
1.42
(CCTV) 1.13
FENNY STRATFORD (4) 1.05
(CCTV)
BOW BRICKHILL (2) 2.05
Pony Crossing (UWC) 3.20
DM
UM
Woodleys Farm (UWC) 3.54
WOBURN SANDS (3) 4.08
(CCTV) 4.11
ASPLEY GUISE (2) 5.04
Berry Lane (UWW) 5.33
Marston Vale SCC (MV)
6.47 M1
RIDGMONT (3) 6.59
(CCTV) 6.61
LIDLINGTON (3) 8.49
(CCTV)
Marston (AHBC-X) 9.02
MILLBROOK (Beds) 10.05 (3)
(CCTV) 10.02
STEWARTBY 11.17 (2)
Green Lane (AHBC-X)
Stewartby Brickworks (CCTV) 11.33
Local Distribution Centre DBS
Forders Sidings
Maintenance
NBS
New Ballast Stockpile
Loading Dock Sdg
11.55
ARR&DEP
DN MAIN
UP MAIN
Shanks & McEwan Waste Disposal Terminal
CR
LC
SPUR
12.05
Wootton Broadmead (CCTV) 12.08
(AHBC-X) 12.77
DN BED
UP BED
KEMPSTON HARDWICK 12.76
2C : to Bedford

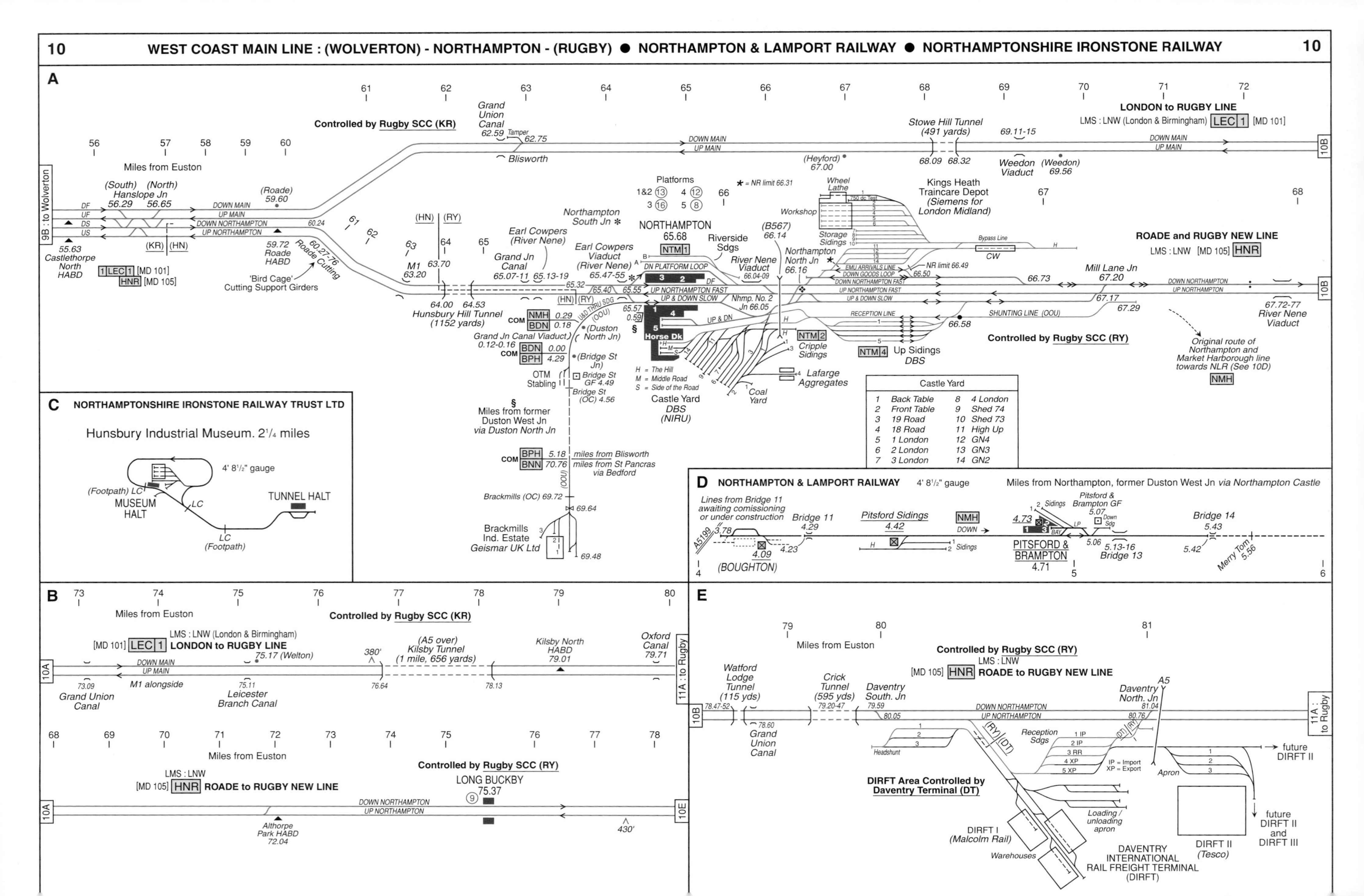
A
Controlled by Rugby SCC (KR)
LONDON to RUGBY LINE
LMS : LNW (London & Birmingham) LEC 1 [MD 101]
Miles from Euston
(South) (North)
Hanslope Jn
56.29 56.65
9B : to Wolverton
DF
UF
DS
US
DOWN MAIN
UP MAIN
DOWN NORTHAMPTON
UP NORTHAMPTON
55.63
Castlethorpe
North
HABD
1 LEC 1 [MD 101]
HNR [MD 105]
(KR) (HN)
(Roade)
59.60
60.24
59.72
Roade
HABD
60.27-76
Roade Cutting
'Bird Cage'
Cutting Support Girders
Grand
Union
Canal
62.59
Tamper
62.75
Blisworth
(Heyford)
67.00
Stowe Hill Tunnel
(491 yards)
68.09 68.32
69.11-15
Weedon
Viaduct
(Weedon)
69.56
10B
(HN) (RY)
M1 63.70
63.20
64.00 64.53
Hunsbury Hill Tunnel
(1152 yards)
Earl Cowpers
(River Nene)
Grand Jn
Canal
65.07-11 65.13-19
Earl Cowpers
Viaduct
(River Nene)
65.47-55
Northampton
South Jn *
65.32
65.40
65.55
Platforms
1&2 (13) 4 (12)
3 (16) 5 (8)
NORTHAMPTON
65.68
NTM 1
Riverside
Sdgs
* = NR limit 66.31
(B567)
66.14
River Nene
Viaduct
66.04-09
Northampton
North Jn
66.16
DN PLATFORM LOOP
UP NORTHAMPTON FAST
UP & DOWN SLOW
Nhmp. No. 2
Jn 66.05
UP & DN
UP & DN THRU SDG
(OOU)
65.57
0.59
Horse Dk
H = The Hill
M = Middle Road
S = Side of the Road
Castle Yard
DBS
(NIRU)
NTM 2
Cripple
Sidings
NTM 4
Up Sidings
DBS
Lafarge
Aggregates
Coal
Yard
COM NMH 0.29
BDN 0.18
(Duston
North Jn)
Grand Jn Canal Viaduct
0.12-0.16
COM BDN 0.00
BPH 4.29
(Bridge St
Jn)
OTM
Stabling
Bridge St
GF 4.49
Bridge St
(OC) 4.56
§
Miles from former
Duston West Jn
via Duston North Jn
COM BPH 5.18 miles from Blisworth
BNN 70.76 miles from St Pancras
via Bedford
(OOU)
Brackmills (OC) 69.72
69.64
69.48
Brackmills
Ind. Estate
Geismar UK Ltd
Wheel
Lathe
750 dc Test
Workshop
Storage
Sidings
Kings Heath
Traincare Depot
(Siemens for
London Midland)
Bypass Line
CW
EMU ARRIVALS LINE
DOWN GOODS LOOP
DOWN NORTHAMPTON FAST
UP NORTHAMPTON FAST
UP & DOWN SLOW
RECEPTION LINE
NR limit 66.49
66.50
66.73
SHUNTING LINE (OOU)
66.58
Mill Lane Jn
67.20
67.17
67.29
ROADE and RUGBY NEW LINE
LMS : LNW [MD 105] HNR
DOWN NORTHAMPTON
UP NORTHAMPTON
67.72-77
River Nene
Viaduct
Controlled by Rugby SCC (RY)
Original route of
Northampton and
Market Harborough line
towards NLR (See 10D)
NMH
Castle Yard
1 Back Table 8 4 London
2 Front Table 9 Shed 74
3 19 Road 10 Shed 73
4 18 Road 11 High Up
5 1 London 12 GN4
6 2 London 13 GN3
7 3 London 14 GN2
C NORTHAMPTONSHIRE IRONSTONE RAILWAY TRUST LTD
Hunsbury Industrial Museum. 2¼ miles
4' 8½" gauge
(Footpath) LC
MUSEUM
HALT
LC
LC
(Footpath)
TUNNEL HALT
D NORTHAMPTON & LAMPORT RAILWAY 4' 8½" gauge
Miles from Northampton, former Duston West Jn via Northampton Castle
Lines from Bridge 11
awaiting comissioning
or under construction
A5199
3.78
4.09
(BOUGHTON)
4.23
Bridge 11
4.29
Pitsford Sidings
4.42
H
Sidings
NMH
DOWN
4.73
Sidings
Pitsford &
Brampton GF
5.07
Down
Sdg
LP
BAY
PITSFORD &
BRAMPTON
4.71
5.06
5.13-16
Bridge 13
Bridge 14
5.43
5.42
Merry Tom
5.56
B
Miles from Euston
Controlled by Rugby SCC (KR)
LMS : LNW (London & Birmingham)
[MD 101] LEC 1 LONDON to RUGBY LINE
75.17 (Welton)
380'
(A5 over)
Kilsby Tunnel
(1 mile, 656 yards)
Kilsby North
HABD
79.01
Oxford
Canal
79.71
10A
DOWN MAIN
UP MAIN
11A : to Rugby
73.09
Grand Union
Canal
M1 alongside
75.11
Leicester
Branch Canal
76.64
78.13
Miles from Euston
LMS : LNW
[MD 105] HNR ROADE to RUGBY NEW LINE
Controlled by Rugby SCC (RY)
LONG BUCKBY
(9) 75.37
DOWN NORTHAMPTON
UP NORTHAMPTON
Althorpe
Park HABD
72.04
430'
10E
E
Miles from Euston
Controlled by Rugby SCC (RY)
LMS : LNW
[MD 105] HNR ROADE to RUGBY NEW LINE
Watford
Lodge
Tunnel
(115 yds)
78.47-52
78.60
Grand
Union
Canal
Crick
Tunnel
(595 yds)
79.20-47
Daventry
South. Jn
79.59
80.05
DOWN NORTHAMPTON
UP NORTHAMPTON
Daventry
North. Jn
81.04
80.76
A5
11A : to Rugby
Headshunt
Reception
Sdgs
1 IP
2 IP
3 RR
4 XP
5 XP
IP = Import
XP = Export
Apron
future
DIRFT II
future
DIRFT II
and
DIRFT III
DIRFT Area Controlled by
Daventry Terminal (DT)
Loading /
unloading
apron
DIRFT I
(Malcolm Rail)
Warehouses
DAVENTRY
INTERNATIONAL
RAIL FREIGHT TERMINAL
(DIRFT)
DIRFT II
(Tesco)

A

ELR and Line name changes, Hillmorton Jn and Rugby South Flyover

Ref	Mileage LEC1	Mileage HNR	Description
a	81.29		Change of line name; Dn Main to Dn Fast; Up Fast to Up Main
b	81.75	84.22	Change of ELR; Change of line name; Dn N/Hampton to Dn Coventry; Dn N/Hampton to Dn Slow
c	82.13	84.40	Change of ELR

ELR and Line name changes, Rugby Trent Valley Jn

Ref	Mileage LEC2	Description
d	83.18	Change of ELR, LEC1 to LEC2, conn. RBS1
e	83.19	Connection LEC2 to RTS
f	83.19	Change of line name; Up Trent Valley Fast to Up Fast; Up Coventry to Up N/Hampton
g	83.28	Change of line name; Dn Fast to Dn Trent Valley Fast

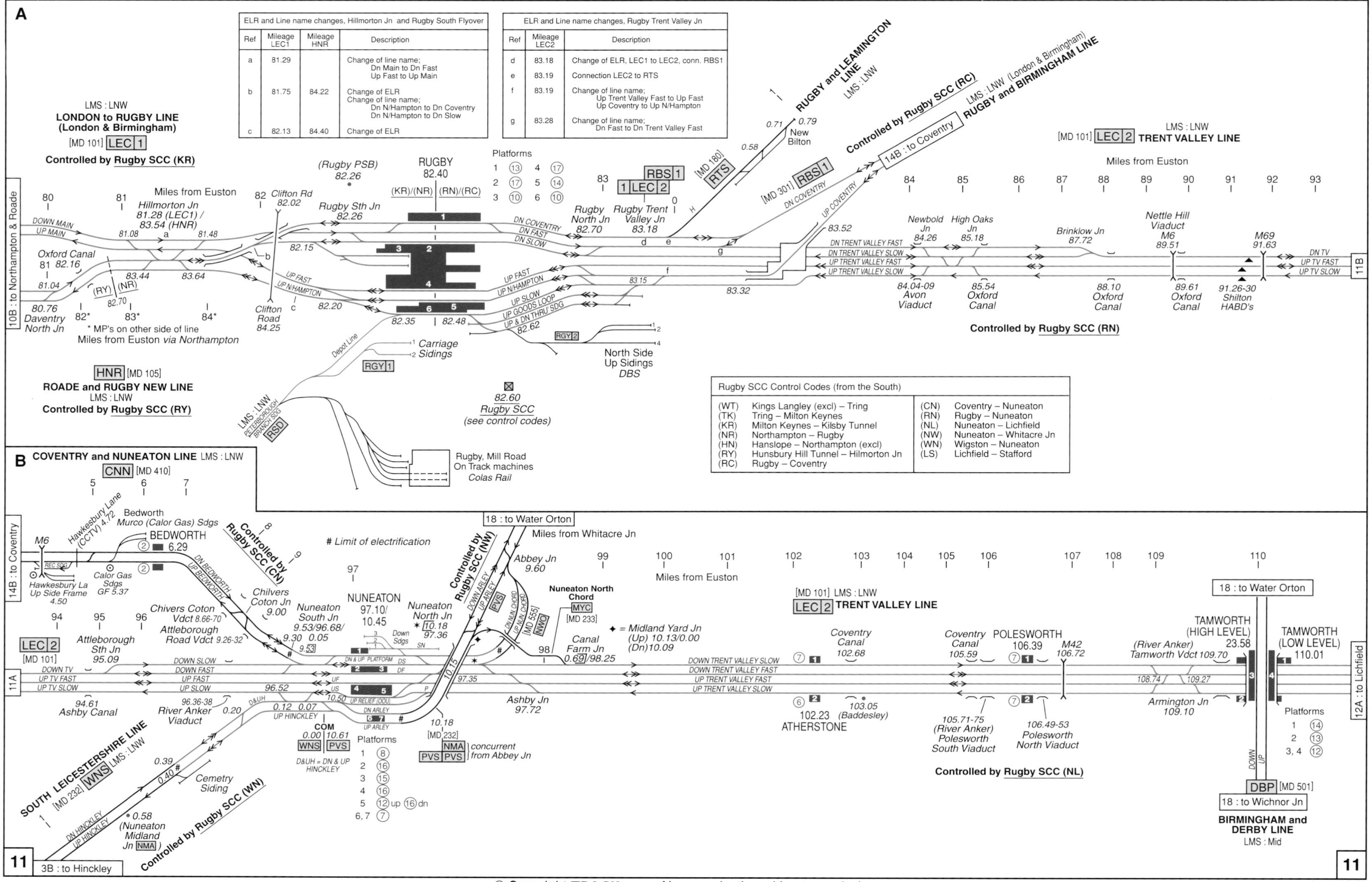

LMS : LNW
LONDON to RUGBY LINE (London & Birmingham)
[MD 101] LEC 1
Controlled by Rugby SCC (KR)

Miles from Euston

10B : to Northampton & Roade

80 — 81 — 82 — 83 — 84 — 85 — 86 — 87 — 88 — 89 — 90 — 91 — 92 — 93

DOWN MAIN / UP MAIN

Hillmorton Jn 81.28 (LEC1) / 83.54 (HNR)

81.08 a 81.48

Oxford Canal 81 82.16

81.04

(RY) (NR) 83.44 83.64 82.70

80.76 Daventry North Jn

82* 83* 84*

* MP's on other side of line
Miles from Euston via Northampton

HNR [MD 105]
ROADE and RUGBY NEW LINE
LMS : LNW
Controlled by Rugby SCC (RY)

Clifton Rd 82.02

b c

Clifton Road 84.25

(Rugby PSB) 82.26

Rugby Sth Jn 82.26

82.15 82.20

UP FAST / UP N/HAMPTON

RUGBY 82.40
(KR)/(NR) (RN)/(RC)

Platforms 1 (13) 4 (17) 2 (17) 5 (14) 3 (10) 6 (10)

82.35 82.48

Depot Line

Carriage Sidings

RGY 1

LMS : LNW PETERBOROUGH BRANCH SDG RSD

82.60 Rugby SCC (see control codes)

Rugby, Mill Road On Track machines Colas Rail

DN COVENTRY / DN FAST / DN SLOW

UP FAST / UP N/HAMPTON / UP SLOW / UP GOODS LOOP / UP & DN THRU SDG

82.62

RGY 2

North Side Up Sidings DBS

83

Rugby North Jn 82.70

RBS 1
1 LEC 2

Rugby Trent Valley Jn 83.18

d e g f 0 H

83.15

[MD 180] RTS

0.58 0.71 0.79 New Bilton

RUGBY and LEAMINGTON LINE
LMS : LNW

[MD 301] RBS 1

DN COVENTRY / UP COVENTRY

Controlled by Rugby SCC (RC)

14B : to Coventry

LMS : LNW (London & Birmingham)
RUGBY and BIRMINGHAM LINE

83.52 83.32

DN TRENT VALLEY FAST / DN TRENT VALLEY SLOW / UP TRENT VALLEY FAST / UP TRENT VALLEY SLOW

LMS : LNW
[MD 101] LEC 2 **TRENT VALLEY LINE**

Miles from Euston

Newbold Jn 84.26

High Oaks Jn 85.18

Brinklow Jn 87.72

Nettle Hill Viaduct M6 89.51

M69 91.63

84.04-09 Avon Viaduct

85.54 Oxford Canal

88.10 Oxford Canal

89.61 Oxford Canal

91.26-30 Shilton HABD's

DN TV / UP TV FAST / UP TV SLOW

11B

Controlled by Rugby SCC (RN)

Rugby SCC Control Codes (from the South)

(WT)	Kings Langley (excl) – Tring	(CN)	Coventry – Nuneaton
(TK)	Tring – Milton Keynes	(RN)	Rugby – Nuneaton
(KR)	Milton Keynes – Kilsby Tunnel	(NL)	Nuneaton – Lichfield
(NR)	Northampton – Rugby	(NW)	Nuneaton – Whitacre Jn
(HN)	Hanslope – Northampton (excl)	(WN)	Wigston – Nuneaton
(RY)	Hunsbury Hill Tunnel – Hilmorton Jn	(LS)	Lichfield – Stafford
(RC)	Rugby – Coventry		

B

COVENTRY and NUNEATON LINE LMS : LNW
CNN [MD 410]

5 — 6 — 7 — 8 — 9

14B : to Coventry

M6

REC SDG

Hawkesbury La Up Side Frame 4.50

Hawkesbury Lane (CCTV) 4.72

Bedworth Murco (Calor Gas) Sdgs

BEDWORTH (2) 6.29 (2)

Calor Gas Sdgs GF 5.37

DN BEDWORTH / UP BEDWORTH

Controlled by Rugby SCC (CN)

Chilvers Coton Jn 9.00

Chilvers Coton Vdct 8.66-70

Attleborough Road Vdct 9.26-32

Limit of electrification

18 : to Water Orton

Miles from Whitacre Jn

Controlled by Rugby SCC (NW)

Abbey Jn 9.60

DOWN ARLEY / UP ARLEY PVS

DN NUN CHORD / UP NUN CHORD [MD 555] NWO

Nuneaton North Chord MYC [MD 233]

✦ = Midland Yard Jn (Up) 10.13/0.00 (Dn) 10.09

Canal Farm Jn 0.69/98.25

98

97

NUNEATON 97.10/ 10.45

Nuneaton South Jn 9.53/96.68/ 9.30 0.05 9.53

Nuneaton North Jn * 10.18 97.36

Down Sdgs SN

DN & UP PLATFORM DS DF UF US UP RELIEF (OOU) DN ARLEY UP ARLEY P

10.15 97.35 10.50

10.18 [MD 232] NMA PVS PVS concurrent from Abbey Jn

COM 0.00 10.61 WNS PVS

D&UH = DN & UP HINCKLEY

Platforms 1 (8) 2 (16) 3 (15) 4 (16) 5 (12) up (16) dn 6, 7 (7)

LEC 2 [MD 101]

11A

DOWN TV / UP TV FAST / UP TV SLOW

94 — 95 — 96

Attleborough Sth Jn 95.09

DOWN SLOW / DOWN FAST / UP FAST / UP SLOW

94.61 Ashby Canal

96.52

96.36-38 River Anker Viaduct

0.20 D&UH 0.12 0.07 UP HINCKLEY

SOUTH LEICESTERSHIRE LINE [MD 232] WNS LMS : LNW

0.39 0.40 #

Cemetery Siding

0.58 (Nuneaton Midland Jn NMA)

DN HINCKLEY / UP HINCKLEY

Controlled by Rugby SCC (WN)

3B : to Hinckley

99 — 100 — 101 — 102 — 103 — 104 — 105 — 106 — 107 — 108 — 109 — 110

Miles from Euston

Ashby Jn 97.72

[MD 101] LMS : LNW
LEC 2 **TRENT VALLEY LINE**

DOWN TRENT VALLEY SLOW / DOWN TRENT VALLEY FAST / UP TRENT VALLEY FAST / UP TRENT VALLEY SLOW

(7) 1 (6) 2

102.23 ATHERSTONE

Coventry Canal 102.68

103.05 (Baddesley)

Coventry Canal 105.59

POLESWORTH 106.39 (7) 1 (7) 2

M42 106.72

105.71-75 (River Anker) Polesworth South Viaduct

106.49-53 Polesworth North Viaduct

Controlled by Rugby SCC (NL)

(River Anker) Tamworth Vdct 109.70

108.74 109.27

Armington Jn 109.10

18 : to Water Orton

TAMWORTH (HIGH LEVEL) 23.58

TAMWORTH (LOW LEVEL) 110.01

Platforms 1 (14) 2 (13) 3, 4 (12)

DOWN UP

DBP [MD 501]

18 : to Wichnor Jn

BIRMINGHAM and DERBY LINE
LMS : Mid

12A : to Lichfield

August 2013

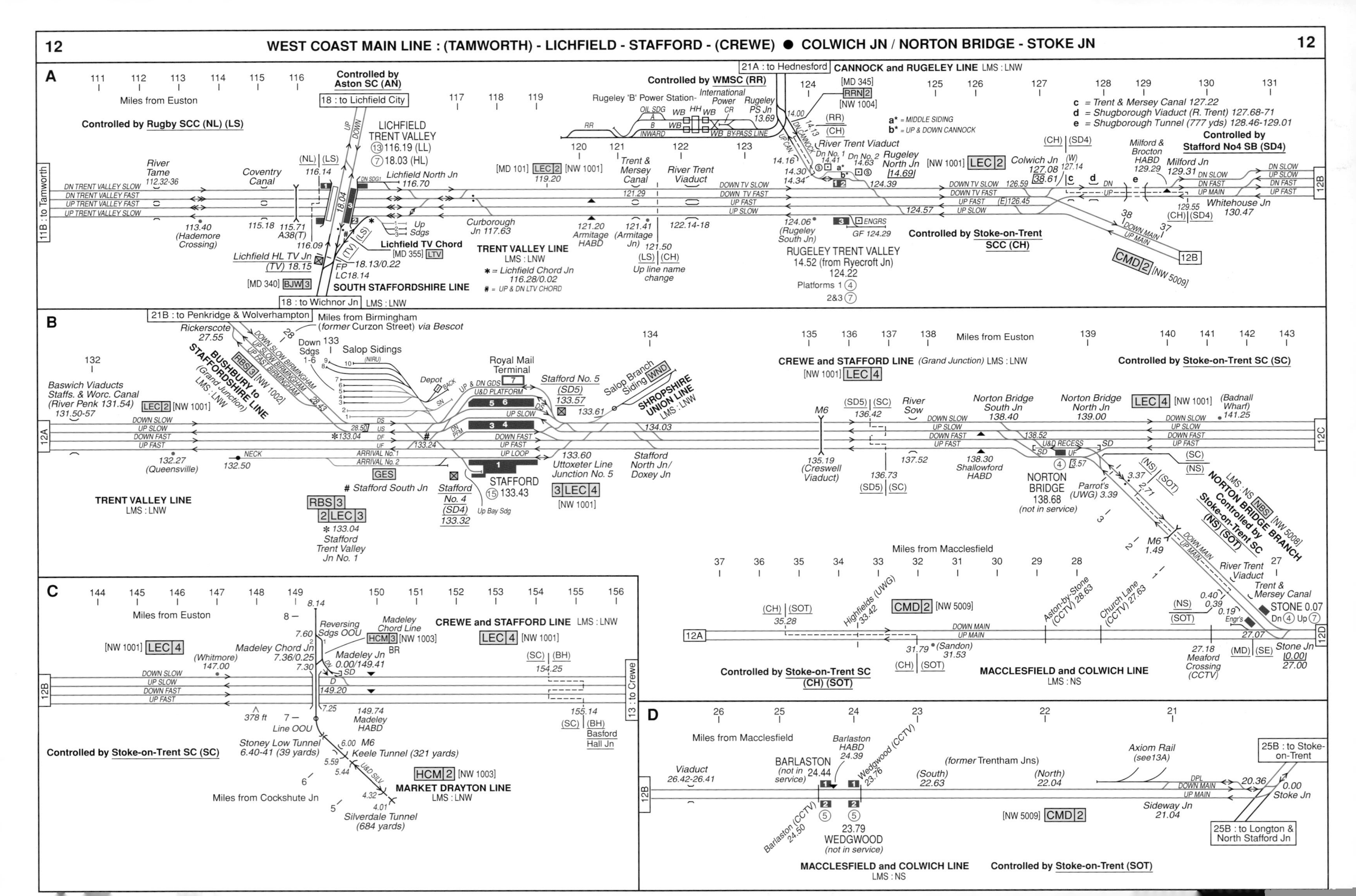
A
Miles from Euston
Controlled by Rugby SCC (NL) (LS)
Controlled by Aston SC (AN)
18 : to Lichfield City
11B : to Tamworth
DN TRENT VALLEY SLOW
DN TRENT VALLEY FAST
UP TRENT VALLEY FAST
UP TRENT VALLEY SLOW
River Tame 112.32-36
113.40 (Hademore Crossing)
Coventry Canal
115.18
115.71 A38(T)
(NL) | (LS) 116.14
LICHFIELD TRENT VALLEY
13 116.19 (LL)
7 18.03 (HL)
Lichfield North Jn 116.70
Up Sdgs
Lichfield HL TV Jn (TV) 18.15
116.09
FP LC18.14
18.13/0.22
Lichfield TV Chord [MD 355] LTV
[MD 340] BJW 3
SOUTH STAFFORDSHIRE LINE
18 : to Wichnor Jn LMS : LNW
[MD 101] LEC 2 [NW 1001] 119.20
Curborough Jn 117.63
TRENT VALLEY LINE LMS : LNW
* = Lichfield Chord Jn 116.28/0.02
# = UP & DN LTV CHORD
Controlled by WMSC (RR)
Rugeley 'B' Power Station-
International Power
Rugeley PS Jn 13.69
Trent & Mersey Canal 121.29
121.20 Armitage HABD
121.41 (Armitage Jn)
121.50 (LS) | (CH) Up line name change
River Trent Viaduct 122.14-18
21A : to Hednesford
CANNOCK and RUGELEY LINE LMS : LNW
[MD 345] RRN 2 [NW 1004]
(RR) (CH)
River Trent Viaduct
a* = MIDDLE SIDING
b* = UP & DOWN CANNOCK
Rugeley North Jn 14.69
124.39
124.06 (Rugeley South Jn)
RUGELEY TRENT VALLEY 14.52 (from Ryecroft Jn) 124.22
Platforms 1 4
2&3 7
GF 124.29
124.57
[NW 1001] LEC 2
Colwich Jn 127.08 38.61
Controlled by Stoke-on-Trent SCC (CH)
c = Trent & Mersey Canal 127.22
d = Shugborough Viaduct (R. Trent) 127.68-71
e = Shugborough Tunnel (777 yds) 128.46-129.01
Controlled by Stafford No4 SB (SD4)
Milford & Brocton HABD 129.29
Milford Jn 129.31
Whitehouse Jn 130.47
129.55 (CH) | (SD4)
CMD 2 [NW 5009]
12B
B
21B : to Penkridge & Wolverhampton
Miles from Birmingham (former Curzon Street) via Bescot
Rickerscote 27.55
BUSHBURY to STAFFORDSHIRE LINE (Grand Junction) LMS : LNW
RBS 3 [NW 1002]
Baswich Viaducts Staffs. & Worc. Canal (River Penk 131.54) 131.50-57
LEC 2 [NW 1001]
12A
132.27 (Queensville)
132.50
Salop Sidings
Down Sdgs 1-6
Royal Mail Terminal
Stafford No. 5 (SD5) 133.57
133.61
STAFFORD 15 133.43
Stafford No. 4 (SD4) 133.32
Stafford South Jn
RBS 3
2 LEC 3
* 133.04 Stafford Trent Valley Jn No. 1
GES
133.60 Uttoxeter Line Junction No. 5
3 LEC 4 [NW 1001]
Salop Branch Siding WND
SHROPSHIRE UNION LINE LMS : LNW
134.03
Stafford North Jn/ Doxey Jn
TRENT VALLEY LINE LMS : LNW
CREWE and STAFFORD LINE (Grand Junction) LMS : LNW
[NW 1001] LEC 4
M6
135.19 (Creswell Viaduct)
(SD5) | (SC) 136.42
136.73 (SD5) | (SC)
River Sow
137.52
Norton Bridge South Jn 138.40
138.30 Shallowford HABD
Norton Bridge North Jn 139.00
NORTON BRIDGE 138.68 (not in service)
Parrot's (UWG) 3.39
LEC 4 [NW 1001]
(Badnall Wharf) 141.25
Controlled by Stoke-on-Trent SC (SC)
12C
LMS : NS NBS [NW 5008]
NORTON BRIDGE BRANCH Controlled by Stoke-on-Trent SC (NS) (SOT)
M6 1.49
River Trent Viaduct
Trent & Mersey Canal
STONE 0.07
Dn 4 Up 7
Stone Jn 0.00 27.00
12D
Miles from Macclesfield
(CH) | (SOT) 35.28
Highfields (UWG) 33.42
CMD 2 [NW 5009]
31.79 (Sandon) 31.53
Aston-by-Stone (CCTV) 28.63
Church Lane (CCTV) 27.63
27.18 Meaford Crossing (CCTV)
(MD) | (SE)
Controlled by Stoke-on-Trent SC (CH) (SOT)
MACCLESFIELD and COLWICH LINE LMS : NS
C
Miles from Euston
[NW 1001] LEC 4
(Whitmore) 147.00
12B
378 ft
Madeley Chord Jn 7.36/0.25
Reversing Sdgs OOU
Madeley Chord Line HCM 3 [NW 1003]
Madeley Jn 0.00/149.41
149.20
149.74 Madeley HABD
Line OOU
Stoney Low Tunnel 6.40-41 (39 yards)
Keele Tunnel (321 yards)
HCM 2 [NW 1003]
MARKET DRAYTON LINE LMS : LNW
Silverdale Tunnel (684 yards)
Miles from Cockshute Jn
CREWE and STAFFORD LINE LMS : LNW
LEC 4 [NW 1001]
(SC) | (BH) 154.25
155.14 (SC) | (BH) Basford Hall Jn
13 : to Crewe
Controlled by Stoke-on-Trent SC (SC)
D
Miles from Macclesfield
Viaduct 26.42-26.41
BARLASTON (not in service) 24.44
Barlaston HABD 24.39
Barlaston (CCTV) 24.50
Wedgwood (CCTV) 23.76
23.79 WEDGWOOD (not in service)
(former Trentham Jns)
(South) 22.63
(North) 22.04
[NW 5009] CMD 2
Axiom Rail (see13A)
Sideway Jn 21.04
20.36
0.00 Stoke Jn
25B : to Stoke-on-Trent
25B : to Longton & North Stafford Jn
MACCLESFIELD and COLWICH LINE LMS : NS
Controlled by Stoke-on-Trent (SOT)

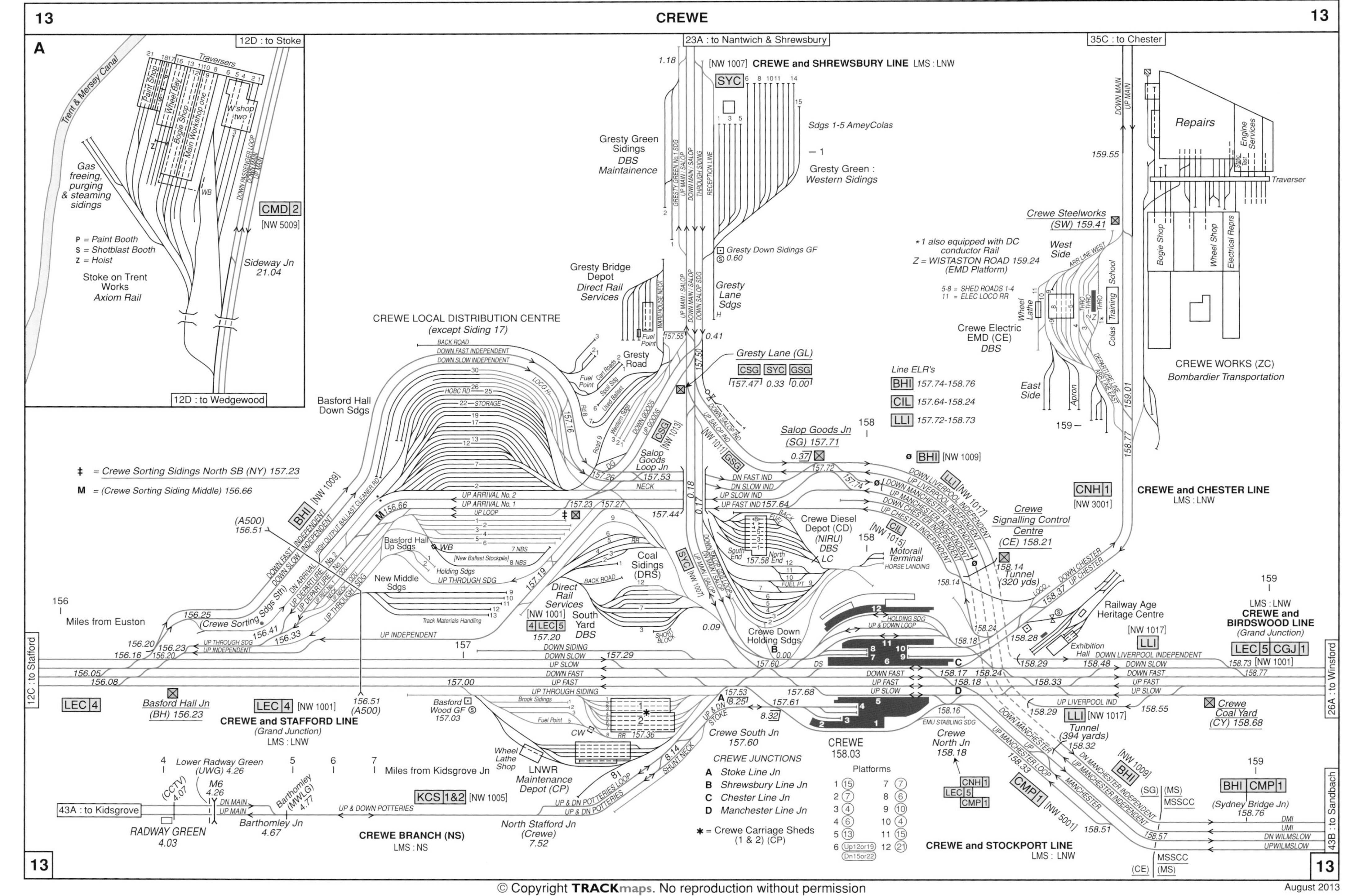
A
12D : to Stoke
Trent & Mersey Canal
Traversers
Paint Shop
Wheel Bay
Bogie Shop
Main Workshop one
W'shop two
Gas freeing, purging & steaming sidings
P = Paint Booth
S = Shotblast Booth
Z = Hoist
Stoke on Trent Works
Axiom Rail
CMD 2
[NW 5009]
Sideway Jn
21.04
12D : to Wedgewood
23A : to Nantwich & Shrewsbury
[NW 1007] CREWE and SHREWSBURY LINE LMS : LNW
SYC
Sdgs 1-5 AmeyColas
Gresty Green : Western Sidings
Gresty Green Sidings
DBS
Maintainence
Gresty Down Sidings GF
0.60
Gresty Lane Sdgs
Gresty Bridge Depot
Direct Rail Services
CREWE LOCAL DISTRIBUTION CENTRE
(except Siding 17)
Basford Hall Down Sdgs
Gresty Road
Gresty Lane (GL)
CSG SYC GSG
157.47 0.33 0.00
Salop Goods Jn
(SG) 157.71
Salop Goods Loop Jn
Line ELR's
BHI 157.74-158.76
CIL 157.64-158.24
LLI 157.72-158.73
‡ = Crewe Sorting Sidings North SB (NY) 157.23
M = (Crewe Sorting Siding Middle) 156.66
Basford Hall Up Sdgs
New Middle Sdgs
Holding Sdgs
UP THROUGH SDG
Track Materials Handling
Coal Sidings (DRS)
Direct Rail Services
South Yard
DBS
[NW 1001]
4 LEC 5
157.20
Crewe Diesel Depot (CD)
(NIRU)
DBS
LC
Motorail Terminal
HORSE LANDING
Crewe Down Holding Sdgs
Crewe Signalling Control Centre
(CE) 158.21
Tunnel
(320 yds)
35C : to Chester
Repairs
Engine Services
Traverser
Bogie Shop
Wheel Shop
Electrical Repairs
Crewe Steelworks
(SW) 159.41
*1 also equipped with DC conductor Rail
Z = WISTASTON ROAD 159.24
(EMD Platform)
5-8 = SHED ROADS 1-4
11 = ELEC LOCO RR
West Side
East Side
Wheel Lathe
Crewe Electric EMD (CE)
DBS
Colas Training School
CREWE WORKS (ZC)
Bombardier Transportation
CNH 1
[NW 3001]
CREWE and CHESTER LINE
LMS : LNW
Railway Age Heritage Centre
Exhibition Hall
LMS : LNW
CREWE and BIRDSWOOD LINE
(Grand Junction)
LEC 5 CGJ 1
[NW 1001]
26A : to Winsford
Crewe Coal Yard
(CY) 158.68
Tunnel
(394 yards)
LLI [NW 1017]
BHI [NW 1009]
BHI CMP 1
(Sydney Bridge Jn)
158.76
43B : to Sandbach
CMP 1 [NW 5001]
CREWE and STOCKPORT LINE
LMS : LNW
Crewe North Jn
158.18
CREWE
158.03
Crewe South Jn
157.60
12C : to Stafford
156
Miles from Euston
LEC 4
Basford Hall Jn
(BH) 156.23
LEC 4 [NW 1001]
CREWE and STAFFORD LINE
(Grand Junction)
LMS : LNW
Basford Wood GF
157.03
LNWR Maintenance Depot (CP)
Wheel Lathe Shop
KCS 1&2 [NW 1005]
Miles from Kidsgrove Jn
43A : to Kidsgrove
RADWAY GREEN
4.03
Lower Radway Green
(UWG) 4.26
M6
4.26
Barthomley Jn
4.67
CREWE BRANCH (NS)
LMS : NS
North Stafford Jn
(Crewe)
7.52
CREWE JUNCTIONS
A Stoke Line Jn
B Shrewsbury Line Jn
C Chester Line Jn
D Manchester Line Jn
* = Crewe Carriage Sheds
(1 & 2) (CP)
Platforms
DOWN SLOW
UP SLOW
DOWN FAST
UP FAST
UP THROUGH SIDING
DOWN SIDING
UP INDEPENDENT

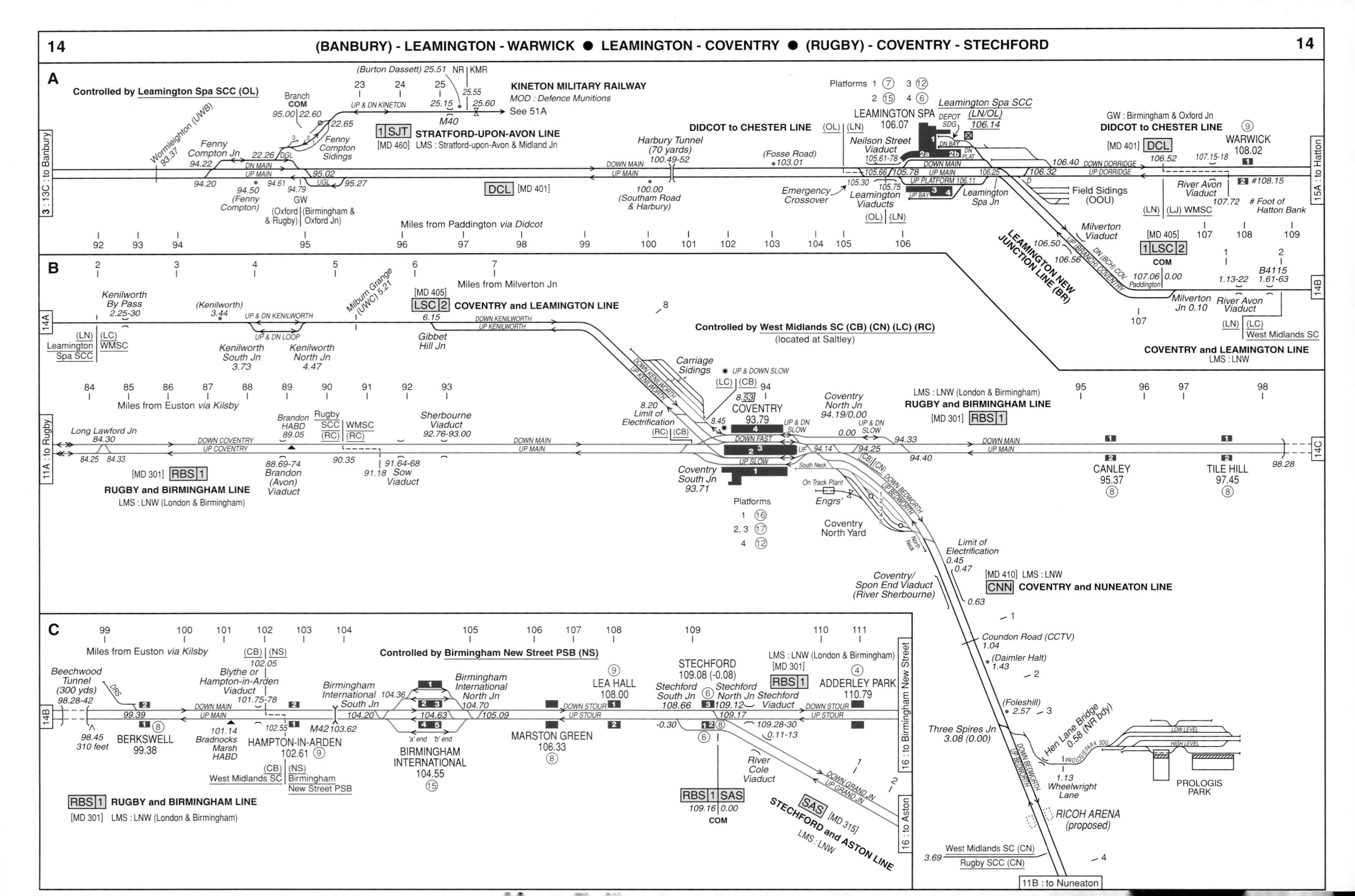

14
(BANBURY) - LEAMINGTON - WARWICK ● LEAMINGTON - COVENTRY ● (RUGBY) - COVENTRY - STECHFORD
14
A
Controlled by Leamington Spa SCC (OL)
3 : 13C : to Banbury
Wormleighton (UWB) 93.37
Fenny Compton Jn 94.22
Branch COM 95.00 | 22.60
22.65
Fenny Compton Sidings
94.50 (Fenny Compton)
GW (Oxford | (Birmingham & Rugby) | Oxford Jn)
(Burton Dassett) 25.51
NR | KMR
UP & DN KINETON
25.15
25.55
25.60
M40
KINETON MILITARY RAILWAY
MOD : Defence Munitions
See 51A
1 SJT STRATFORD-UPON-AVON LINE
[MD 460] LMS : Stratford-upon-Avon & Midland Jn
DCL [MD 401]
Miles from Paddington via Didcot
Harbury Tunnel (70 yards) 100.49-52
100.00 (Southam Road & Harbury)
DIDCOT to CHESTER LINE
(Fosse Road) 103.01
Emergency Crossover
Platforms 1 (7) 3 (12) 2 (15) 4 (6)
LEAMINGTON SPA 106.07
Leamington Spa SCC (LN/OL) 106.14
Neilson Street Viaduct 105.61-78
Leamington Viaducts 105.75
Leamington Spa Jn
Field Sidings (OOU)
GW : Birmingham & Oxford Jn
DIDCOT to CHESTER LINE
[MD 401] DCL 106.52
WARWICK 108.02
River Avon Viaduct 107.72
Foot of Hatton Bank
15A : to Hatton
Milverton Viaduct
LEAMINGTON NEW JUNCTION LINE (BR)
[MD 405] 1 LSC 2 COM
107.06 | 0.00 Paddington
Milverton Jn 0.10
River Avon Viaduct
B4115 1.61-63
(LN) | (LC) West Midlands SC
COVENTRY and LEAMINGTON LINE
LMS : LNW
B
14A
Kenilworth By Pass 2.25-30
(LN) | (LC) Leamington Spa SCC | WMSC
(Kenilworth) 3.44
UP & DN KENILWORTH
UP & DN LOOP
Kenilworth South Jn 3.73
Kenilworth North Jn 4.47
Milburn Grange (UWC) 5.21
[MD 405] LSC 2 COVENTRY and LEAMINGTON LINE
Miles from Milverton Jn
Gibbet Hill Jn 6.15
Controlled by West Midlands SC (CB) (CN) (LC) (RC)
(located at Saltley)
Carriage Sidings
UP & DOWN SLOW
COVENTRY 93.79
Coventry North Jn 94.19/0.00
Coventry South Jn 93.71
8.20 Limit of Electrification
Platforms 1 (16) 2, 3 (17) 4 (12)
Engrs'
Coventry North Yard
11A : to Rugby
Long Lawford Jn 84.30
Miles from Euston via Kilsby
[MD 301] RBS 1
RUGBY and BIRMINGHAM LINE
LMS : LNW (London & Birmingham)
Brandon HABD 89.05
88.69-74 Brandon (Avon) Viaduct
Rugby SCC (RC) | WMSC (RC)
91.64-68 Sow Viaduct
Sherbourne Viaduct 92.76-93.00
LMS : LNW (London & Birmingham)
RUGBY and BIRMINGHAM LINE
[MD 301] RBS 1
CANLEY 95.37 (8)
TILE HILL 97.45 (8)
14C
Limit of Electrification 0.45
Coventry/ Spon End Viaduct (River Sherbourne)
[MD 410] LMS : LNW
CNN COVENTRY and NUNEATON LINE
Coundon Road (CCTV) 1.04
(Daimler Halt) 1.43
(Foleshill) 2.57
Three Spires Jn 3.08 (0.00)
Hen Lane Bridge 0.58 (NR bdy)
1.13 Wheelwright Lane
PROLOGIS PARK
RICOH ARENA (proposed)
West Midlands SC (CN) | Rugby SCC (CN) 3.69
11B : to Nuneaton
C
14B
Miles from Euston via Kilsby
Beechwood Tunnel (300 yds) 98.28-42
98.45 310 feet
BERKSWELL 99.38
Blythe or Hampton-in-Arden Viaduct 101.75-78
(CB) | (NS) 102.05
101.14 Bradnocks Marsh HABD
HAMPTON-IN-ARDEN 102.61 (9)
M42 103.62
(CB) | (NS) West Midlands SC | Birmingham New Street PSB
Controlled by Birmingham New Street PSB (NS)
Birmingham International South Jn 104.20
Birmingham International North Jn 104.70
BIRMINGHAM INTERNATIONAL 104.55 (15)
MARSTON GREEN 106.33 (8)
LEA HALL 108.00 (9)
STECHFORD 109.08 (-0.08)
Stechford South Jn 108.66
Stechford North Jn 109.12
Stechford Viaduct
LMS : LNW (London & Birmingham) [MD 301] RBS 1
ADDERLEY PARK 110.79 (4)
16 : to Birmingham New Street
River Cole Viaduct
RBS 1 SAS 109.16 | 0.00 COM
SAS [MD 315] STECHFORD and ASTON LINE
LMS : LNW
16 : to Aston
RBS 1 RUGBY and BIRMINGHAM LINE
[MD 301] LMS : LNW (London & Birmingham)

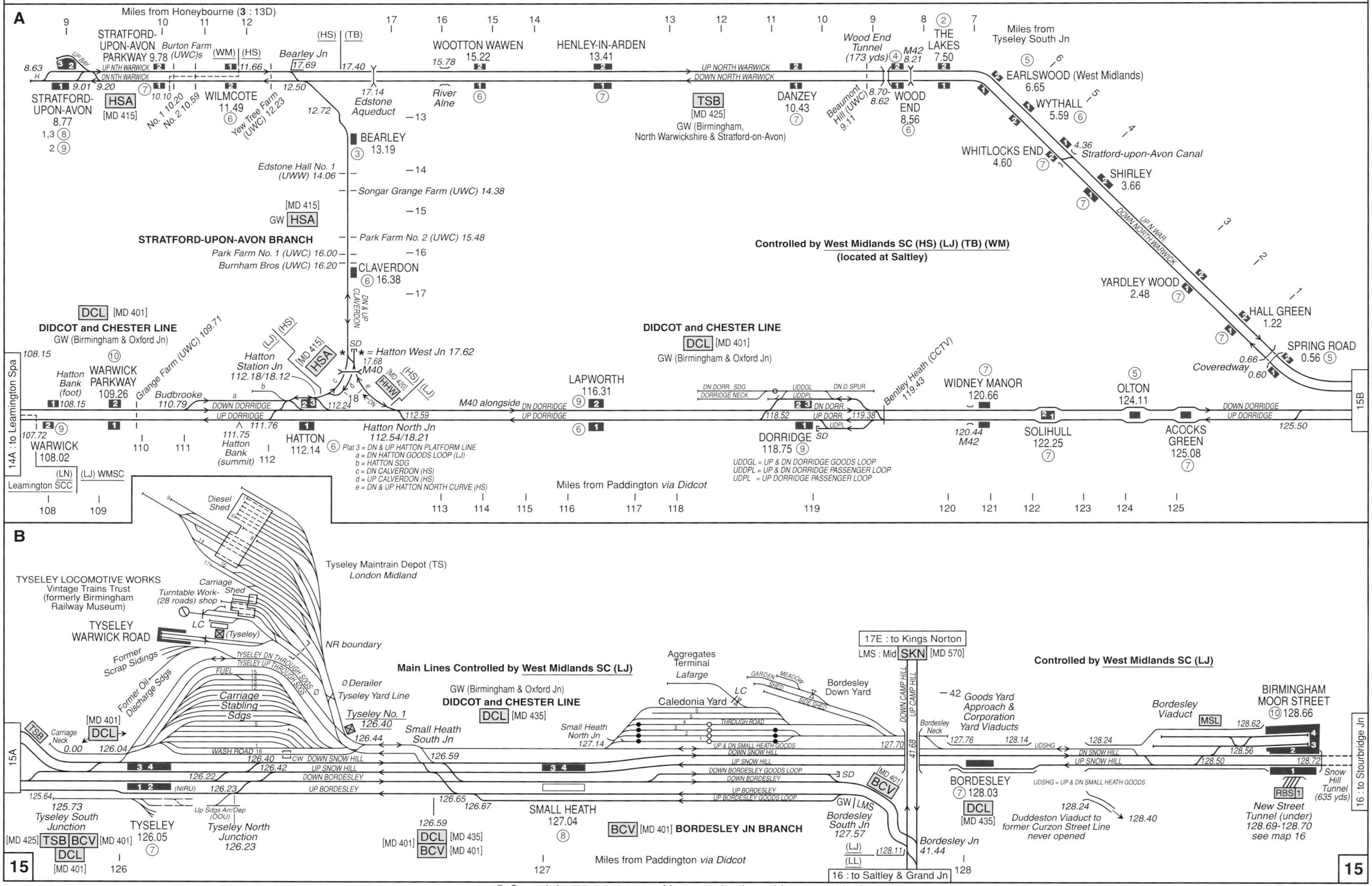

A

Miles from Honeybourne (3 : 13D)

STRATFORD-UPON-AVON 8.77
1,3 (8)
2 (9)
8.63
9.01
9.20
UP BAY
UP NTH WARWICK
DN NTH WARWICK
HSA [MD 415]
STRATFORD-UPON-AVON PARKWAY 9.78 (7)
Burton Farm (UWC)s
No. 1 10.20
No. 2 10.59
10.10
(WM) (HS)
11.66
WILMCOTE 11.49 (6)
Yew Tree Farm (UWC) 12.23
Bearley Jn 17.69
(HS) (TB)
12.50
12.72
17.40
17.14 Edstone Aqueduct
WOOTTON WAWEN 15.22 (6)
15.78
River Alne
HENLEY-IN-ARDEN 13.41 (7)
UP NORTH WARWICK
DOWN NORTH WARWICK
TSB [MD 425]
GW (Birmingham, North Warwickshire & Stratford-on-Avon)
DANZEY 10.43 (7)
Beaumont Hill (UWC) 9.11
Wood End Tunnel (173 yds) (4)
8.70-8.62
M42 8.21
WOOD END 8.56 (6)
THE LAKES 7.50 (2)
Miles from Tyseley South Jn
EARLSWOOD (West Midlands) 6.65 (5)
WYTHALL 5.59 (6)
WHITLOCKS END 4.60 (7)
4.36 Stratford-upon-Avon Canal
SHIRLEY 3.66 (7)
UP N WAR
DOWN NORTH WARWICK
YARDLEY WOOD 2.48 (7)
HALL GREEN 1.22 (7)
SPRING ROAD 0.56 (5)
0.66
Coverdway 0.60
15B

BEARLEY 13.19 (3)
Edstone Hall No. 1 (UWW) 14.06
Songar Grange Farm (UWC) 14.38
GW HSA [MD 415]
STRATFORD-UPON-AVON BRANCH
Park Farm No. 2 (UWC) 15.48
Park Farm No. 1 (UWC) 16.00
Burnham Bros (UWC) 16.20
CLAVERDON (6) 16.38
DN & UP CLAVERDON

Controlled by West Midlands SC (HS) (LJ) (TB) (WM)
(located at Saltley)

DCL [MD 401]
DIDCOT and CHESTER LINE
GW (Birmingham & Oxford Jn)
(10)
108.15
14A : to Leamington Spa
Hatton Bank (foot) 108.15
WARWICK PARKWAY 109.26
Grange Farm (UWC) 109.71
Budbrooke 110.79
107.72
WARWICK 108.02 (9)
(LN) Leamington SCC
(LJ) WMSC
DOWN DORRIDGE
UP DORRIDGE
111.76
111.75 Hatton Bank (summit)
Hatton Station Jn 112.18/18.12
(LJ) (HS)
HSA [MD 415]
SD
* = Hatton West Jn 17.62
17.68
M40
HHW [MD 420]
(HS) (LJ)
112.24
HATTON 112.14 (6)
Hatton North Jn 112.54/18.21
112.59
Plat 3 = DN & UP HATTON PLATFORM LINE
a = DN HATTON GOODS LOOP (LJ)
b = HATTON SDG
c = DN CALVERDON (HS)
d = UP CALVERDON (HS)
e = DN & UP HATTON NORTH CURVE (HS)
M40 alongside
LAPWORTH 116.31 (9) (6)
DIDCOT and CHESTER LINE
DCL [MD 401]
GW (Birmingham & Oxford Jn)
DN DORR. SDG
DORRIDGE NECK
UDDGL
UDDPL
DN D. SPUR
DN DORR.
UP DORR.
UDPL
118.52
119.38
SD
DORRIDGE 118.75 (9)
UDDGL = UP & DN DORRIDGE GOODS LOOP
UDDPL = UP & DN DORRIDGE PASSENGER LOOP
UDPL = UP DORRIDGE PASSENGER LOOP
Bentley Heath (CCTV) 119.43
WIDNEY MANOR 120.66 (7)
120.44 M42
SOLIHULL 122.25 (7)
OLTON 124.11 (5)
ACOCKS GREEN 125.08 (7)
125.50
Miles from Paddington via Didcot
108 109 110 111 112 113 114 115 116 117 118 119 120 121 122 123 124 125

B

TYSELEY LOCOMOTIVE WORKS
Vintage Trains Trust
(formerly Birmingham Railway Museum)
Turntable (28 roads)
Work-shop
Carriage Shed
Diesel Shed
Tyseley Maintrain Depot (TS)
London Midland
LC
(Tyseley)
TYSELEY WARWICK ROAD
NR boundary
Former Scrap Sidings
Former Oil Discharge Sdgs
TYSELEY DN THROUGH SDGS
TYSELEY UP THROUGH SDGS
FUEL
Carriage Stabling Sdgs
Ø Derailer
Tyseley Yard Line
Tyseley No. 1 126.40
126.44
WASH ROAD
CW DOWN SNOW HILL
UP SNOW HILL
DOWN BORDESLEY
UP BORDESLEY
15A
TSB
Carriage Neck 0.00
[MD 401] DCL
126.04
126.40
126.42
126.22
(NIRU)
126.23
125.64
125.73 Tyseley South Junction
[MD 425] TSB BCV [MD 401]
DCL [MD 401]
TYSELEY 126.05 (7)
Up Sdgs Arr/Dep (OOU)
Tyseley North Junction 126.23
Small Heath South Jn
126.59
126.65
126.67
126.59
[MD 401] DCL [MD 435]
BCV [MD 401]
Main Lines Controlled by West Midlands SC (LJ)
GW (Birmingham & Oxford Jn)
DIDCOT and CHESTER LINE
DCL [MD 435]
SMALL HEATH 127.04 (8)
BCV [MD 401] **BORDESLEY JN BRANCH**
Miles from Paddington via Didcot
Small Heath North Jn 127.14
Aggregates Terminal Lafarge
Caledonia Yard
LC
THROUGH ROAD
GARDEN MEADOW SHED
SIDE SHED
Bordesley Down Yard
UP & DN SMALL HEATH GOODS
DOWN SNOW HILL
UP SNOW HILL
DOWN BORDESLEY GOODS LOOP
DOWN BORDESLEY
UP BORDESLEY
UP BORDESLEY GOODS LOOP
SD
127.70
17E : to Kings Norton
LMS : Mid SKN [MD 570]
DOWN CAMP HILL
UP CAMP HILL
41.68
BCV [MD 401]
GW | LMS
Bordesley South Jn 127.57
(LJ)
(LL)
128.11
Bordesley Jn 41.44
16 : to Saltley & Grand Jn
Bordesley Neck
127.76
– 42 Goods Yard Approach & Corporation Yard Viaducts
128.14
UDSHG
BORDESLEY (7) 128.03
DCL [MD 435]
UDSHG = UP & DN SMALL HEATH GOODS
128.24 Duddeston Viaduct to former Curzon Street Line never opened
128.40
Controlled by West Midlands SC (LJ)
128.24
DN SNOW HILL
UP SNOW HILL
Bordesley Viaduct
MSL
128.62
128.56
128.50
128.72
BIRMINGHAM MOOR STREET (10) 128.66
RBS1
New Street Tunnel (under) 128.69-128.70 see map 16
Snow Hill Tunnel (635 yds)
16 : to Stourbridge Jn
126 127 128

August 2013

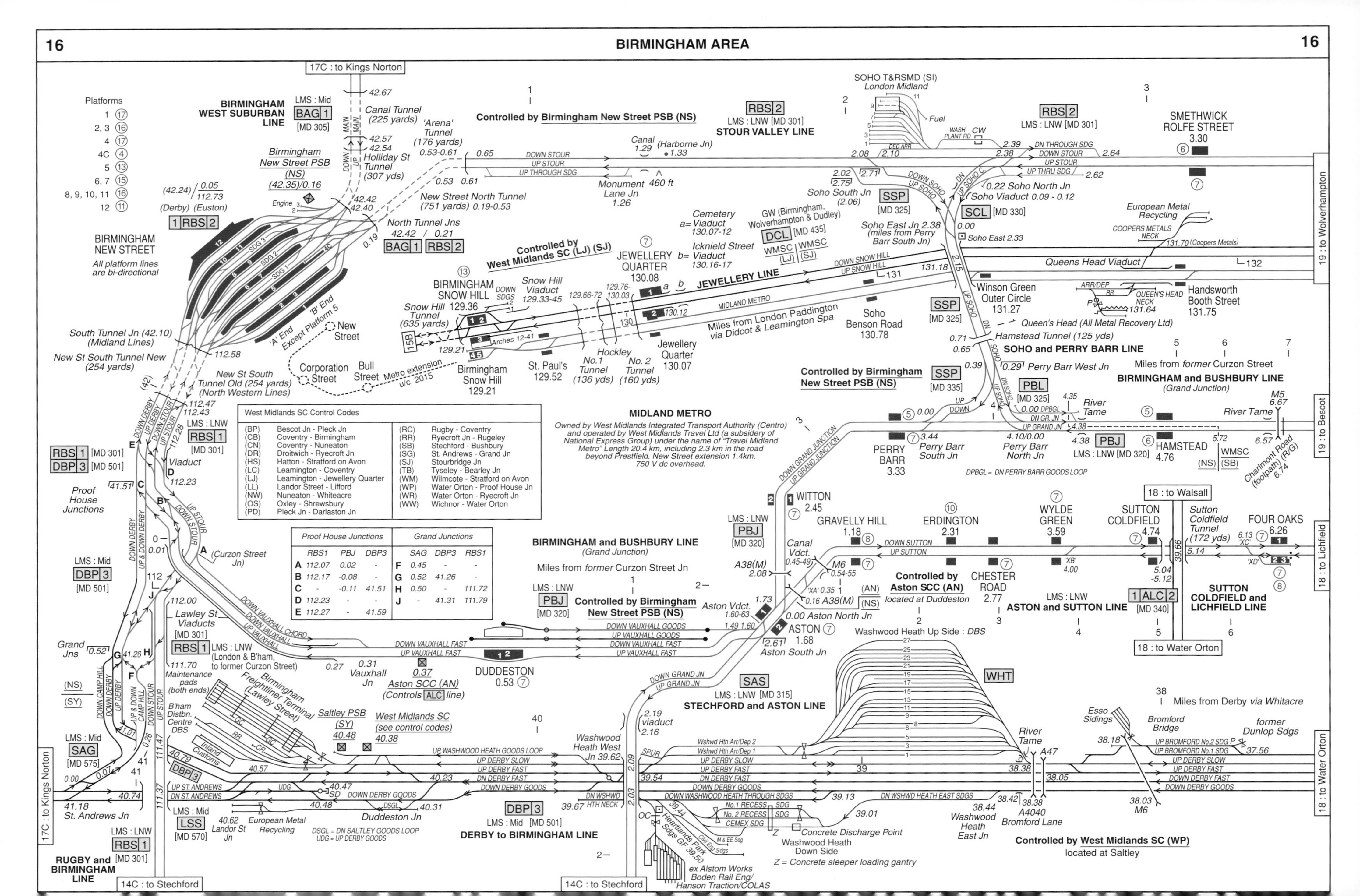

West Midlands SC Control Codes

(BP)	Bescot Jn - Pleck Jn	(RC)	Rugby - Coventry
(CB)	Coventry - Birmingham	(RR)	Ryecroft Jn - Rugeley
(CN)	Coventry - Nuneaton	(SB)	Stechford - Bushbury
(DR)	Droitwich - Ryecroft Jn	(SG)	St. Andrews - Grand Jn
(HS)	Hatton - Stratford on Avon	(SJ)	Stourbridge Jn
(LC)	Leamington - Coventry	(TB)	Tyseley - Bearley Jn
(LJ)	Leamington - Jewellery Quarter	(WM)	Wilmcote - Stratford on Avon
(LL)	Landor Street - Lifford	(WP)	Water Orton - Proof House Jn
(NW)	Nuneaton - Whiteacre	(WR)	Water Orton - Ryecroft Jn
(OS)	Oxley - Shrewsbury	(WW)	Wichnor - Water Orton
(PD)	Pleck Jn - Darlaston Jn		

Proof House Junctions	RBS1	PBJ	DBP3	Grand Junctions	SAG	DBP3	RBS1
A	112.07	0.02	-	F	0.45	-	-
B	112.17	-0.08	-	G	0.52	41.26	-
C	-	-0.11	41.51	H	0.50	-	111.72
D	112.23	-	-	J	-	41.31	111.79
E	112.27	-	41.59				

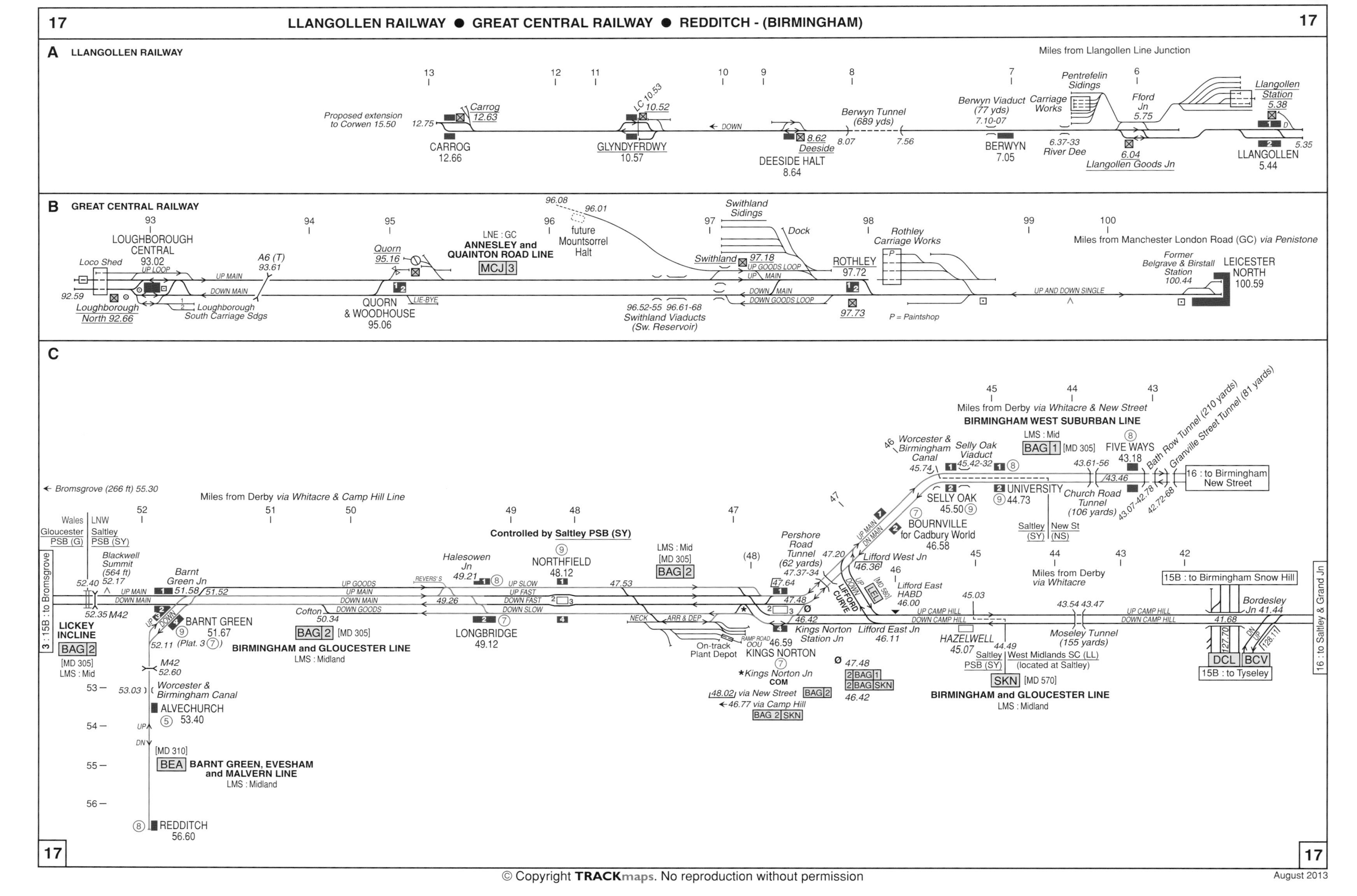
A LLANGOLLEN RAILWAY
Miles from Llangollen Line Junction
Proposed extension to Corwen 15.50
12.75
Carrog 12.63
CARROG 12.66
LC 10.53
10.52
GLYNDYFRDWY 10.57
DOWN
8.62 Deeside
DEESIDE HALT 8.64
8.07
Berwyn Tunnel (689 yds)
7.56
Berwyn Viaduct (77 yds) 7.10-07
BERWYN 7.05
Carriage Works
Pentrefelin Sidings
6.37-33 River Dee
Fford Jn 5.75
6.04 Llangollen Goods Jn
Llangollen Station 5.38
LLANGOLLEN 5.44
5.35
B GREAT CENTRAL RAILWAY
LOUGHBOROUGH CENTRAL 93.02
Loco Shed
UP LOOP
92.59
Loughborough North 92.66
Loughborough South Carriage Sdgs
UP MAIN
DOWN MAIN
A6 (T) 93.61
Quorn 95.16
LIE-BYE
QUORN & WOODHOUSE 95.06
LNE : GC
ANNESLEY and QUAINTON ROAD LINE
MCJ 3
96.08
96.01
future Mountsorrel Halt
96.52-55 96.61-68 Swithland Viaducts (Sw. Reservoir)
Swithland Sidings
Dock
Swithland 97.18
UP GOODS LOOP
DOWN GOODS LOOP
ROTHLEY 97.72
97.73
Rothley Carriage Works
P = Paintshop
UP AND DOWN SINGLE
Miles from Manchester London Road (GC) via Penistone
Former Belgrave & Birstall Station 100.44
LEICESTER NORTH 100.59
C
← Bromsgrove (266 ft) 55.30
Miles from Derby via Whitacre & Camp Hill Line
3 : 15B : to Bromsgrove
Wales | LNW
Gloucester PSB (G) | Saltley PSB (SY)
Blackwell Summit (564 ft) 52.17
52.40
52.35 M42
LICKEY INCLINE
BAG 2
[MD 305]
LMS : Mid
Barnt Green Jn 51.58
51.52
BARNT GREEN 51.67
52.11 (Plat. 3)
M42 52.60
53.03
Worcester & Birmingham Canal
ALVECHURCH 53.40
[MD 310]
BEA BARNT GREEN, EVESHAM and MALVERN LINE
LMS : Midland
REDDITCH 56.60
UP GOODS
UP MAIN
DOWN MAIN
DOWN GOODS
Cofton 50.34
BAG 2 [MD 305]
BIRMINGHAM and GLOUCESTER LINE
LMS : Midland
Halesowen Jn 49.21
49.26
REVERS'S
UP SLOW
UP FAST
DOWN FAST
DOWN SLOW
LONGBRIDGE 49.12
Controlled by Saltley PSB (SY)
NORTHFIELD 48.12
47.53
LMS : Mid
[MD 305]
BAG 2
NECK
ARR & DEP
On-track Plant Depot
Pershore Road Tunnel (62 yards) 47.37-34
47.64
47.48
47.20
46.42
Kings Norton Station Jn
KINGS NORTON 46.59
*Kings Norton Jn
COM
48.02 via New Street BAG 2
← 46.77 via Camp Hill BAG 2 SKN
Ø 47.48
2 BAG 1
2 BAG SKN
46.42
LIFFORD CURVE
Lifford West Jn 46.36
[MD 580] LEL
Lifford East HABD 46.00
Lifford East Jn 46.11
UP MAIN
DN MAIN
BOURNVILLE for Cadbury World 46.58
SELLY OAK 45.50
Worcester & Birmingham Canal 45.74
Selly Oak Viaduct 45.42-32
UNIVERSITY 44.73
Saltley (SY) | New St (NS)
Miles from Derby via Whitacre & New Street
BIRMINGHAM WEST SUBURBAN LINE
LMS : Mid
BAG 1 [MD 305]
FIVE WAYS 43.18
43.61-56
43.46
Church Road Tunnel (106 yards)
43.07-42.78
42.72-68
Bath Row Tunnel (210 yards)
Granville Street Tunnel (81 yards)
16 : to Birmingham New Street
UP CAMP HILL
DOWN CAMP HILL
45.03
HAZELWELL 45.07
44.49
Saltley PSB (SY) | West Midlands SC (LL) (located at Saltley)
SKN [MD 570]
BIRMINGHAM and GLOUCESTER LINE
LMS : Midland
Miles from Derby via Whitacre
Moseley Tunnel (155 yards)
43.54 43.47
15B : to Birmingham Snow Hill
Bordesley Jn 41.44
41.68
127.70
128.11
DCL BCV
15B : to Tyseley
16 : to Saltley & Grand Jn

Miles from Dudley Junction 13 14 15 16 17

Controlled by Aston SSC (AN) located at Duddeston

Quattro Group Lichfield Depot
Anglesea Sidings
12.15 12.34 12.64 12.66 M6 (Toll)
(OOU)
BJW 3 [MD 350]
SOUTH STAFFORDSHIRE LINE
Fosseway (AHBC) 15.32
UP & DOWN BRANCH
LICHFIELD CITY 16.70 (7)
16.47 XF
Lichfield City Jn 13.33
13.37 (11)
STABLING
Engineers' Sdg

12A : to Rugeley
Up Sidings
18
Lichfield Chord Jn 116.28/0.02
Lichfield TV Chord [MD 355] LTV
(LS) (TV)
Lichfield TV Jn 0.22/18.13
18.04
LICHFIELD TRENT VALLEY (HL)18.05/ 116.19(LL)
FP LC18.14
Lichfield TV HL Jn (TV) 18.15
18.05
Aston (AN) | (TV)
Hollands (Streethay) 18.41
Corks Farm No. 2 18.66
LEC 2 [MD 101]
WEST COAST MAIN LINE

Miles from Dudley Jn 19 20 21 22
SOUTH STAFFORDSHIRE LINE
LMS : LNW
BJW 3
[MD 340] [LN 3340]
19.00
DOWN WALSALL
UP WALSALL
LNW EM
Brookhay (AHBC) 19.74
Fine Lane (MCG) 20.52
Alrewas (AS) 22.09
22.12
Waterworks (UWC) 20.13
Rodidge (MCG) 21.16
(MCB)
17 18 19 20 21 22 23
Miles from Derby
WMSC (WW) | Derby PSB (DY)
21.27

(AS) | (DY)
(R. Trent) Little Viaduct 22.53-54
Wichnor Viaduct 22.65-78
Wichnor Jn
23.33 15.65
16.22 15.73 Barton South Jn
Wichnor Viaduct (Rivers Tame & Trent) 16.79-58
23 16 15 14
Miles from Derby
Central Rivers Depot **see below**
UP MN DOWN MN
14.55
14.50 Barton North Jn
25C : to Burton-on-Trent
DERBY to BIRMINGHAM LINE
DBP 1
[LN 3501]
LMS : Mid
Controlled by Derby PSB (DY)

UP MAIN DN MAIN DGL
19.31
Elford GF 19.40
Elford Loop
20.17
20.50
22.30 Tamworth HABD
[MD 501] [LN 3501]
LNW EM
24 25 26
TAMWORTH (LOW LEVEL) 110.01
23.55
23.30
(12) TAMWORTH (HIGH LEVEL) 23.58
Tamworth Viaduct (River Anker) 24.16-05
11B : to Nuneaton
WILNECOTE 25.47 (4)
LMS : Mid
[MD 501] DBP 1
DERBY to BIRMINGHAM LINE
Controlled by WMSC (WW)
M42 27.63
27 28 29 30

19 : to Walsall
46 45 44 43 42 41
Aldridge 44.73
DOWN SUTTON PARK
UP SUTTON PARK
Miles from Aston North Jn 7 8 9 10 11 12 13
LMS : LNW
SUTTON COLDFIELD and LICHFIELD LINE
DOWN SUTTON
UP SUTTON
[MD 340] ALC 2
11.38 M6 (Toll)
10.75-11.00 Shenstone Viaduct
SHENSTONE (7) 10.53
Controlled by Aston SCC (AN)
8.04
BLAKE STREET (7) 8.15
BUTLERS LANE (7) 7.27
FOUR OAKS 6.26 (7)(8)
6.13
6
SUTTON PARK 40.09
40
39.65
5.14
5.12
5.04
Sutton Coldfield Tunnel (172 yds)
16 : to Aston
SUTTON COLDFIELD 4.74 (7)

WATER ORTON, WALSALL and WOLVERHAMPTON LINE
LMS : Mid CBR 2 [MD 565]
Controlled by WMSC (WR)
39 38 37
Miles from Derby via Whitacre Jn
UP SUTTON PARK
DOWN SUTTON PARK
Park Lane Jn 36.15
Water Orton Curve
CBR 1 WOP [MD 560]
36.04
Birmingham & Fazeley Canal 36.47
Miles from Derby via Whitacre
Heartlands: Power Station Oil Discharge Sdg (OOU)
37
Jaguar Terminal
37.10 Ramps
36.04 0.00
1 CBR 2 [MD 565]
Castle Bromwich Curve
0.55
36.08
DN (WR) UP
36 UP DBY SLOW
UP (WR) DN
UP DERBY SLOW
UP DERBY FAST
DOWN DERBY FAST
DOWN DERBY GOODS
DOWN DERBY
UP DBY FAST
36.12
36.22 Castle Bromwich Jn
35.43-40 Park Hall Viaduct River Tame
35.10 Water Orton West Jn
35.15
35
33.34
WATER ORTON 34.54 (5)
33.22
DN WHITACRE
Water Orton East Jn 34.43
(WP) | (WW)
34.43 3 DBP 3 34.43
2 33.22
COM
16 : to Saltley
[MD 501] DBP 3 LMS : Mid
DERBY to BIRMINGHAM LINE
Controlled by WMSC (WP)

River Tame Flood Arches
M42
33 34
32.37 32.40 32.54
Coleshill East Jn 33.04
M42 33.74
Coleshill West Jn 33.16
COLESHILL PARKWAY 33.10 (6)
Controlled by WMSC (WW)
KINGSBURY to WATER ORTON LINE
LMS : Mid DBP 2 [MD 501]
Controlled by WMSC (WW)
31 32
Adam Dales Viaduct 30.64-62
UP DERBY
DOWN DERBY
HAMS HALL National Distribution Park Associated British Ports
Loading Pad
Hams Hall Control Centre (HH)
(33.05)
LC
TRANSFER LINE
CR
DEP R/R
E. ARR
W. ARR
(32.58)
UP WHITACRE
DOWN WHITACRE
32.26-22 River Blythe Viaduct
H 32.15
32.10
32.00
H
#
31
Whitacre West Jn 31.69/0.00
DBP 3 KJW
NW0
[MD 555]
(WW) | (NW)
Whitacre East Jn 0.28
= Hams Hall Jn 32.03

Kingsbury Branch Jn 28.35 -0.02
28.40
SHUNTING
Down Sidings
European Metal Recycling
Kingsbury SF (KY) 28.26/0.03
KINGSBURY
Oil Sdgs
Warwickshire Oil Storage Co.
Branch Sidings
0.35 DOWN → LMS : Mid
KBC KINGSBURY BRANCH
29.27 Kingsbury Jn
29.39
1 DBP KJW 2
LMS : Mid
[MD 545]
KJW
DERBY to BIRMINGHAM LINE
Controlled by WMSC (WW)
UP DERBY DOWN DERBY
UP WHITACRE DOWN WHITACRE
DAGL = DOWN ARLEY GOODS LOOP
UP NUNEATON
DOWN
DAGL
Hall End Jn 2.20
1 2 3
Exchange Sdgs ARRIVAL
LC
LC
H
Birmingham International Freight Terminal (BIFT) (Birch Coppice)
VW Group Logistics (CEVA)
Travelling Cranes

1 2 3 4 5 6 7 8 9
Daw Mill Colliery UK Coal
Colliery Control Room (DM)
Loading Pad
Bunker
T & G Discharge Hopper
T & G = Tare & Gross
Reception/ Departure
2.07
Daw Mill West Jn 2.05
Daw Mill East Jn 2.36
Windridge (UWC) 3.03
UP ARLEY
DOWN ARLEY
5.60 Arley HABD
Arley Tunnel (709 yards) 6.22 6.55
(Stockingford)
8.34
8.71
WMSC (NW) | Rugby SCC (NW)
(NW) | (NW)
11B : to Nuneaton
[MD 555] NWO LMS : Mid
WHITACRE and NUNEATON LINE
Controlled by West Midlands SC (NW) located at Saltley

CENTRAL RIVERS DEPOT (CZ)

Bombardier Transportation for CrossCountry Trains

Wheel Lathe
Heavy Maintenance
Stores
Light Maintenance
Servicing
LC
22 21 18 17
16c 15c 14c 13c 12c
16b 15b 14b 13b 12b
16a 15a 14a 13a 11a
UC
UC = Underframe Cleaning
● = Push button control point
11c 11b 11a
10c 10b 10a
Cleaning Platforms
8c 8b 8a
7c 7b 7a
6c 6b 6a
3d 3c 3b 3a
2d 2c 2b 2a
Refuelling points
SOUTH ARRIVAL ROAD
NORTH ARRIVAL ROAD
NR limit
NR limit
CW H
SD H
Barton South Jn 15.65
Barton North Jn 14.55
UP MAIN
DOWN MAIN
15.73
14.50

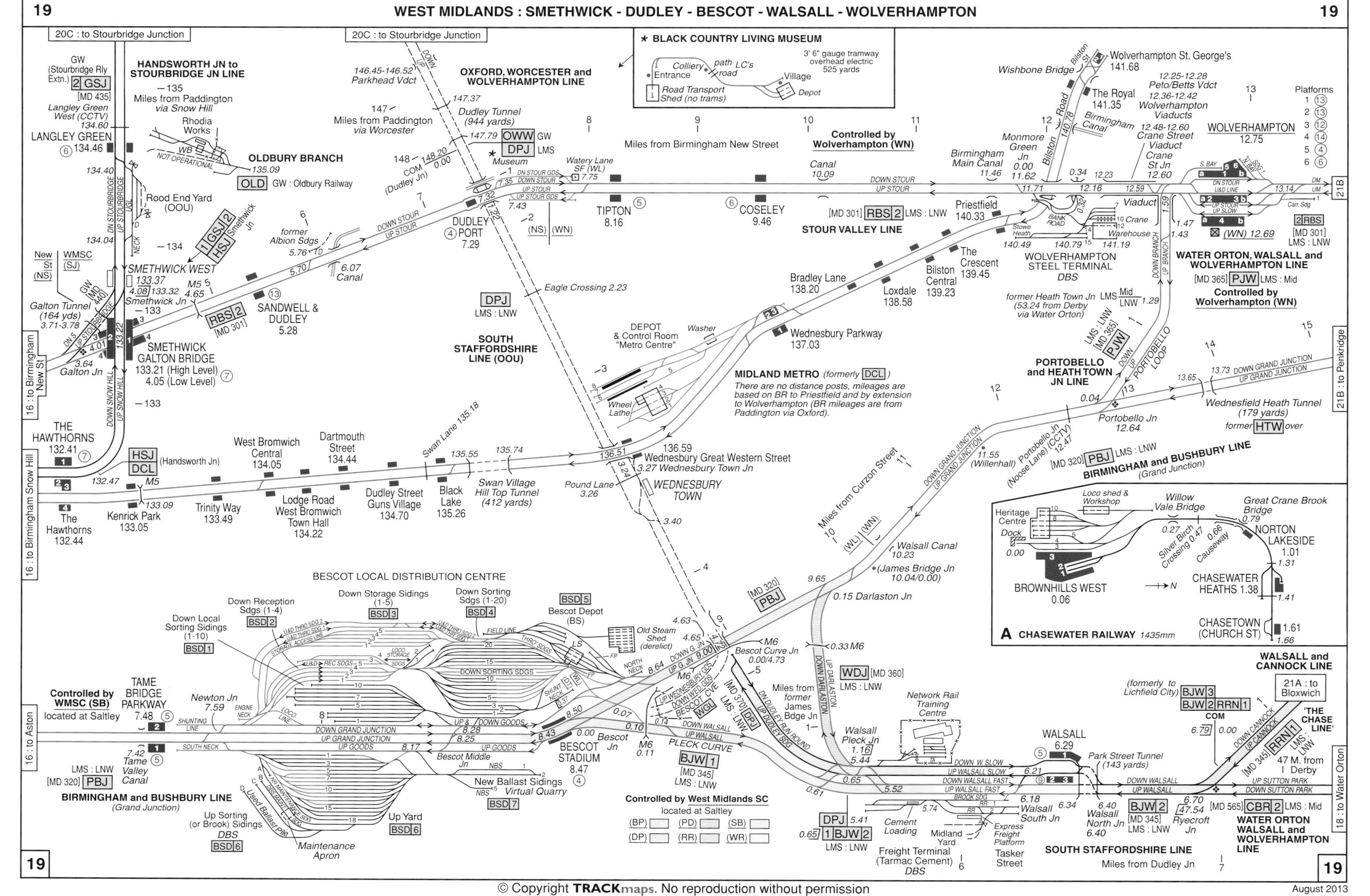

20C : to Stourbridge Junction
HANDSWORTH JN to STOURBRIDGE JN LINE
Miles from Paddington via Snow Hill
Rhodia Works
LANGLEY GREEN 134.46
Langley Green West (CCTV) 134.60
OLDBURY BRANCH
OLD GW : Oldbury Railway
Rood End Yard (OOU)
SMETHWICK WEST
Smethwick Jn
Galton Tunnel (164 yds) 3.71-3.78
Galton Jn
SMETHWICK GALTON BRIDGE 133.21 (High Level) 4.05 (Low Level)
THE HAWTHORNS 132.41
The Hawthorns 132.44
Kenrick Park 133.05
Trinity Way 133.49
West Bromwich Central 134.05
Lodge Road West Bromwich Town Hall 134.22
Dartmouth Street 134.44
Dudley Street Guns Village 134.70
Black Lake 135.26
Swan Village Hill Top Tunnel (412 yards)
Wednesbury Great Western Street
Wednesbury Town Jn
WEDNESBURY TOWN
Pound Lane 3.26
SANDWELL & DUDLEY 5.28
former Albion Sdgs
DUDLEY PORT 7.29
TIPTON 8.16
COSELEY 9.46
OXFORD, WORCESTER and WOLVERHAMPTON LINE
Miles from Paddington via Worcester
Parkhead Vdct 146.45-146.52
Dudley Tunnel (944 yards)
Museum
Watery Lane SF (WL)
SOUTH STAFFORDSHIRE LINE (OOU)
Eagle Crossing 2.23
BLACK COUNTRY LIVING MUSEUM
3' 6" gauge tramway overhead electric 525 yards
Colliery Entrance
Road Transport Shed (no trams)
Village
Depot
Miles from Birmingham New Street
Controlled by Wolverhampton (WN)
STOUR VALLEY LINE
MIDLAND METRO (formerly DCL)
There are no distance posts, mileages are based on BR to Priestfield and by extension to Wolverhampton (BR mileages are from Paddington via Oxford).
DEPOT & Control Room "Metro Centre"
Washer
Wheel Lathe
Bradley Lane 138.20
Wednesbury Parkway 137.03
Loxdale 138.58
Bilston Central 139.23
The Crescent 139.45
Priestfield 140.33
WOLVERHAMPTON STEEL TERMINAL DBS
Wolverhampton St. George's 141.68
The Royal 141.35
Wishbone Bridge
Birmingham Canal
Birmingham Main Canal
Monmore Green Jn
Peto/Betts Vdct
Wolverhampton Viaducts
Crane Street Viaduct
Crane St Jn
WOLVERHAMPTON 12.75
Platforms
21B
WATER ORTON, WALSALL and WOLVERHAMPTON LINE
Controlled by Wolverhampton (WN)
PORTOBELLO and HEATH TOWN JN LINE
former Heath Town Jn
PORTOBELLO LOOP
Portobello Jn 12.64
Wednesfield Heath Tunnel (179 yards)
21B : to Penkridge
BIRMINGHAM and BUSHBURY LINE (Grand Junction)
Miles from Curzon Street
Walsall Canal
James Bridge Jn
Darlaston Jn
Bescot Curve Jn
CHASEWATER RAILWAY 1435mm
Heritage Centre
Loco shed & Workshop
BROWNHILLS WEST 0.06
Willow Vale Bridge
Great Crane Brook Bridge
NORTON LAKESIDE 1.01
CHASEWATER HEATHS 1.38
CHASETOWN (CHURCH ST) 1.61
BESCOT LOCAL DISTRIBUTION CENTRE
Down Local Sorting Sidings (1-10)
Down Reception Sdgs (1-4)
Down Storage Sidings (1-5)
Down Sorting Sdgs (1-20)
Bescot Depot (BS)
Old Steam Shed (derelict)
Controlled by WMSC (SB) located at Saltley
TAME BRIDGE PARKWAY 7.48
Newton Jn 7.59
Tame Valley Canal
Up Sorting (or Brook) Sidings DBS
Maintenance Apron
Up Yard
New Ballast Sidings
Virtual Quarry
Bescot Middle Jn
BESCOT STADIUM 8.47
Bescot Jn
PLECK CURVE
Controlled by West Midlands SC located at Saltley
Walsall Pleck Jn
Network Rail Training Centre
Cement Loading
Freight Terminal (Tarmac Cement) DBS
Midland Yard
Express Freight Platform
Tasker Street
Walsall South Jn
WALSALL 6.29
Park Street Tunnel (143 yards)
Walsall North Jn
Ryecroft Jn
SOUTH STAFFORDSHIRE LINE
Miles from Dudley Jn
WALSALL and CANNOCK LINE
21A : to Bloxwich
'THE CHASE LINE'
47 M. from Derby
WATER ORTON WALSALL and WOLVERHAMPTON LINE
16 : to Birmingham New St
16 : to Birmingham Snow Hill
16 : to Aston
18 : to Water Orton

A

BATTLEFIELD STEAM RAILWAY

Miles from Moira West Jn

Coalville 8.09
SHACKERSTONE 8.25
8.34
Moira
Shackerstone Jn 8.18
Loco Shed
UP →
MARKET BOSWORTH 10.61
10.68
SHENTON 12.49
12.55
9 10 11 12
former Ashby & Nuneaton Joint (LNW/Mid)
ASE

B

FAIRBOURNE and BARMOUTH STEAM RAILWAY

NORTH WALES COAST LIGHT RAILWAY CO. LTD

12¼" gauge

BATHING BEACH
PASSING LOOP
Jack Steele Tunnel
(OOU)
GORSAFAWDDACHÁIDRAIG-DDANHEDDOGLEDDOLON-PENRHYNAREURDRAETHCEREDIGION (GOLF HALT)
LC
PENRHYN POINT (BARMOUTH FERRY)
GORSAF NEWYDD (FAIRBOURNE)
Loco Shed
Traverser

M = Moveable sectors
S = Sector plate
W = Workshop

C

SEVERN VALLEY RAILWAY Plc

Miles from Paddington via Worcester & Stourport

Castle Hill
Bridgnorth Cliff Railway
3' 8" gauge
201 ft long
1 in 1.8

Loco shed
Boiler shop
150.09
150
BRIDGNORTH 149.73
149.76
Oldbury Viaduct (87 yards) 149.28-32
148.60
149.04-06 Knowlesands Tunnel (44 yards)
EARDINGTON 147.57
145.72 Sterns
HAMPTON LOADE 145.33
145.31
DOWN →
COUNTRY PARK HALT 144.07
HIGHLEY 143.20
Engine House Museum
Borle Viaduct (43 yards) 142.28-30
142.34
ARLEY 140.74
Victoria Bridge (River Severn) 140.33-38
(AOCL) 138.75
NORTHWOOD HALT 138.78
BEWDLEY 137.28
Bewdley North 137.32
Carriage shed
Sandbourne Viaduct 137.02-05
P.W. Sidings
137.39
137.33-38 Wribbenhall (Bewdley) Viaduct
Bewdley South 137.14
DN MAIN
UP MAIN
COM
138.21/137.12 (Bewdley South Jn)
SVB
BYK
Bewdley Tunnel (486 yards) 136.69-137.11
— 137 miles from Paddington via Worcester & Kidderminster (reverse)
Carr. sheds
Branch mileage reverses from Main Line at 135.21
(Foley Park) 136.32
Falling Sands (Kidderminster) Viaduct (132 yards) River Stour & Canal 135.77-136.03
(DR) (KR)
Kidderminster/Hoobrook Viaduct (371 yards) 134.36-53
KIDDERMINSTER TOWN (SVR) 135.40
C&W Shed
UP & DN LP
UP & DN MN
DKiddGL
KiddTB
134.59
135.28
KIDDERMINSTER 135.46
* = Kidderminster Stn (SVR) (KR) 135.28

OXFORD, WORCESTER and WOLVERHAMPTON LINE
OWW
GW [MD 430]

HARTLEBURY 131.68
Hartlebury (CCTV) 131.72
DN KIDDERMINSTER
UP KIDDERMINSTER
LNW WR
Cutnall Green 130.40
[GW 370]

DN KIDDERMINSTER
UP KIDDERMINSTER
Blakedown (CCTV) 138.51
138.17-25 Blakedown (or Churchill) Viaduct (173 yards)
BLAKEDOWN 138.54
OWW
GW [MD 430]
HAGLEY 140.29
PMOL Depot Pre Metro Operations Ltd
(DR) (SJ)
2 & 3
STOURBRIDGE JUNCTION 142.16
SJS
GW [MD 445]
UP & DN
GF 142.24
142.78
STOURBRIDGE TOWN

SDS = Stourbridge Dn Sdg
SDTS = Stourbridge Dn Thru Sdg
SDGL = Stourbridge Dn Goods Loop
✻ = Stourbridge North Jn 142.51
✱ = Stourbridge Middle Jn 142.25

Chiltern Railways LMD
142.68-77
(SJ) (DR)
DOWN DUDLEY
UP DUDLEY
Stourbridge Viaduct (190 yards)
(SJ) (DR)
NR / DBS Bdy
Kingswinford Jn GF 144.56 (OOU)
Brierley Hill Terminal: DBS
Stone Stockpile
DISCHARGE RD
RUN ROUND
DOWN/UP BRANCH
NR limit 145.60
145.73
146.30
PENSNETT London & Cambridge Properties Ltd
KWD
GW [MD 455]
KINGSWINFORD BRANCH (OOU)

144.40
OWW
GW [MD 450]
OXFORD, WORCESTER and WOLVERHAMPTON LINE
Miles from Paddington via Worcester
DOWN ROUND OAK SDG 1
UP ROUND OAK SDG 2
RONH
ROS3
ROS3 = ROUND OAK SDG 3
RONH = ROUND OAK NORTH HEADSHUNT
Round Oak Steel Terminal
Tata Steel Europe
146.13 Stop Blocks
19 : to Walsall

Miles from Paddington via Didcot, Oxford & Worcester
Controlled by West Midlands SC (DR) (SJ)

✻ 142.51
[MD 430] OWW OWW [MD 450]
GSJ 2 [MD 435]
141.06
LYE 140.14
139.04
(CCTV) 138.65
River Stour
CRADLEY HEATH 138.70
137.01
OLD HILL 137.30
Old Hill (or Blackheath) Tunnel (896 yards)
GSJ 2 [MD 435]
GW
Stourbridge Railway | Stourbridge Railway Extension
ROWLEY REGIS 136.14
136.40
Miles from Paddington via Oxford & B. (Snow Hill)
URRGL
DRRGL
136.09
135.61-58 M5
UP STOURBRIDGE
DOWN STOURBRIDGE
URRGL = Up Rowley Regis Goods Loop
DRRGL = Down Rowley Regis Goods Loop
19 : to Smethwick

3 : 14A : to Droitwich Spa

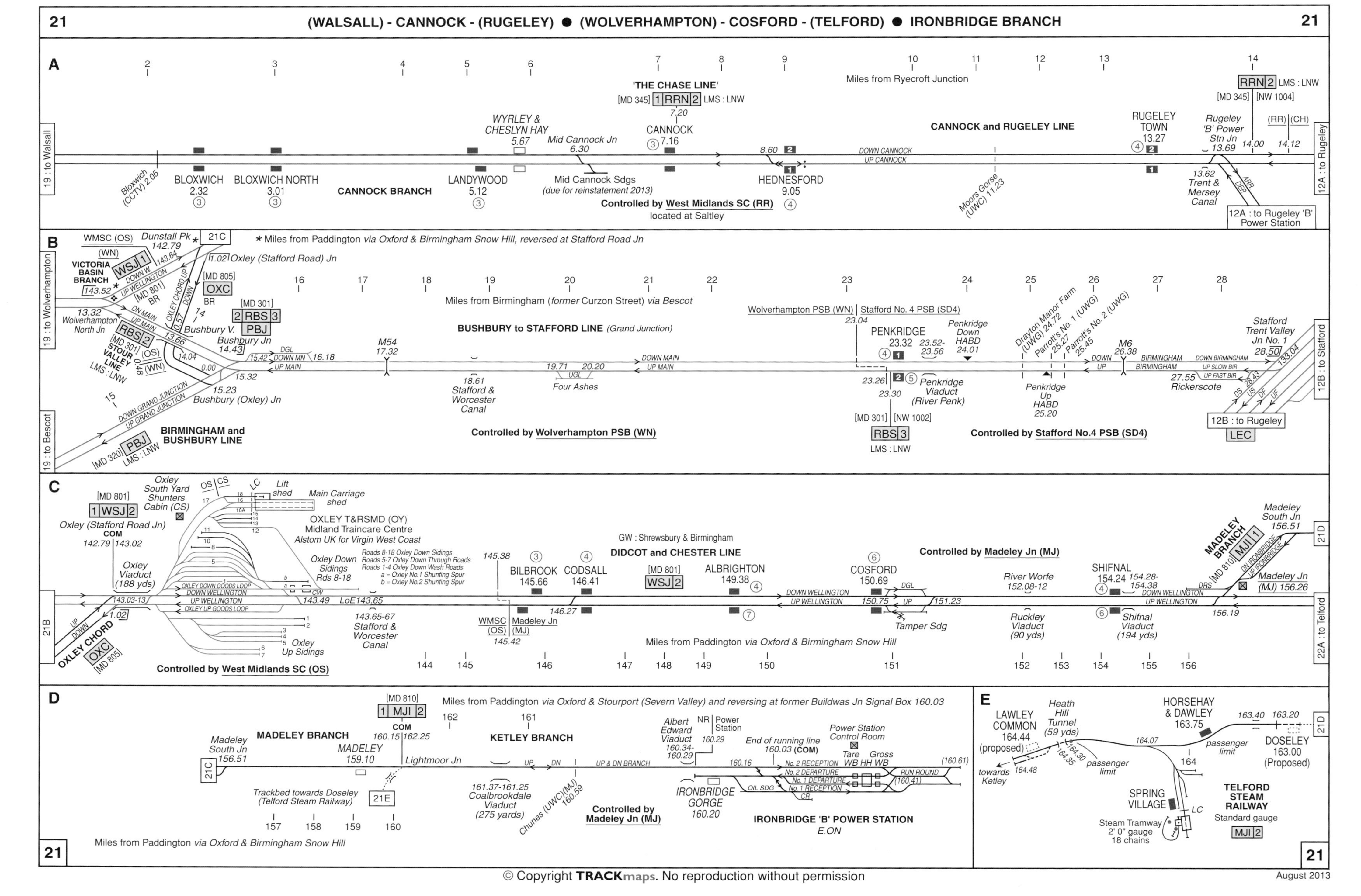
A
Miles from Ryecroft Junction
'THE CHASE LINE'
[MD 345] 1 RRN 2 LMS : LNW
CANNOCK BRANCH
CANNOCK and RUGELEY LINE
19 : to Walsall
Bloxwich (CCTV) 2.05
BLOXWICH 2.32
BLOXWICH NORTH 3.01
LANDYWOOD 5.12
WYRLEY & CHESLYN HAY 5.67
Mid Cannock Jn 6.30
Mid Cannock Sdgs (due for reinstatement 2013)
CANNOCK 7.16
HEDNESFORD 9.05
DOWN CANNOCK
UP CANNOCK
Moors Gorse (UWC) 11.23
RUGELEY TOWN 13.27
Rugeley 'B' Power Stn Jn 13.69
13.62 Trent & Mersey Canal
12A : to Rugeley 'B' Power Station
12A : to Rugeley
Controlled by West Midlands SC (RR) located at Saltley
B
★ Miles from Paddington via Oxford & Birmingham Snow Hill, reversed at Stafford Road Jn
WMSC (OS)
Dunstall Pk 142.79
VICTORIA BASIN BRANCH
Oxley (Stafford Road) Jn
Wolverhampton North Jn
STOUR VALLEY LINE
Bushbury V.
Bushbury Jn 14.43
Bushbury (Oxley) Jn
Miles from Birmingham (former Curzon Street) via Bescot
BUSHBURY to STAFFORD LINE (Grand Junction)
BIRMINGHAM and BUSHBURY LINE
M54 17.32
Stafford & Worcester Canal
Four Ashes
Wolverhampton PSB (WN)
Stafford No. 4 PSB (SD4)
PENKRIDGE 23.32
Penkridge Down HABD 24.01
Penkridge Viaduct (River Penk)
Drayton Manor Farm (UWG) 24.72
Parrott's No. 1 (UWG) 25.27
Parrott's No. 2 (UWG) 25.45
Penkridge Up HABD 25.20
M6 26.38
27.55 Rickerscote
Stafford Trent Valley Jn No. 1 28.50
19 : to Wolverhampton
19 : to Bescot
12B : to Stafford
12B : to Rugeley
Controlled by Wolverhampton PSB (WN)
Controlled by Stafford No.4 PSB (SD4)
C
Oxley (Stafford Road Jn)
Oxley Viaduct (188 yds)
Oxley South Yard Shunters Cabin (CS)
Lift shed
Main Carriage shed
OXLEY T&RSMD (OY)
Midland Traincare Centre
Alstom UK for Virgin West Coast
Oxley Down Sidings Rds 8-18
Oxley Up Sidings
OXLEY CHORD
GW : Shrewsbury & Birmingham
DIDCOT and CHESTER LINE
BILBROOK 145.66
CODSALL 146.41
ALBRIGHTON 149.38
COSFORD 150.69
Tamper Sdg
River Worfe 152.08-12
Ruckley Viaduct (90 yds)
SHIFNAL 154.24
Shifnal Viaduct (194 yds)
MADELEY BRANCH
Madeley South Jn 156.51
Madeley Jn (MJ) 156.26
Miles from Paddington via Oxford & Birmingham Snow Hill
Controlled by West Midlands SC (OS)
Controlled by Madeley Jn (MJ)
21B
22A : to Telford
D
Miles from Paddington via Oxford & Stourport (Severn Valley) and reversing at former Buildwas Jn Signal Box 160.03
MADELEY BRANCH
MADELEY 159.10
Lightmoor Jn
Trackbed towards Doseley (Telford Steam Railway)
KETLEY BRANCH
161.37-161.25 Coalbrookdale Viaduct (275 yards)
Chunes (UWC)(MJ) 160.59
Albert Edward Viaduct 160.34-160.29
IRONBRIDGE GORGE 160.20
End of running line 160.03 (COM)
Power Station Control Room
IRONBRIDGE 'B' POWER STATION
E.ON
Controlled by Madeley Jn (MJ)
Miles from Paddington via Oxford & Birmingham Snow Hill
E
LAWLEY COMMON 164.44 (proposed)
Heath Hill Tunnel (59 yds)
towards Ketley
HORSEHAY & DAWLEY 163.75
passenger limit
DOSELEY 163.00 (Proposed)
SPRING VILLAGE
Steam Tramway 2' 0" gauge 18 chains
TELFORD STEAM RAILWAY
Standard gauge

August 2013

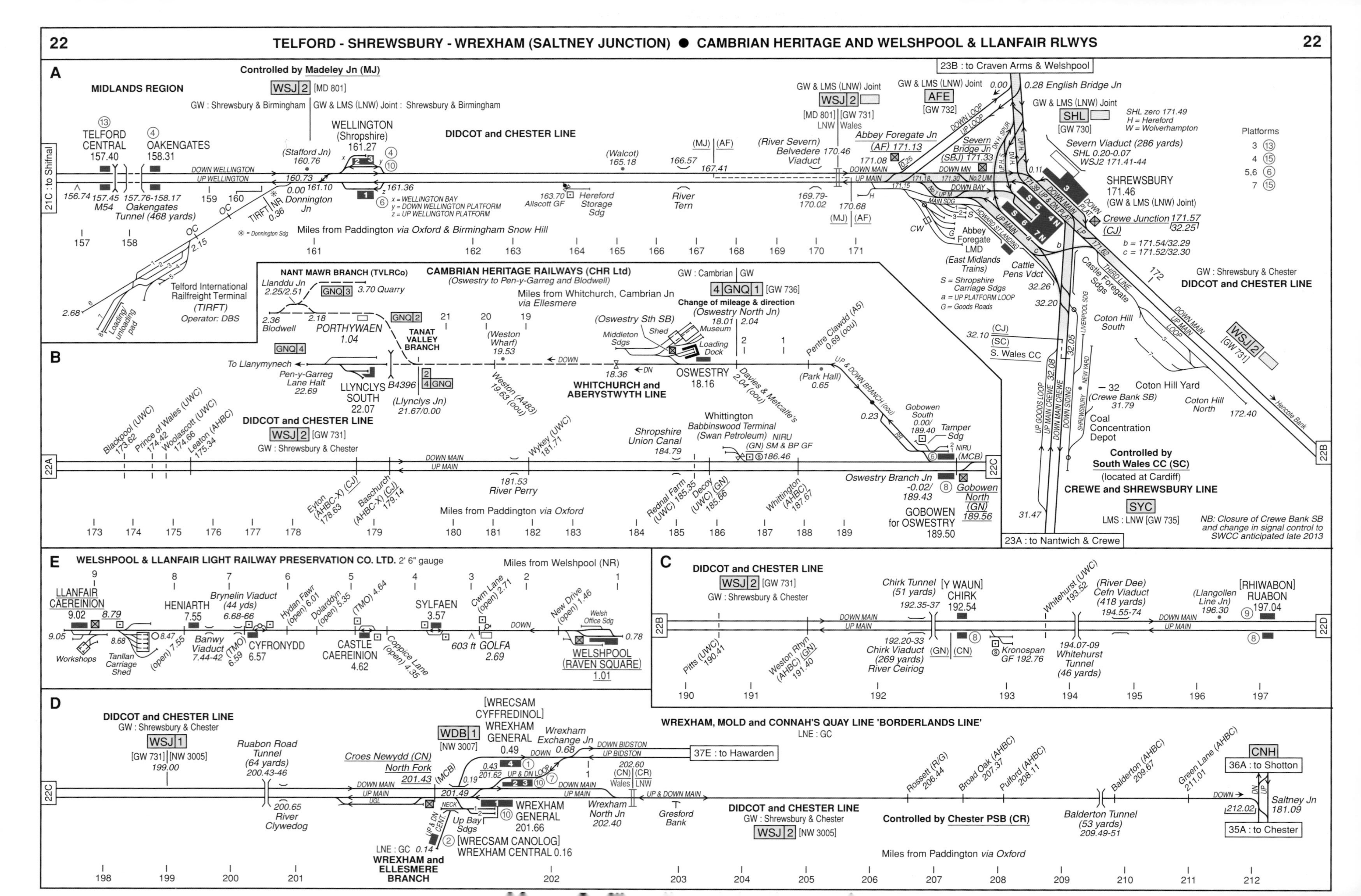
A
Controlled by Madeley Jn (MJ)
MIDLANDS REGION
WSJ 2 [MD 801]
GW : Shrewsbury & Birmingham
GW & LMS (LNW) Joint : Shrewsbury & Birmingham
21C : to Shifnal
TELFORD CENTRAL 157.40
OAKENGATES 158.31
WELLINGTON (Shropshire) 161.27
DIDCOT and CHESTER LINE
(Stafford Jn) 160.76
DOWN WELLINGTON
UP WELLINGTON
156.74 157.45 157.76-158.17
M54 Oakengates Tunnel (468 yards)
0.00 161.10
Donnington Jn
TIRFT 0.36
x = WELLINGTON BAY
y = DOWN WELLINGTON PLATFORM
z = UP WELLINGTON PLATFORM
* = Donnington Sdg
Miles from Paddington via Oxford & Birmingham Snow Hill
Telford International Railfreight Terminal (TIRFT)
Operator: DBS
Loading/unloading pad
(Walcot) 165.18
163.70 Allscott GF
Hereford Storage Sdg
River Tern
(MJ) (AF)
166.57 167.41
(River Severn) Belvedere Viaduct 170.46
169.79-170.02
170.68
GW & LMS (LNW) Joint
WSJ 2 [MD 801] [GW 731]
LNW Wales
Abbey Foregate Jn (AF) 171.13
171.08
AFE [GW 732]
23B : to Craven Arms & Welshpool
0.28 English Bridge Jn
SHL [GW 730]
SHL zero 171.49
H = Hereford
W = Wolverhampton
Severn Viaduct (286 yards)
SHL 0.20-0.07
WSJ2 171.41-44
Severn Bridge Jn (SBJ) 171.33
SHREWSBURY 171.46 (GW & LMS (LNW) Joint)
Crewe Junction 171.57 32.25 (CJ)
b = 171.54/32.29
c = 171.52/32.30
Platforms 3 (13) 4 (15) 5,6 (6) 7 (15)
Abbey Foregate LMD (East Midlands Trains)
S = Shropshire Carriage Sdgs
a = UP PLATFORM LOOP
G = Goods Roads
Cattle Pens Vdct 32.26 32.20
Castle Foregate Sdgs
Coton Hill South
Coton Hill Yard
Coton Hill North
172.40
Hencote Bank
(Crewe Bank SB) 31.79
Coal Concentration Depot
32.10 (CJ) (SC) S. Wales CC
GW : Shrewsbury & Chester
DIDCOT and CHESTER LINE
WSJ 2 [GW 731]
Controlled by South Wales CC (SC) (located at Cardiff)
CREWE and SHREWSBURY LINE
SYC
LMS : LNW [GW 735]
NB: Closure of Crewe Bank SB and change in signal control to SWCC anticipated late 2013
23A : to Nantwich & Crewe
31.47
B
NANT MAWR BRANCH (TVLRCo)
Llanddu Jn 2.25/2.51
GNQ 3 3.70 Quarry
2.36 Bldwell
PORTHYWAEN 1.04
GNQ 2
GNQ 4
TANAT VALLEY BRANCH
CAMBRIAN HERITAGE RAILWAYS (CHR Ltd) (Oswestry to Pen-y-Garreg and Blodwell)
Miles from Whitchurch, Cambrian Jn via Ellesmere
GW : Cambrian | GW
4 GNQ 1 [GW 736]
Change of mileage & direction (Oswestry North Jn) 18.01 2.04
To Llanymynech
Pen-y-Garreg Lane Halt 22.69
LLYNCLYS SOUTH 22.07
B4396
(Llynclys Jn) 21.67/0.00
(Weston Wharf) 19.53
Weston (A483) 19.63 (oou)
(Oswestry Sth SB)
Middleton Sdgs
Shed
Museum
Loading Dock
OSWESTRY 18.16
WHITCHURCH and ABERYSTWYTH LINE
Davies & Metcalfe's 2.04 (oou)
Pentre Clawdd (A5) 0.69 (oou)
(Park Hall) 0.65
UP & DOWN BRANCH (oou)
Gobowen South 0.00/189.40
Tamper Sdg
Oswestry Branch Jn -0.02/189.43
GOBOWEN for OSWESTRY 189.50
Gobowen North (GN) 189.56
DIDCOT and CHESTER LINE
WSJ 2 [GW 731]
GW : Shrewsbury & Chester
22A
Blackpool (UWC) 173.62
Prince of Wales (UWC) 174.42
Woolascott (UWC) 174.66
Leaton (AHBC) 175.34
Eyton (AHBC-X) (CJ) 178.63
Baschurch (AHBC-X) (CJ) 179.14
Wykey (UWC) 181.71
181.53 River Perry
Shropshire Union Canal 184.79
Whittington Babbinswood Terminal (Swan Petroleum)
(GN) SM & BP GF 186.46
Rednal Farm (UWC) 185.35
Decoy (UWC) (GN) 185.66
Whittington (AHBC) 187.67
Miles from Paddington via Oxford
E
WELSHPOOL & LLANFAIR LIGHT RAILWAY PRESERVATION CO. LTD. 2' 6" gauge
Miles from Welshpool (NR)
LLANFAIR CAEREINION 9.02
Workshops
Tanllan Carriage Shed
HENIARTH 7.55
Brynelin Viaduct (44 yds) 6.68-66
Banwy Viaduct 7.44-42
CYFRONYDD 6.57
Hydan Fawr (open) 6.01
Dolarddyn (open) 5.35
CASTLE CAEREINION 4.62
Coppice Lane (open) 4.35
SYLFAEN 3.57
Cwm Lane (open) 2.71
603 ft GOLFA 2.69
New Drive (open) 1.46
Welsh Office Sdg
WELSHPOOL (RAVEN SQUARE) 1.01
C
DIDCOT and CHESTER LINE
WSJ 2 [GW 731]
GW : Shrewsbury & Chester
22B
Pitts (UWC) 190.41
Weston Rhyn (AHBC) (GN) 191.40
Chirk Tunnel (51 yards) 192.35-37
[Y WAUN] CHIRK 192.54
192.20-33 Chirk Viaduct (269 yards) River Ceiriog
(GN) (CN)
Kronospan GF 192.76
Whitehurst (UWC) 193.52
194.07-09 Whitehurst Tunnel (46 yards)
(River Dee) Cefn Viaduct (418 yards) 194.55-74
(Llangollen Line Jn) 196.30
[RHIWABON] RUABON 197.04
22D
D
DIDCOT and CHESTER LINE
GW : Shrewsbury & Chester
WSJ 1 [GW 731] [NW 3005] 199.00
Ruabon Road Tunnel (64 yards) 200.43-46
200.65 River Clywedog
Croes Newydd (CN) North Fork 201.43
WDB 1 [NW 3007]
[WRECSAM CYFFREDINOL] WREXHAM GENERAL 0.49
Wrexham Exchange Jn 0.68
DOWN BIDSTON
UP BIDSTON
37E : to Hawarden
WREXHAM GENERAL 201.66
Up Bay Sdgs
[WRECSAM CANOLOG] WREXHAM CENTRAL 0.16
LNE : GC 0.14
WREXHAM and ELLESMERE BRANCH
Wrexham North Jn 202.40
202.60 (CN) (CR) Wales LNW
Gresford Bank
WREXHAM, MOLD and CONNAH'S QUAY LINE 'BORDERLANDS LINE'
LNE : GC
DIDCOT and CHESTER LINE
GW : Shrewsbury & Chester
WSJ 2 [NW 3005]
Controlled by Chester PSB (CR)
Rossett (R/G) 206.44
Broad Oak (AHBC) 207.37
Pulford (AHBC) 208.11
Balderton Tunnel (53 yards) 209.49-51
Balderton (AHBC) 209.67
Green Lane (AHBC) 211.01
CNH
36A : to Shotton
Saltney Jn 181.09
212.02
35A : to Chester
Miles from Paddington via Oxford

A

31 30 29 28 27 26 25 24 23 22 21 20 19 18 17 16 15 14 13 12 11 10 9 8 7 6 5 4 3 2

Miles from Crewe South Junction

22A : to Shrewsbury

Harlescott (MCB-OD) 30.29
Bridgeway (UWC) 28.35
YORTON 25.14
Lyons Wood Farm (UWC) 23.54
21.77 21.69
WEM 21.57
Wem (MCB-OD) 21.57
Creamore Farm (UWC) 20.50
Farm Crossing (UWC) 19.36
Prees (MCB-OD) 18.39
PREES 18.36
DOWN MAIN
UP MAIN
[GW 735] SYC LMS : LNW
CREWE and SHREWSBURY LINE
Controlled by South Wales Control Centre (SC)
located at Cardiff
Darlington's (UWC) 14.32
WHITCHURCH 13.44
Kynaston (UWC) 12.30
Brick Kiln Lane (UWC) 12.50
Marley Green (UWC) 10.10
WRENBURY 8.48
Wrenbury (MCB-OD) 8.52
Young's Farm Crossing (UWC) 8.23
Reed's Farm (UWC) 6.51
Shropshire Union Canal 5.30
Green Lane (UWC) 4.74
Fields Farm (UWC) 4.57
Shrewbridge Road 4.32 (AHBC-X)
River Weaver 4.40
(MCB-OD) 4.14 NANTWICH
Newcastle Rd (AHBC-X) 3.46
3.10
2.60
Willaston (CCTV) (Gresty Lane) 2.41
Gresty Green
DOWN MAIN
UP MAIN 1.18
Limit of electrification 1.41
(SC) (GL)
[GW 735] Wales | LNW [NW 1007]
13 : to Crewe

NB: Signal Boxes at Harlescott, Wem, Prees, Wrenbury and Nantwich are shown as closed. Change in control to SWCC is scheduled for late 2013.

B

18 17 16 15 14 13 12 11 10 9 8 7 6 5 4 3 2

3 : 27A : to Craven Arms

Miles from Shrewsbury Stn.
Zero = 171.49 (Paddington mileage)

(MCB)
Marsh Brook (MB) 15.29
Old Mill (UWC) 15.06
Woodlands (UWC) 14.66
Marsh Farm HABD 14.33
13.35
CHURCH STRETTON 12.63
613 ft
UP MAIN
DOWN MAIN
All Stretton No. 1 (UWC) 11.38
New House Farm (UWC) 8.45
Micklewood No. 2 (UWC) 7.67
Dorrington (DR) 6.25

SHREWSBURY to HEREFORD LINE
SHL [GW 730] GW : LMS (LNW) Joint : Shrewsbury & Hereford

Tarmac GF 2.77
Hopper (OOU)
Bayston Hill Tarmac
1.31
UP GOODS LOOP
UP MAIN
DOWN MAIN
0.72
0.68
0.00
0.65
Sutton Bridge Jn (SUB)
23C : to Dovey Jn
DOWN
WELSHPOOL SINGLE
UP
GW & LMS (LNW) Jt : Shrewsbury & Welshpool
[GW 733] SBA 1
Sidings: 1 & 2 ETRMS
4 & 5 OTM
Servicing Shed
Loading Docks
Coleham Depot
0.39-32 Abbey Foregate Viaduct
22A : to Shrewsbury

C

44 43 42 41 40 39 38 37 36 35 34 33 32 16 15 14 13 12 11 10 9 8 7 6 5 4 3 2 1

23D

Miles from Whitchurch *via* Oswestry

44.04 Court Farm (UWC)
43.63 Abermule (AHBC)
43.26 The Bryn (UWC)
42.60 Upper Llegodig (UWC)
Cherry Orchard (UWC) 41.18
MONTGOMERY 40.18
Rhydwhimen (R/G) 39.68
38.20 Forden (AOCL)
38.06 Munllyn (UWC)
36.39 Fron (UWC)
36.57 Fron Jn
35.71 Kilkewydd Viaduct (74 yds)
Glanhafren Viaduct (31 yds) R. Severn 35.60
Glanhafren (UWC) 35.50
Coed y Dinas (UWC) 34.79
UP LOOP GF 34.00
DN LOOP
34.02 DRS 33.55
WELSHPOOL 33.70
GW : Cambrian [GW 733]
Buttington Crossing Flood Opening (38 yds) 32.30-32
32.39 Malt House (UWC)
32.27 Buttington (AHBC)
31.60 Buttington Hall (UWC)
31.25 Parry Green (UWC)
15.72 Smiths Lower Cefn (UWC)
31.20 | 16.19 (Buttington Jn)
2 SBA 1 COM

Miles from Sutton Bridge Junction
GW & LMS (LNW) Jt : Shrewsbury & Welshpool [GW 733]
Plas-y-Court (AHBC) 12.41
10.25 Westbury (AHBC)
8.76 Stretton Heath (AHBC)
7.17 Hanselmans 1 (UWC)
DOWN & UP SHREWSBURY
5.13 Bridge 22
4.09 Hanwood (UWC)
3.73 Hanwood Yard (UWC)
(Hookagate) 2.03
A5 2.10 1.49
(MH) Machynlleth SC (Limit of ETRMS
(SUB) Sutton Bridge Jn
23B

Controlled by ERTMS level 2 from Machynlleth SC (MH)

WHITCHURCH and ABERYSTWYTH LINE

SHREWSBURY and WELSHPOOL LINE

D

73 72 71 70 69 68 67 66 65 64 63 62 61 60 59 58 57 56 55 54 53 52 51 50 49 48 47 46 45

23E

Miles from Whitchurch *via* Oswestry

72.03-02 Bridge 223
71.51 Coedd Ddol (UWC)
Cemmes Road (R/G) 70.05
DN UP & DOWN SHREWSBURY UP
[GW 733] SBA 2
GW : Cambrian
66.49 Durn (UWC)
66.10 Mywars No. 2 (UWC)
Ty Pella (UWC) 65.57
65.36 Pentre Mawr (UWC)
64.06 Coed Cae No. 1 (UWC)
Caetwpa (UWC) 63.13
63.05 Tyn-yr-Wtre No. 2 (UWC)
Talerddig 61.26
UL URS DL
61.36 61.08
Ystrad Fawr (UWC) 61.25
Tyddyn-y-Pwll (UWC) 60.50
60.78 Rallt (UWC)
60.35 Pikins (UWC)
59.46 Sarn Pile Viaduct (19 yds)
59.42 Sarn (UWC)
59.17 Carno (AHBC)
58.73 Post Office No. 2 (UWC)
58.72 No. 1
58.42 Village Viaduct (18 yds)
57.76 Plas Newydd (UWC)
57.15 Oerffrwyd (UWC)
55.78 Plasau Clatter No. 1 (UWC)
54.50 Craigfryn (UWC)
Weig La (CCTV) 54.26
CAERSWS 53.31
(CCTV)
River Carno & River Severn, Bridge 171 53.20-16
53.11 Football Field (UWC)
52.70 Llanidloes Road (CCTV)
Ty Mawr Fm (UWC) 51.18
51.40 Red Ho. Fm No. 1 (UWC)
Penstrowed (UWC) 50.25
Doughty's Viaduct (62 yds)
50.12 49.42 River Severn
NEWTOWN (Powys) 47.58
UL DL
47.79 47.47
Newtown GF 47.65
TROLLEY SDG
DN BAY SDG
Pen-y-gelli No. 2 (UWC) 46.34
Pen-y-gelli No. 1 (UWC) 46.29
Red House (UWC) 44.63
23C

Controlled by ERTMS level 2 from Machynlleth SC (MH)

WHITCHURCH and ABERYSTWYTH LINE

E

93 92 91 90 89 88 87 86 85 84 83 82 81 80 79 78 77 76 75 74

WHITCHURCH and ABERYSTWYTH LINE
[GW 733] SBA 1
GW : Cambrian

Controlled by ERTMS level 2 from Machynlleth SC (MH)

Platforms 3 (2), 4 & 5 (OOU)
ABERYSTWYTH 95.60 (0.16)
Up Sdgs
SDG 1
Aberystwyth No. 1 GF 95.30
H (Plas Crug)
No. 2 GF 95.56
UP & DOWN
PIT
Vale of Rheidol GF 0.25
95 94
Llanbadarn (ABCL) 94.56
Llanbadarn (AOCL) 1.18
LLANBADARN 1.15
1.34 Rheidol River Bridge
GLANYRAFON 2.26
New Glanyrafon (ABCL) 2.02
Pant Y Peron (UWC) 90.64
Llandre Vicarage (R/G) 90.02
Llandre (ABCL) 89.58
← DOWN
Borth Capel Soar (AOCL) 87.59
BORTH 87.27
Borth Capel Seion (UWC) 87.35
Miles from Whitchurch *via* Oswestry
CAPEL BANGOR 4.57
4.53 c 75 ft
Tanyrallt (OC) 5.34
86.04 Aberleri (AHBC)
85.32-85.30 Leri Viaduct (Bridge 250) (49 yds)
85.29 Leri Bdge (UWC)
85.21 Ynyslas (AHBC)
Brickyard No. 3 (UWC) 84.66
Nantyronen (OC) 6.55
NANTYRONEN (197 ft) 6.58
83.31
x UP & DN ABERYSTWYTH
Trer'ddol River Viaduct (Bridge 247) (28 yds)
Aberffrwd (OC) 7.55
ABERFFRWD 7.51
c 280 ft
x 82.48 Bridge 246
y 79.18 Bridge 242
GW : Cambrian
SBA 2 [GW 733]
Cottage Pie Viaduct (Bridge 243) (24 yds)
80.19
425 ft
RHEIDOL FALLS 9.21
(Mileposts are on the north (up) side)
24A : to Tywyn
y
Dovey Jn 78.60
79.11
78.58
DOVEY JUNCTION (CYFFORDD DYFI) 79.03
(Quay Ward) 78.08 No. 4 (UWC)
77.71 No. 3 (UWC)
77.61 No. 2 (UWC)
77.44 No. 1 (UWC)
Dolydfi (UWC) 77.13
76.78 Rhiwlas HallNo. 4 (UWC)
c 590 ft
RHIWFRON 10.69
75.70 Rhosfach (UWC)
UP & DN DOVEY
GF 11.65
11.70
DEVIL'S BRIDGE (PONTARFYNACH)
680 ft above sea level
MACHYNLLETH 75.11
UP MAIN
DN MAIN
75.21
AB
74.72
TANK SDG
Shed
AB = ABERYSTWYTH SIDING
* Machynlleth SC (MH) 75.08
Machynlleth LMD (MN)
Arriva Trains Wales
Llanglan Fechan No. 4 74.54
UP & DOWN SHREWSBURY
Llanglan Fechan No. 2 (UWC) 74.05
DN UP
23D

Vale of Rheidol Light Railway (1' 11½" gauge)
The Phyllis Rampton Narrow Gauge Railway Trust

1 2 3 4 5 6 7 8 9 10 11

August 2013

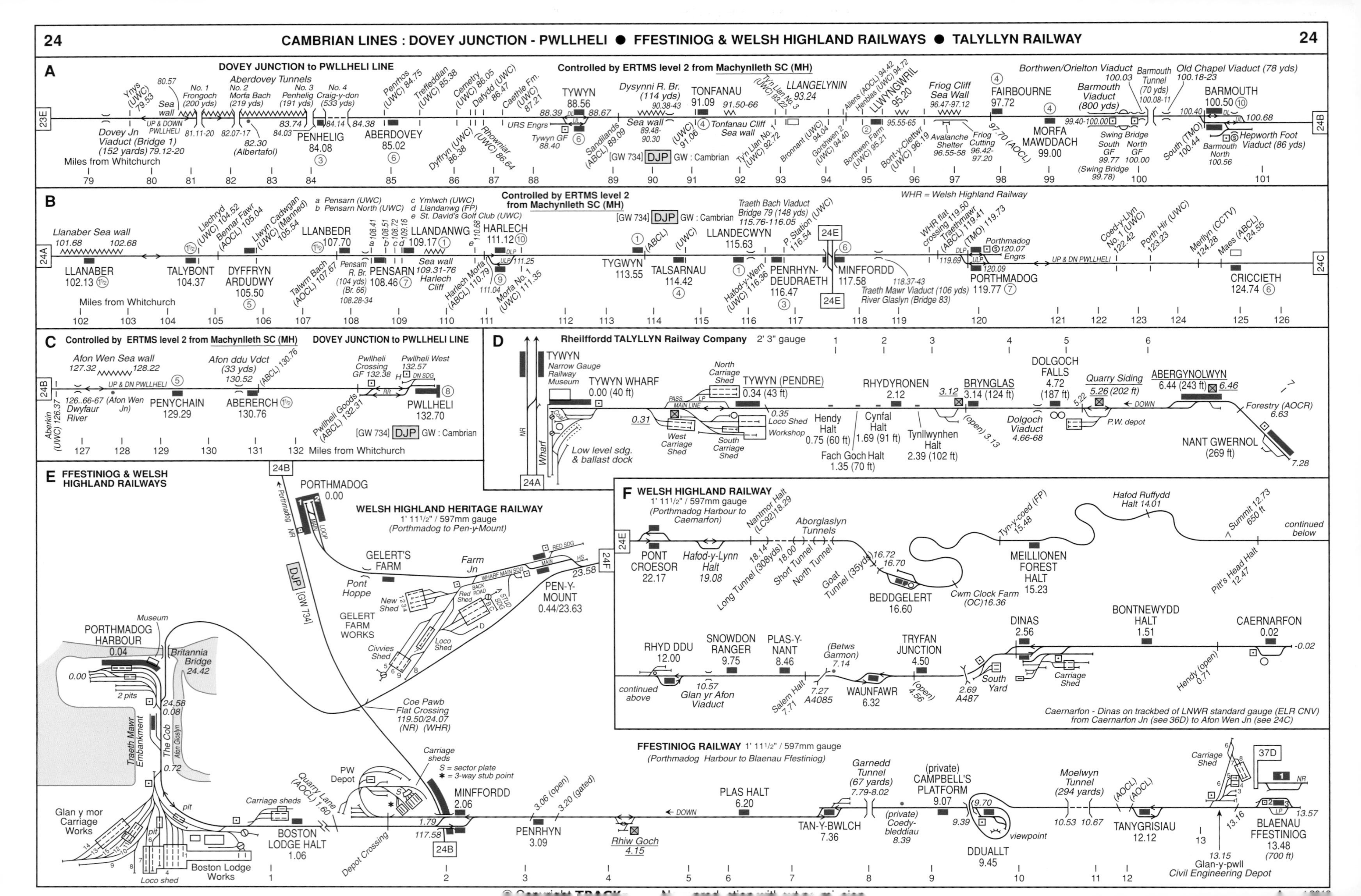
24
CAMBRIAN LINES : DOVEY JUNCTION - PWLLHELI ● FFESTINIOG & WELSH HIGHLAND RAILWAYS ● TALYLLYN RAILWAY
24
A
DOVEY JUNCTION to PWLLHELI LINE
Controlled by ERTMS level 2 from Machynlleth SC (MH)
Ynys (UWC) 79.53
80.57
Sea wall
No. 1 Frongoch (200 yds)
Aberdovey Tunnels
No. 2 Morfa Bach (219 yds)
No. 3 Penhelig (191 yds)
No. 4 Craig-y-don (533 yds)
UP & DOWN PWLLHELI
Dovey Jn Viaduct (Bridge 1) (152 yards) 79.12-20
81.11-20
82.07-17
82.30 (Albertafol)
83.74
84.03
84.14
84.38
PENHELIG 84.08 ③
Penrhos (UWC) 84.75
Treffeddian (UWC) 85.38
ABERDOVEY 85.02 ⑥
Cemetry (UWC) 86.05
Dafydd (UWC) 86.47
Caethle Fm. (UWC) 87.21
Dyffryn (UWC) 86.38
Rhowniar (UWC) 86.64
URS Engrs
TYWYN 88.56
88.39
88.67
Tywyn GF 88.40
⑥
Sandilands (ABCL) 89.09
Dysynni R. Br. (114 yds) 90.38-43
Sea wall 89.48-90.30
[GW 734] DJP GW : Cambrian
TONFANAU 91.09
91.50-66
(UWC) 91.06
④ Tonfanau Cliff Sea wall
Tyn Llan No. 3 (UWC) 93.22
LLANGELYNIN 93.24
Tyn Llan No. 1 (UWC) 92.72
Bronnant (UWC) 94.04
Gorshwen 2 (UWC) 94.40
Allens (AOCL) 94.42
Henblas (UWC) 94.72
LLWYNGWRIL 95.20
②
95.55-65
Borthwen Farm (UWC) 95.21
Bont-y-Cleltwr (UWC) 96.19
Frieg Cliff Sea Wall 96.47-97.12
Avalanche Shelter 96.55-58
Friog Cutting 96.42-97.20
④ FAIRBOURNE 97.72
97.70 (AOCL)
Borthwen/Orielton Viaduct 100.03
Barmouth Viaduct (800 yds)
④
MORFA MAWDDACH 99.00
99.40-100.00
Swing Bridge South GF 99.77
North GF 100.00
(Swing Bridge 99.78)
Barmouth Tunnel (70 yds) 100.08-11
Old Chapel Viaduct (78 yds) 100.18-23
BARMOUTH 100.50 ⑩
100.40
100.68
South (TMO) 100.44
Barmouth North 100.56
Hepworth Foot Viaduct (86 yds)
Miles from Whitchurch
79 80 81 82 83 84 85 86 87 88 89 90 91 92 93 94 95 96 97 98 99 100 101
23E
24B
B
Controlled by ERTMS level 2 from Machynlleth SC (MH)
a Pensarn (UWC)
b Pensarn North (UWC)
c Ymlwch (UWC)
d Llandanwg (FP)
e St. David's Golf Club (UWC)
WHR = Welsh Highland Railway
Llanaber Sea wall 101.68 102.68
LLANABER 102.13 ①½
Llechryd (UWC) 104.52
Bennar Fawr (AOCL) 105.04
Llwyn Cadwgan (UWC) (Manned) 105.54
TALYBONT 104.37
DYFFRYN ARDUDWY 105.50 ⑤
LLANBEDR 107.70
Talwrn Bach (AOCL) 107.67
Pensarn R. Br. (104 yds) (Br. 66) 108.28-34
PENSARN 108.46 ⑦
108.41 108.51 108.72 109.16
LLANDANWG 109.17 ①
Sea wall 109.31-76 Harlech Cliff
110.88
HARLECH 111.12 ⑩
DLP ULP 111.25
Harlech Morfa (ABCL) 110.79
⑨
111.04
Morfa No. 1 (UWC) 111.35
[GW 734] DJP GW : Cambrian
TYGWYN 113.55
① (ABCL)
(UWC)
TALSARNAU 114.42 ④
LLANDECWYN 115.63
Traeth Bach Viaduct Bridge 79 (148 yds) 115.76-116.05
P. Station (UWC) 116.54
Hafod-y-Wern (UWC) 116.36
PENRHYN-DEUDRAETH 116.47 ③
24E
⑥
MINFFORDD 117.58
118.37-43
Traeth Mawr Viaduct (106 yds) River Glaslyn (Bridge 83)
WHR flat crossing 119.50
Traethmawr (ABCL) 119.41
(TMO) 119.73
119.69
Porthmadog 120.07 Engrs
120.09
PORTHMADOG 119.77 ⑦
UP & DN PWLLHELI
Coed-y-Llyn No. 1 (UWC) 122.42
Porth Hir (UWC) 123.23
Merllyn (CCTV) 124.28
Maes (ABCL) 124.55
CRICCIETH 124.74 ⑥
Miles from Whitchurch
102 103 104 105 106 107 108 109 110 111 112 113 114 115 116 117 118 119 120 121 122 123 124 125 126
24A
24C
C
Controlled by ERTMS level 2 from Machynlleth SC (MH)
DOVEY JUNCTION to PWLLHELI LINE
Afon Wen Sea wall 127.32 128.22
UP & DN PWLLHELI
Aberkin (UWC) 126.37
126.66-67 Dwyfaur River
(Afon Wen Jn)
PENYCHAIN 129.29
⑤
Afon ddu Vdct (33 yds) 130.52
(ABCL) 130.76
ABERERCH 130.76 ①½
Pwllheli Crossing GF 132.38
Pwllheli West 132.57
DN SDG
RR
Pwllheli Goods (ABCL) 132.31
PWLLHELI 132.70 ⑧
[GW 734] DJP GW : Cambrian
127 128 129 130 131 132 Miles from Whitchurch
24B
D
Rheilffordd TALYLLYN Railway Company 2' 3" gauge
TYWYN Narrow Gauge Railway Museum
TYWYN WHARF 0.00 (40 ft)
NR
Wharf
Low level sdg. & ballast dock
0.31
PASS. MAIN LINE
LP
North Carriage Shed
TYWYN (PENDRE) 0.34 (43 ft)
West Carriage Shed
South Carriage Shed
0.35 Loco Shed
Workshop
Hendy Halt 0.75 (60 ft)
Fach Goch Halt 1.35 (70 ft)
RHYDYRONEN 2.12
Cynfal Halt 1.69 (91 ft)
Tynllwynhen Halt 2.39 (102 ft)
3.12
BRYNGLAS 3.14 (124 ft)
(open) 3.13
DOLGOCH FALLS 4.72 (187 ft)
Dolgoch Viaduct 4.66-68
5.22
Quarry Siding 5.26 (202 ft)
P.W. depot
DOWN
ABERGYNOLWYN 6.44 (243 ft) 6.46
Forestry (AOCR) 6.63
NANT GWERNOL (269 ft)
7.28
1 2 3 4 5 6
24A
E FFESTINIOG & WELSH HIGHLAND RAILWAYS
24B
Porthmadog NR
PORTHMADOG 0.00
MAIN LOOP
WELSH HIGHLAND HERITAGE RAILWAY
1' 11½" / 597mm gauge
(Porthmadog to Pen-y-Mount)
GELERT'S FARM
Pont Hoppe
Farm Jn
WHARF MAIN SDG
RED SDG
MAIN
HS
24F
23.58
New Shed
Red Shed
BACK ROAD
STUD SDG
GELERT FARM WORKS
Civvies Shed
Loco Shed
PEN-Y-MOUNT 0.44/23.63
DJP [GW 734]
Museum
PORTHMADOG HARBOUR 0.04
0.00
2 pits
Britannia Bridge 24.42
24.58
0.08
The Cob
Afon Glaslyn
0.72
Traeth Mawr Embankment
Coe Pawb Flat Crossing 119.50/24.07 (NR) (WHR)
Glan y mor Carriage Works
pit
Loco shed
Boston Lodge Works
Carriage sheds
BOSTON LODGE HALT 1.06
Quarry Lane (AOCL) 1.60
PW Depot
Depot Crossing
Carriage sheds
S = sector plate
✱ = 3-way stub point
MINFFORDD 2.06
1.79
117.58
24B
PENRHYN 3.09
3.06 (open)
3.20 (gated)
Rhiw Goch 4.15
DOWN
F WELSH HIGHLAND RAILWAY
1' 11½" / 597mm gauge
(Porthmadog Harbour to Caernarfon)
24E
PONT CROESOR 22.17
Hafod-y-Lynn Halt 19.08
Nantmor Halt (LC92)18.29
Aberglaslyn Tunnels
18.14 Long Tunnel (308yds)
18.00 Short Tunnel
North Tunnel
Goat Tunnel (35yds)
16.72
16.70
BEDDGELERT 16.60
Cwm Clock Farm (OC)16.36
Tyn-y-coed (FP) 15.48
MEILLIONEN FOREST HALT 15.23
Hafod Ruffydd Halt 14.01
Summit 12.73 650 ft
continued below
Pitt's Head Halt 12.47
RHYD DDU 12.00
continued above
10.57 Glan yr Afon Viaduct
SNOWDON RANGER 9.75
PLAS-Y-NANT 8.46
Salem Halt 7.71
7.27 A4085
(Betws Garmon) 7.14
WAUNFAWR 6.32
TRYFAN JUNCTION 4.50
(open) 4.56
2.69 A487
South Yard
DINAS 2.56
Carriage Shed
BONTNEWYDD HALT 1.51
Hendy (open) 0.71
CAERNARFON 0.02
-0.02
Caernarfon - Dinas on trackbed of LNWR standard gauge (ELR CNV) from Caernarfon Jn (see 36D) to Afon Wen Jn (see 24C)
FFESTINIOG RAILWAY 1' 11½" / 597mm gauge
(Porthmadog Harbour to Blaenau Ffestiniog)
PLAS HALT 6.20
Garnedd Tunnel (67 yards) 7.79-8.02
TAN-Y-BWLCH 7.36
(private) Coedy-bleddiau 8.39
(private) CAMPBELL'S PLATFORM 9.07
9.39
9.70
viewpoint
DDUALLT 9.45
Moelwyn Tunnel (294 yards)
10.53 10.67
(AOCL)
(AOCL)
TANYGRISIAU 12.12
13
13.15 Glan-y-pwll Civil Engineering Depot
13.16
Carriage Shed
37D
NR
LP
13.57
BLAENAU FFESTINIOG 13.48 (700 ft)
1 2 3 4 5 6 7 8 9 10 11 12

A

FOXFIELD RAILWAY

BLYTHE BRIDGE (CAVERSWALL ROAD) 2.70
Loco Shed
2.72
Running Shed
25B
3.27 3
Blythe Bridge West
← DOWN
NR
3.32
(CCTV) 5.19
BLYTHE BRIDGE 5.23
Creswell Ford 2.13
Cash Heath Jn 2.61
Forsbrook Road 2.55
Hegarty's or Blakeley-bank Wood 1.67
DILHORNE PARK 0.72
Near 0.50 NIRU
Foxfield Bank 1/31, 1/25, 1/19, 1/28
FOXFIELD COLLIERY 0.00
All level crossing are "open"

LEEK LINE

LMS : NS [NW 5010]
SCQ 2 / SCQ 1 (Milton Jn) 0.00 / 3.51
(ELR origin at -0.22)
Controlled by (SOT)
Change of mileage
0.40 (Milton)
Abbey (TMO) 3.20
2.60, 2.22, 1.73 River Trent
Stockton Brook Tunnel (72 yds) 2.09-2.12
Endon (AOCL) 3.11
LEEK LINE LMS : NS SCQ 2 [NW 5010]
Non operational (leased to Moorland & City Railways Ltd)
CVL
(Birchall Tunnel 18.09-18.12 towards Leek)
River Churnet 6.58/17.50
17.62
GF
6.65/0.00 Leekbrook Jn
17.57
17.49 NR/CVR
17.45 (Leek Brook Halt)
17.28
Leekbrook Jn 6.58/17.50 (OOU)
RR
Cheddleton Tunnel (531 yds) 17.04
DN UP
Carriage Shed
Cheddleton (TMO) 16.45
CHEDDLETON 16.43
LS Pit Diesel Road
CHURNET VALLEY RAILWAY
CVL
CONSALL 14.19
Miles from Uttoxeter
KINGSLEY & FROGHALL 12.17
RR
12.00 Froghall Jn
Stock Sdg with road access
UP DOWN
No passenger availability
10.40
OAKAMOOR
10.21
WB
10.08
Diesel Workshop
1.54 Bradnop Tunnel 2.17-19
3.69
Apesford (MG) 3.20
Ipstones Summit 1063 ft 5.73
DOWN →
Caldon Low GF 7.62
7.77
CALDON LOW
[NW 5010] SCQ 3 LMS : NS
WATERHOUSES BRANCH
(leased to Moorland & City Railways Ltd, operated by Churnet Valley Railway)

B

MACCLESFIELD and COLWICH LINE

43A : to Longport
UP GOODS, UP MAIN, DOWN MAIN, DOWN GOODS
18.64 (Etruria)
Cockshute Sdgs
19.12 Cliffe Vale Jn
Miles from Macclesfield
DBS for Imerys Minerals
Cliff Vale Terminal
London North Western Yard
UP & DN THRO.S, UG
19.44
19.35 Newcastle Jn
19.45 Trent & Mersey Canal
LMS : NS CMD 2 [NW 5009]
Stoke-on-Trent SCC (SOT) 19.60
STOKE-ON-TRENT 19.78
Stoke North Jn 19.61
UP MAIN, DN & UP MAIN, BAY
20.10 Glebe Street Jn
Stoke/Seven Arches Viaduct 20.22 - 20.26
20.36 Stoke Jn
12D : to Wedgwood
Controlled by Stoke-on-Trent SCC (SOT)
UP/DN LEEK BROOK BCH
No. 1 VDCT SDG
0.68 0.63
0.00 20.33
0.00 → UP DERBY, DOWN DERBY

BIDDULPH VALLEY LINE

Non operational
Fenton Manor Tunnel (106 yds) (SOT) (FY)
LONGTON 1.71
(FY) Foley Crossing 1.56
1.75-2.05 Longton Vdct A50(T)
1.40 LNW EM [NW 5012] [LN 3505]
NSS LMS : NS
3.12 3.49
Meir Tunnel (814 yds)
4.13
Caverswall (CL) 4.20
(MCB)
4.54 UGL UP DOWN DGL 4.58
25A
BLYTHE BRIDGE 5.23
Calverleigh Farm (UWS) 4.59
(CCTV) 5.19
Stallington (CCTV) (CL) 5.42
5.74 Jacksons (UWC)
6.07 Bennetts (UWC)
6.45 Critchlows (UWC)
6.76 Cresswell (AHBC) (CL)
Newton (farm) (UWW) 7.61
Colliers (UWC) 9.39
Baileys (UWC) 10.06
Leigh (AHBC-X) (CL) 10.24
Upper Leigh (CL) (AHBC-X) 9.57
UP STOKE, DOWN STOKE
NSS [LN 3505] LMS : NS
DERBY LINE
13.32 Bramshall (AHBC-X)
13.52 Serieants (UWC)
13.71 Westons (UWC)
14.11 Loxley Lane (AHBC-X)
14.50 Stathams (UWC)
15.27 Bakers (UWC)
25C

C

25B
Hockley (CCTV) 15.61
Pinfold (MCB) 16.00
Bridge St Vdct 16.17
Uttoxeter Racecourse (UWC) 16.33
DGL
Engrs
A518
Uttoxeter (UR) 16.00
UTTOXETER 16.29
UP STOKE, DOWN STOKE
17.20 Tunnicliffs No. 1 (UWC)
17.75 Langridge No. 2 (UWC)
Marchington Old Stn (UWC) 19.01
MARCHINGTON 18.78
19.62 Dovefields (R/G)
Sudbury 20.67 (SY)
21.20 Nash's (UWC)
(MCB)
21.15-19 Sudbury Vdct River Dove
(MCG)
22.41 Archers No. 1 (UWC)
Scropton 22.53
22.75 Scropton Mill Ln (UWC)
23.23 Brandons (UWC)
23.43 Weer Lane (UWC)
Tutbury Crossing (MCB) 24.13
TUTBURY & HATTON 24.13
24.33 Rocks (UWC)
24.57 Rowes (UWC)
25.28 Marston-on-Dove (AHBC)
25.45 Hayside (UWC)
26.06 Spurrier's No.2 (UWC)
DERBY LINE
NSS [LN 3505] LMS : NS
Miles from Stoke Jn
26.67
Egginton Jn (EN) 26.69
Hilton (MCG) 27.08
Egginton (AHBC-X) 27.50
Miles from Derby, London Road Jn

DERBY to BIRMINGHAM LINE

[LN 3501] DBP 1 LMS : Mid
18 : to Wichor Jn & Tamworth
Branston Up HABD 13.44
13.31 Dunstalls (UWC)
Boultons (UWC) 12.47
UP MAIN, DOWN MAIN
Branston Jn 12.15
127.19
UP THROUGH SDG, DOWN THROUGH SDG
Branston (OOU) 127.13
BIRMINGHAM CURVE
BCJ [LN 3535] LMS : Mid
LMS : Mid [LN 3525] KSL
DN LEICESTER GDS, UP LEICESTER GDS
Cambridge Street (UWC) 126.60
Birmingham Curve Jn 126.40 (miles from St. Pancras)
7C : to Coalville
LEICESTER and BURTON LINE
Leicester Jn 11.17 127.00 11.02
M. St GF 11.00
NIRU
Mosley Street Sdgs
BURTON ON TRENT 10.67
Horninglow Bridge Jn 10.33
10.25
New Wetmore Sdgs
Depot Nemesis Rail
UP GOODS, UP MAIN, DOWN MAIN, DOWN GOODS
DEP ARR
West Yard
Horninglow Sdgs Steel Terminal Maurice Hill (Road & Rail Ltd)
East Yard
9.51 9.42
9.46
9.51
9.60 Wetmore Jn
Controlled by Derby PSB (DY)
Clay Mills Jn (CCTV) 8.54
8.17 Wiltshires (UWC)
8.13 Bromleys (UWC)
River Dove Viaduct 7.79-7.76
(EN) (DY)
6.01 Willington Down HABD
WILLINGTON 6.03
UP STOKE, DOWN STOKE
Willington (AHBC) 29.19
Findern (AHBC) 29.49
29.51
Trent & M. Canal 30.10
5.14 North Stafford Jn
Stenson Jn 4.56
4.58 132.18
UP MAIN, DOWN MAIN
UP CHELLASTON, DN CHELLASTON
SSJ 2 [LN 3520] LMS : Mid
6C : to Sheet Stores Jn
STENSON BRANCH
Stenson Raynors (UWC) 4.16
DERBY to BIRMINGHAM LINE
DBP 1 LMS : Mid [LN 3501]
2.08 UGL UP MAIN, DOWN MAIN, DOWN GOODS
2.34
Sunny Hill
1.31 1.44 1.02
Melbourne Jn 131.15 1.27
PEARTREE 1.16
(OOU) RAMSLINE HALT 0.51
ø St. Andrews Sidings 1 & 2
UP MAIN WEST, DN MAIN WEST, UP GDS WEST, DN GDS WEST
4B : to Derby
L & NW Jn 0.75
131
S & T Sdg GF 0.27
SINFIN NORTH 130.73
Sinfin No. 1 GF 130.69
Sinfin No. 2 GF 130.56
RR
DERBY to MELBOURNE LINE
SINFIN CENTRAL 130.37
Rolls Royce Ltd (Oil Terminal)
Sinfin No. 3 GF 130.31
130.20 (miles from 129.79 St. Pancras)
LMS : Mid [LN 3515] MJS 1

August 2013

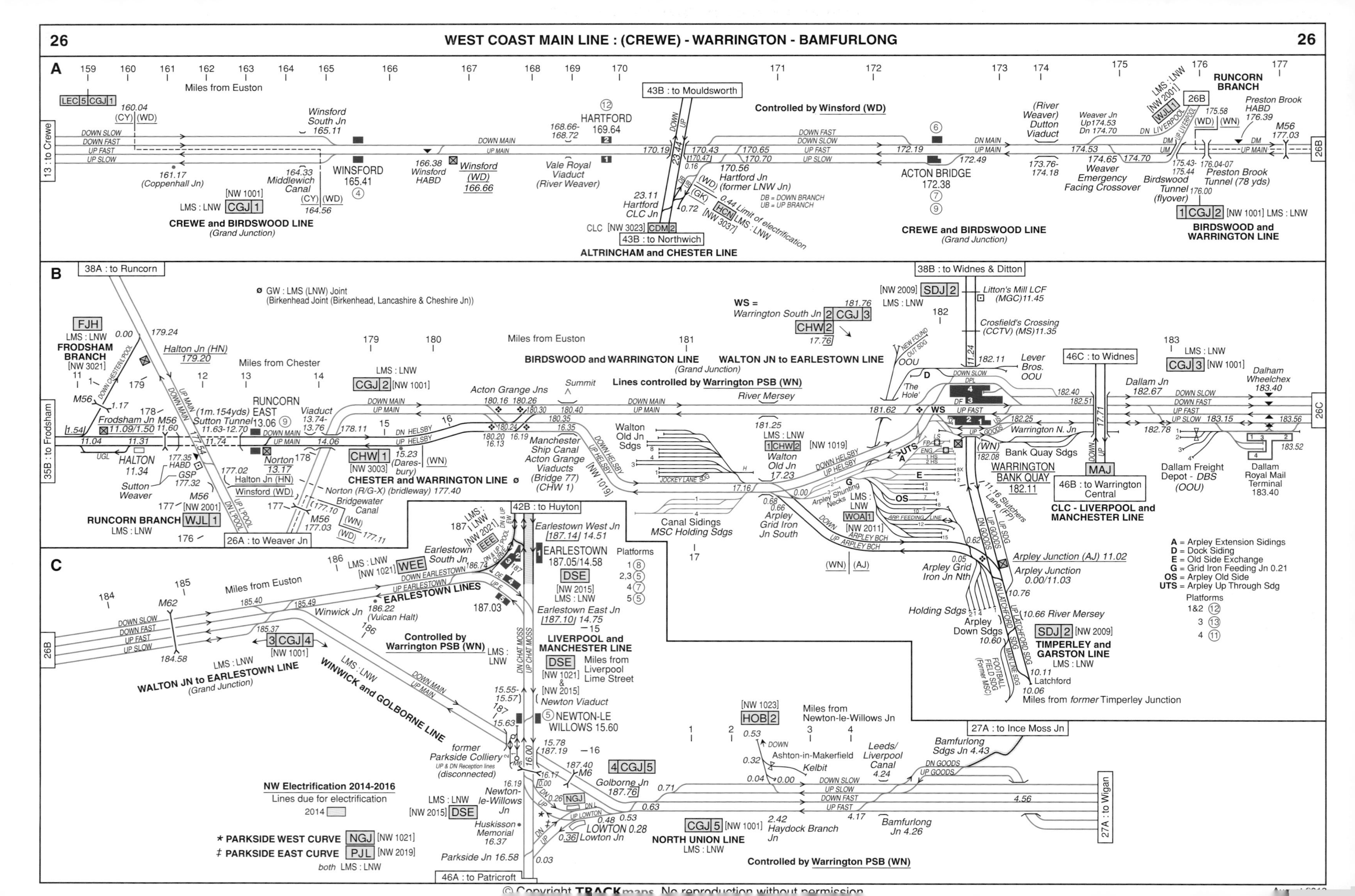
26
WEST COAST MAIN LINE : (CREWE) - WARRINGTON - BAMFURLONG
26
A
Miles from Euston
13 : to Crewe
LEC 5 CGJ 1
160.04 (CY) (WD)
DOWN SLOW
DOWN FAST
UP FAST
UP SLOW
161.17 (Coppenhall Jn)
Winsford South Jn 165.11
164.33 Middlewich Canal
(CY) (WD) 164.56
WINSFORD 165.41
[NW 1001] LMS : LNW CGJ 1
CREWE and BIRDSWOOD LINE
(Grand Junction)
166.38 Winsford HABD
Winsford (WD) 166.66
DOWN MAIN
UP MAIN
168.66-168.72
HARTFORD 169.64
Vale Royal Viaduct (River Weaver)
43B : to Mouldsworth
170.19
23.44
170.47
0.16
170.43
170.56 Hartford Jn (former LNW Jn)
23.11 Hartford CLC Jn
0.72
0.44 Limit of electrification
DB = DOWN BRANCH
UB = UP BRANCH
HCN LMS : LNW [NW 3037]
CLC [NW 3023] CDM 2
43B : to Northwich
ALTRINCHAM and CHESTER LINE
Controlled by Winsford (WD)
DOWN FAST
DOWN SLOW
UP FAST
UP SLOW
170.65
170.70
172.19
172.49
ACTON BRIDGE 172.38
CREWE and BIRDSWOOD LINE
(Grand Junction)
DN MAIN
UP MAIN
(River Weaver) Dutton Viaduct
173.76-174.18
Weaver Jn Up174.53 Dn 174.70
174.53
174.65 Weaver Emergency Facing Crossover
174.70
LMS : LNW [NW 2001] WJL 1
DN LIVERPOOL
UP LIVERPOOL
26B
175.58 (WD) (WN)
175.43-175.44 Birdswood Tunnel (flyover)
176.00
176.04-07 Preston Brook Tunnel (78 yds)
RUNCORN BRANCH
Preston Brook HABD 176.39
M56 177.03
1 CGJ 2 [NW 1001] LMS : LNW
BIRDSWOOD and WARRINGTON LINE
B
38A : to Runcorn
ø GW : LMS (LNW) Joint (Birkenhead Joint (Birkenhead, Lancashire & Cheshire Jn))
FJH LMS : LNW 0.00
FRODSHAM BRANCH [NW 3021]
179.24
Halton Jn (HN) 179.20
Miles from Chester
DOWN CHESTER/POOL
M56 1.17
Frodsham Jn M56 11.09/1.50 11.60
1.54
11.04
11.31
UGL
HALTON 11.34
177.35 HABD
GSP 177.32
Sutton Weaver
177.54
(1m.154yds) Sutton Tunnel 11.63-12.70
11.74
RUNCORN EAST 13.06
Viaduct 13.74-13.76
14.06
DOWN MAIN
UP MAIN
177.02
Halton Jn (HN)
Winsford (WD)
M56 [NW 2001]
RUNCORN BRANCH WJL 1
LMS : LNW
DN L'POOL
UP L'POOL
26A : to Weaver Jn
Norton 13.17
178.11
CHW 1 [NW 3003]
15.23 (Daresbury) (WN)
CHESTER and WARRINGTON LINE ø
Norton (R/G-X) (bridleway) 177.40
Bridgewater Canal
177.10
M56 177.03
(WN) (WD) 177.11
LMS : LNW CGJ 2 [NW 1001]
DN HELSBY
UP HELSBY
Acton Grange Jns 180.16 180.26
180.30
180.24
180.20 16.13
16.19
16.35
180.35
180.40
Summit
Manchester Ship Canal Acton Grange Viaducts (Bridge 77) (CHW 1)
Miles from Euston
BIRDSWOOD and WARRINGTON LINE
(Grand Junction)
WALTON JN to EARLESTOWN LINE
Lines controlled by Warrington PSB (WN)
River Mersey
WS = Warrington South Jn 2 CGJ 3 181.76
CHW 2 17.76
Walton Old Jn Sdgs
JOCKEY LANE SDG
17.16
181.25 LMS : LNW 1 CHW 2 [NW 1019]
Walton Old Jn 17.23
DOWN HELSBY
UP HELSBY
[NW 1019]
Canal Sidings MSC Holding Sdgs
0.00
0.68 0.66 Arpley Grid Iron Jn South
Arpley Shunting Necks
LMS : LNW WOA 1 [NW 2011]
ARPLEY BCH
(WN) (AJ)
38B : to Widnes & Ditton
[NW 2009] SDJ 2 LMS : LNW
Litton's Mill LCF (MGC)11.45
Crossfield's Crossing (CCTV) (MS)11.35
NEW FOUND OUT SDG
OOU
'The Hole'
11.24
182.11
Lever Bros. OOU
DOWN SLOW
DPL
UP FAST
181.62
WS
UTS
A
E
OS
G
182.25
Warrington N. Jn
(WN) 182.08 Bank Quay Sdgs
WARRINGTON BANK QUAY 182.11
11.16 Slutchers Lane (FP)
DN GOODS
UP GOODS
UP SDG
46C : to Widnes
17.71
182.40
182.51
MAJ
46B : to Warrington Central
CLC - LIVERPOOL and MANCHESTER LINE
Dallam Jn 182.67
LMS : LNW CGJ 3 [NW 1001]
DOWN SLOW
DOWN FAST
UP FAST
UP SLOW 183.15
182.78
Dallam Wheelchex 183.40
183.56
26C
183.52
Dallam Freight Depot - DBS (OOU)
Dallam Royal Mail Terminal 183.40
Arpley Junction (AJ) 11.02
Arpley Junction 0.00/11.03
0.62
0.05 Arpley Grid Iron Jn Nth
10.76
DN LATCHFORD
UP LATCHFORD SDG
MAIN LINE SDG
FOOTBALL FIELD SDG (Former MSC)
Holding Sdgs
Arpley Down Sdgs 10.60
10.66 River Mersey
SDJ 2 [NW 2009]
TIMPERLEY and GARSTON LINE
LMS : LNW
10.11 Latchford
10.06 Miles from former Timperley Junction
A = Arpley Extension Sidings
D = Dock Siding
E = Old Side Exchange
G = Grid Iron Feeding Jn 0.21
OS = Arpley Old Side
UTS = Arpley Up Through Sdg
Platforms
1&2 12
3 13
4 11
C
26B
Miles from Euston
M62
184.58
185.40
185.49
185.37
3 CGJ 4 [NW 1001]
LMS : LNW
WALTON JN to EARLESTOWN LINE
(Grand Junction)
Winwick Jn
186.22 (Vulcan Halt)
LMS : LNW
WINWICK and GOLBORNE LINE
DOWN MAIN
UP MAIN
LMS : LNW [NW 1021] WEE
Earlestown South Jn 186.74
DOWN EARLESTOWN
UP EARLESTOWN
EARLESTOWN LINES
LMS : LNW [NW 2021] EEE
42B : to Huyton
Earlestown West Jn 187.14 14.51
EARLESTOWN 187.05/14.58
DSE [NW 2015] LMS : LNW
187.03
Platforms
1 8
2,3 5
4 7
5 5
Earlestown East Jn 187.10 14.75
LIVERPOOL and MANCHESTER LINE
Controlled by Warrington PSB (WN)
LMS : LNW
DN CHAT MOSS
UP CHAT MOSS
DSE [NW 1021] & [NW 2015]
Miles from Liverpool Lime Street
15.55-15.57
Newton Viaduct
15.63
NEWTON-LE WILLOWS 15.60
former Parkside Colliery
UP & DN Reception lines (disconnected)
16.00
15.78 187.19
187.40 M6
16.17 0.00
16.19 Newton-le-Willows Jn
LMS : LNW [NW 2015] DSE
Huskisson Memorial 16.37
Parkside Jn 16.58
0.03
46A : to Patricroft
NGJ
0.26
UP LOWTON
0.48 0.53
LOWTON 0.28
0.36 Lowton Jn
4 CGJ 5
Golborne Jn 187.76
0.71
0.63
CGJ 5 [NW 1001]
NORTH UNION LINE
LMS : LNW
NW Electrification 2014-2016
Lines due for electrification
2014
* PARKSIDE WEST CURVE NGJ [NW 1021]
‡ PARKSIDE EAST CURVE PJL [NW 2019]
both LMS : LNW
[NW 1023] HOB 2
0.53
0.32
0.04 0.00
Ashton-in-Makerfield
Kelbit
Miles from Newton-le-Willows Jn
Leeds/ Liverpool Canal 4.24
2.42 Haydock Branch Jn
4.17
Bamfurlong Jn 4.26
27A : to Ince Moss Jn
Bamfurlong Sdgs Jn 4.43
DN GOODS
UP GOODS
DOWN SLOW
UP SLOW
DOWN FAST
UP FAST
4.56
27A : to Wigan
Controlled by Warrington PSB (WN)
© Copyright TRACKmaps. No reproduction without permission

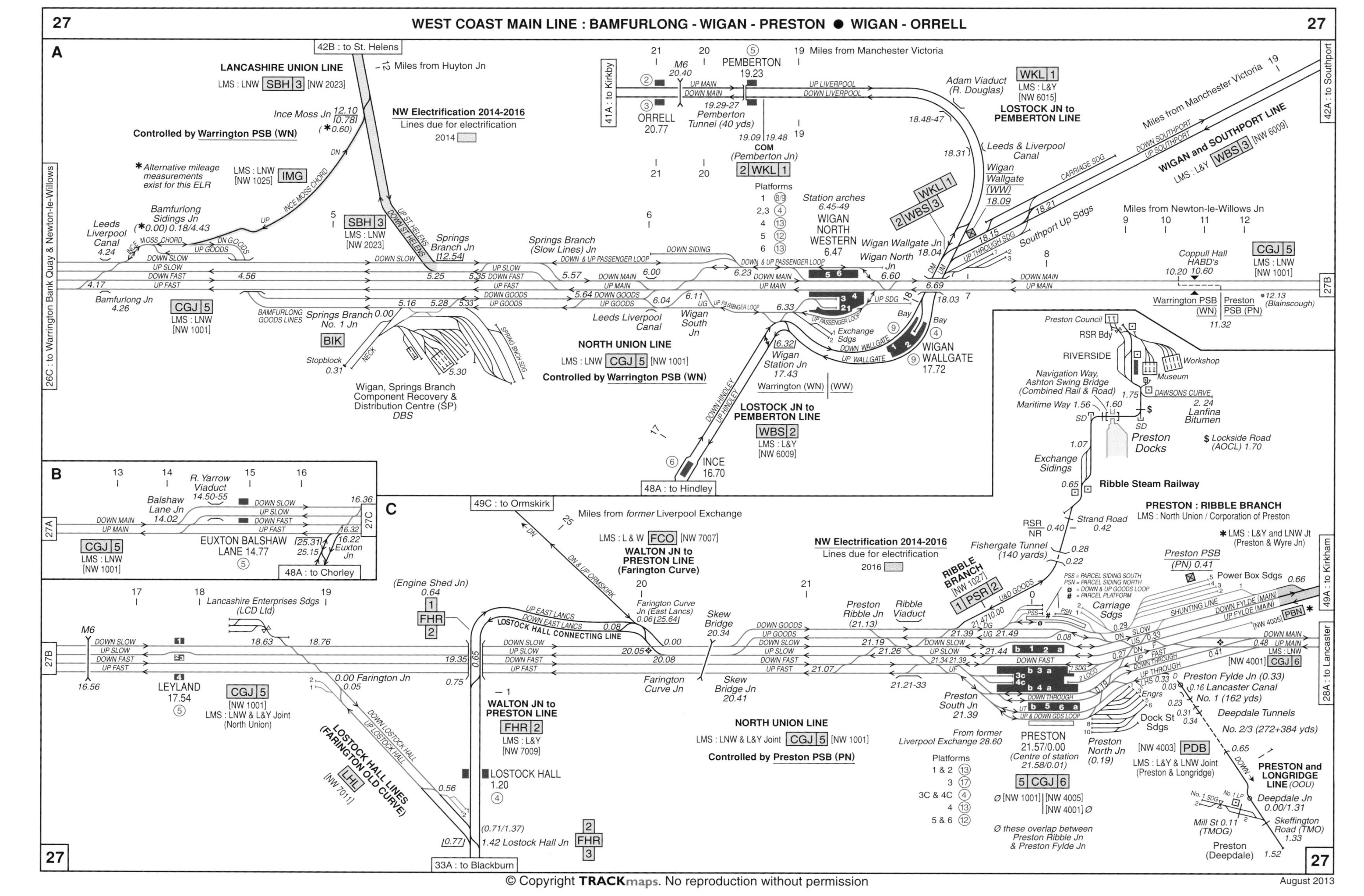
A
42B : to St. Helens
12 Miles from Huyton Jn
LANCASHIRE UNION LINE
LMS : LNW SBH 3 [NW 2023]
Ince Moss Jn 12.10 0.78 (*0.60)
Controlled by Warrington PSB (WN)
NW Electrification 2014-2016
Lines due for electrification
2014
* Alternative mileage measurements exist for this ELR
LMS : LNW [NW 1025] IMG
INCE MOSS CHORD
Bamfurlong Sidings Jn (*0.00) 0.18/4.43
Leeds Liverpool Canal 4.24
Bamfurlong Jn 4.26
CGJ 5
LMS : LNW [NW 1001]
BAMFURLONG GOODS LINES
Springs Branch 0.00 No. 1 Jn
BIK
Stopblock 0.31
Wigan, Springs Branch Component Recovery & Distribution Centre (SP) DBS
SBH 3 LMS : LNW [NW 2023]
Springs Branch Jn 12.54
Springs Branch (Slow Lines) Jn
DOWN SLOW
UP SLOW
DOWN FAST
UP FAST
DOWN GOODS
UP GOODS
DOWN MAIN
UP MAIN
DOWN & UP PASSENGER LOOP
DOWN SIDING
SPRING BNCH SDG
Leeds Liverpool Canal
Wigan South Jn
NORTH UNION LINE
LMS : LNW CGJ 5 [NW 1001]
Controlled by Warrington PSB (WN)
41A : to Kirkby
ORRELL 20.77
M6 20.40
PEMBERTON 19.23
19.29-27 Pemberton Tunnel (40 yds)
19.09 19.48
COM (Pemberton Jn)
2 WKL 1
19 Miles from Manchester Victoria
UP LIVERPOOL
DOWN LIVERPOOL
Platforms
1 8/9
2,3 4
4 13
5 12
6 13
Station arches 6.45-49
WIGAN NORTH WESTERN 6.47
Wigan North Jn 6.60
Wigan Wallgate Jn 18.04
WKL 1
2 WBS 3
Adam Viaduct (R. Douglas)
WKL 1 LMS : L&Y [NW 6015]
LOSTOCK JN to PEMBERTON LINE
Leeds & Liverpool Canal
Wigan Wallgate (WW) 18.09
Southport Up Sdgs
CARRIAGE SDG
Miles from Manchester Victoria
WIGAN and SOUTHPORT LINE
LMS : L&Y WBS 3 [NW 6009]
42A : to Southport
Miles from Newton-le-Willows Jn
Coppull Hall HABD's 10.20 10.60
CGJ 5 LMS : LNW [NW 1001]
Warrington PSB (WN) | Preston PSB (PN) 11.32
12.13 (Blainscough)
27B
WIGAN WALLGATE 17.72
Exchange Sdgs
Wigan Station Jn 17.43
Warrington (WN) | (WW)
LOSTOCK JN to PEMBERTON LINE
WBS 2 LMS : L&Y [NW 6009]
INCE 16.70
48A : to Hindley
26C : to Warrington Bank Quay & Newton-le-Willows
Preston Council
RSR Bdy
RIVERSIDE
Workshop
Museum
DAWSONS CURVE
Navigation Way, Ashton Swing Bridge (Combined Rail & Road)
Maritime Way 1.56
2.24 Lanfina Bitumen
Preston Docks
$ Lockside Road (AOCL) 1.70
Exchange Sidings
Ribble Steam Railway
B
Balshaw Lane Jn 14.02
R. Yarrow Viaduct 14.50-55
EUXTON BALSHAW LANE 14.77
Euxton Jn 16.22
CGJ 5 LMS : LNW [NW 1001]
27A
27C
48A : to Chorley
C
49C : to Ormskirk
Miles from former Liverpool Exchange
LMS : L & W FCO [NW 7007]
WALTON JN to PRESTON LINE (Farington Curve)
Farington Curve Jn (East Lancs) 0.06 25.64
LOSTOCK HALL CONNECTING LINE
(Engine Shed Jn) 0.64
1 FHR 2
Lancashire Enterprises Sdgs (LCD Ltd)
LEYLAND 17.54
CGJ 5 [NW 1001] LMS : LNW & L&Y Joint (North Union)
0.00 Farington Jn 0.05
LOSTOCK HALL LINES (FARINGTON OLD CURVE)
LHL [NW 7011]
WALTON JN to PRESTON LINE
FHR 2 LMS : L&Y [NW 7009]
LOSTOCK HALL 1.20
1.42 Lostock Hall Jn
2 FHR 3
33A : to Blackburn
Farington Curve Jn
Skew Bridge 20.34
Skew Bridge Jn 20.41
NORTH UNION LINE
LMS : LNW & L&Y Joint CGJ 5 [NW 1001]
Controlled by Preston PSB (PN)
Preston Ribble Jn (21.13)
Ribble Viaduct
NW Electrification 2014-2016
Lines due for electrification
2016
RIBBLE BRANCH [NW 1027] 1 PSR 2
Fishergate Tunnel (140 yards)
Strand Road 0.42
PRESTON : RIBBLE BRANCH
LMS : North Union / Corporation of Preston
* LMS : L&Y and LNW Jt (Preston & Wyre Jn)
Preston PSB (PN) 0.41
Power Box Sdgs
PSS = PARCEL SIDING SOUTH
PSN = PARCEL SIDING NORTH
ø = DOWN & UP GOODS LOOP
= PARCEL PLATFORM
Carriage Sdgs
SHUNTING LINE
DOWN FYLDE (MAIN)
UP FYLDE (MAIN)
PBN
49A : to Kirkham
28A : to Lancaster
Preston South Jn 21.39
From former Liverpool Exchange 28.60
PRESTON 21.57/0.00 (Centre of station 21.58/0.01)
5 CGJ 6
Ø [NW 1001] | [NW 4005]
[NW 4001] Ø
Ø these overlap between Preston Ribble Jn & Preston Fylde Jn
Platforms
1 & 2 13
3 17
3C & 4C 4
4 13
5 & 6 12
Preston North Jn (0.19)
Dock St Sdgs
Preston Fylde Jn (0.33)
0.16 Lancaster Canal No. 1 (162 yds)
Deepdale Tunnels No. 2/3 (272+384 yds)
[NW 4003] PDB
LMS : L&Y & LNW Joint (Preston & Longridge)
PRESTON and LONGRIDGE LINE (OOU)
Deepdale Jn 0.00/1.31
Skeffington Road (TMO) 1.33
Mill St 0.11 (TMOG)
Preston (Deepdale) 1.52
[NW 4001] CGJ 6
LMS : LNW

August 2013

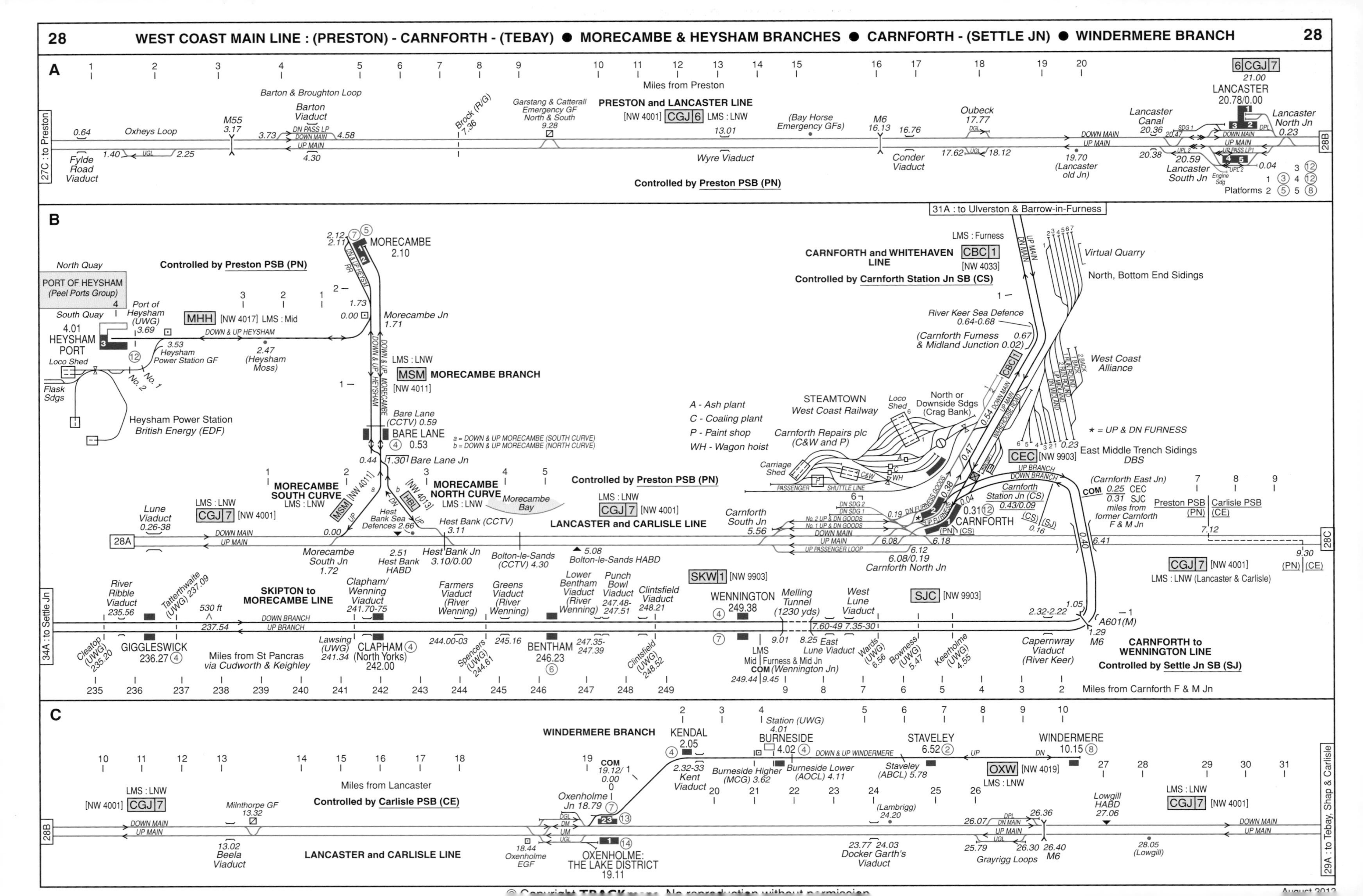
28
WEST COAST MAIN LINE : (PRESTON) - CARNFORTH - (TEBAY) ● MORECAMBE & HEYSHAM BRANCHES ● CARNFORTH - (SETTLE JN) ● WINDERMERE BRANCH
28
A
Miles from Preston
PRESTON and LANCASTER LINE
[NW 4001] CGJ 6 LMS : LNW
Controlled by Preston PSB (PN)
27C : to Preston
Fylde Road Viaduct
Oxheys Loop
M55 3.17
Barton & Broughton Loop
Barton Viaduct
Brock (R/G) 7.36
Garstang & Catterall Emergency GF North & South 9.28
Wyre Viaduct
(Bay Horse Emergency GFs)
M6 16.13
Conder Viaduct
Oubeck 17.77
19.70 (Lancaster old Jn)
Lancaster Canal 20.36
Lancaster South Jn 20.59
6 CGJ 7
21.00
LANCASTER 20.78/0.00
Lancaster North Jn 0.23
Platforms
28B
B
31A : to Ulverston & Barrow-in-Furness
North Quay
PORT OF HEYSHAM (Peel Ports Group)
South Quay
4.01 HEYSHAM PORT
Loco Shed
Flask Sdgs
Port of Heysham (UWG) 3.69
3.53 Heysham Power Station GF
Heysham Power Station British Energy (EDF)
Controlled by Preston PSB (PN)
MHH [NW 4017] LMS : Mid
2.47 (Heysham Moss)
MORECAMBE 2.10
Morecambe Jn 1.71
LMS : LNW
MSM MORECAMBE BRANCH
[NW 4011]
Bare Lane (CCTV) 0.59
BARE LANE 0.53
a = DOWN & UP MORECAMBE (SOUTH CURVE)
b = DOWN & UP MORECAMBE (NORTH CURVE)
1.30 Bare Lane Jn
MORECAMBE SOUTH CURVE LMS : LNW
MORECAMBE NORTH CURVE LMS : LNW
Morecambe Bay
Hest Bank Sea Defences 2.66
Hest Bank (CCTV) 3.11
Controlled by Preston PSB (PN)
LMS : LNW
CGJ 7 [NW 4001]
LANCASTER and CARLISLE LINE
Lune Viaduct 0.26-38
28A
Morecambe South Jn 1.72
2.51 Hest Bank HABD
Hest Bank Jn 3.10/0.00
Bolton-le-Sands (CCTV) 4.30
5.08 Bolton-le-Sands HABD
Carnforth South Jn 5.56
A - Ash plant
C - Coaling plant
P - Paint shop
WH - Wagon hoist
STEAMTOWN West Coast Railway
Carnforth Repairs plc (C&W and P)
Carriage Shed
Loco Shed
North or Downside Sdgs (Crag Bank)
LMS : Furness
CARNFORTH and WHITEHAVEN LINE
CBC 1 [NW 4033]
Controlled by Carnforth Station Jn SB (CS)
River Keer Sea Defence 0.64-0.68
(Carnforth Furness & Midland Junction 0.02)
Virtual Quarry
North, Bottom End Sidings
West Coast Alliance
* = UP & DN FURNESS
East Middle Trench Sidings DBS
CEC [NW 9903]
Carnforth Station Jn (CS) 0.43/0.09
CARNFORTH 0.31
6.08/0.19 Carnforth North Jn
(Carnforth East Jn)
COM 0.25 CEC 0.31 SJC miles from former Carnforth F & M Jn
Preston PSB (PN)
Carlisle PSB (CE)
28C
CGJ 7 [NW 4001]
LMS : LNW (Lancaster & Carlisle)
SKIPTON to MORECAMBE LINE
34A : to Settle Jn
River Ribble Viaduct 235.56
Cleatop (UWG) 235.20
GIGGLESWICK 236.27
Tatterthwaite (UWG) 237.09
530 ft
Miles from St Pancras via Cudworth & Keighley
Lawsing (UWG) 241.34
Clapham/ Wenning Viaduct 241.70-75
CLAPHAM (North Yorks) 242.00
Farmers Viaduct (River Wenning)
Greens Viaduct (River Wenning)
Spencers (UWG) 244.61
BENTHAM 246.23
Lower Bentham Viaduct (River Wenning)
Punch Bowl Viaduct 247.48-247.51
Clintsfield Viaduct 248.21
Clintsfield (UWG) 248.52
SKW 1 [NW 9903]
WENNINGTON 249.38
Melling Tunnel (1230 yds)
West Lune Viaduct
8.25 East Lune Viaduct
LMS Mid | Furness & Mid Jn
COM (Wennington Jn)
Wards (UWG) 6.56
Bowness (UWG) 5.47
Keerholme (UWG) 4.55
SJC [NW 9903]
Capernwray Viaduct (River Keer)
A601(M)
M6
CARNFORTH to WENNINGTON LINE
Controlled by Settle Jn SB (SJ)
Miles from Carnforth F & M Jn
C
[NW 4001] CGJ 7 LMS : LNW
Miles from Lancaster
Controlled by Carlisle PSB (CE)
28B
13.02 Beela Viaduct
Milnthorpe GF 13.32
LANCASTER and CARLISLE LINE
18.44 Oxenholme EGF
Oxenholme Jn 18.79
COM 19.12/1 0.00 0
OXENHOLME: THE LAKE DISTRICT 19.11
WINDERMERE BRANCH
KENDAL 2.05
2.32-33 Kent Viaduct
Burneside Higher (MCG) 3.62
Station (UWG) 4.01
BURNESIDE 4.02
Burneside Lower (AOCL) 4.11
DOWN & UP WINDERMERE
STAVELEY 6.52
Staveley (ABCL) 5.78
OXW [NW 4019]
LMS : LNW
WINDERMERE 10.15
(Lambrigg) 24.20
23.77 24.03 Docker Garth's Viaduct
Grayrigg Loops
M6
Lowgill HABD 27.06
28.05 (Lowgill)
LMS : LNW
CGJ 7 [NW 4001]
29A : to Tebay, Shap & Carlisle
© Copyright TRACKmaps. No reproduction without permission
August 2012

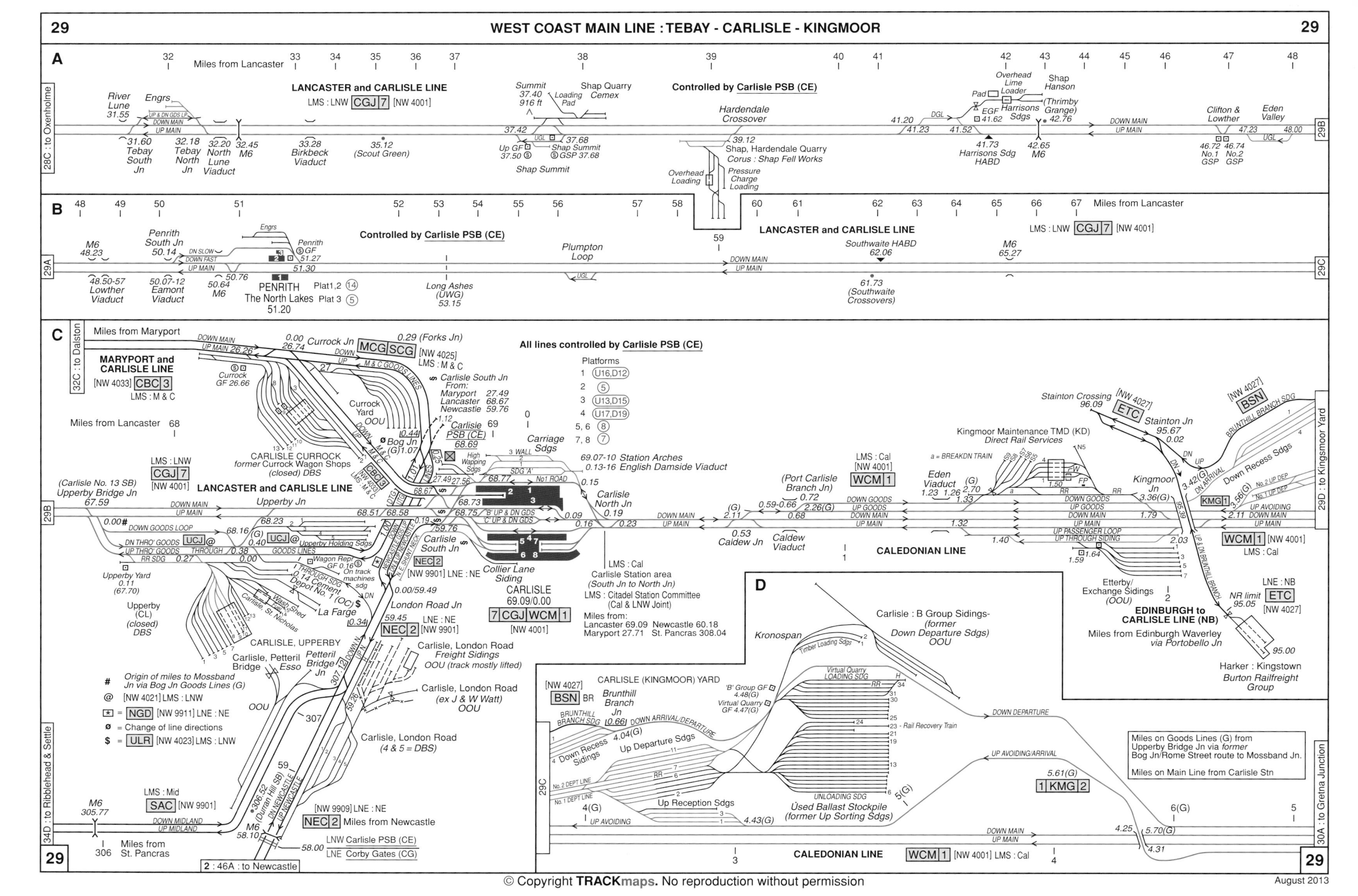
A
Miles from Lancaster
LANCASTER and CARLISLE LINE
LMS : LNW CGJ 7 [NW 4001]
Controlled by Carlisle PSB (CE)
28C : to Oxenholme
River Lune 31.55
Engrs
UP & DN GDS LP
DOWN MAIN
UP MAIN
31.60 Tebay South Jn
32.18 Tebay North Jn
32.20 North Lune Viaduct
32.45 M6
33.28 Birkbeck Viaduct
35.12 (Scout Green)
Summit 37.40 916 ft
Loading Pad
Shap Quarry Cemex
37.42
Up GF 37.50
37.68 Shap Summit GSP 37.68
Shap Summit
Hardendale Crossover
39.12 Shap, Hardendale Quarry
Corus : Shap Fell Works
Overhead Loading
Pressure Charge Loading
41.20
41.23
41.52
DGL
Pad
Overhead Lime Loader
EGF 41.62
Harrisons Sdgs
Shap Hanson (Thrimby Grange) 42.76
41.73 Harrisons Sdg HABD
42.65 M6
Clifton & Lowther
Eden Valley
47.23
48.00
46.72 No.1 GSP
46.74 No.2 GSP
UGL
29B
B
M6 48.23
48.50-57 Lowther Viaduct
Penrith South Jn 50.14
DN SLOW
DOWN FAST
UP MAIN
50.07-12 Eamont Viaduct
50.64 M6
50.76
Engrs
Penrith GF 51.27
51.30
PENRITH The North Lakes 51.20
Plat1,2 14
Plat 3 5
Controlled by Carlisle PSB (CE)
Long Ashes (UWG) 53.15
Plumpton Loop
UGL
59
LANCASTER and CARLISLE LINE
Southwaite HABD 62.06
61.73 (Southwaite Crossovers)
M6 65.27
Miles from Lancaster
LMS : LNW CGJ 7 [NW 4001]
29A
29C
C
Miles from Maryport
32C : to Dalston
MARYPORT and CARLISLE LINE
[NW 4033] CBC 3
LMS : M & C
0.00 26.74 Currock Jn
MCG SCG [NW 4025] LMS : M & C
0.29 (Forks Jn)
M & C GOODS LINES
Currock GF 26.66
Currock Yard OOU
Bog Jn (G) 1.07
0.44
1.12
Carlisle PSB (CE) 68.69
Carlisle South Jn From: Maryport 27.49 Lancaster 68.67 Newcastle 59.76
CARLISLE CURROCK former Currock Wagon Shops (closed) DBS
Miles from Lancaster 68
LMS : LNW CGJ 7 [NW 4001]
LANCASTER and CARLISLE LINE
(Carlisle No. 13 SB) Upperby Bridge Jn 67.59
Upperby Jn
DOWN GOODS LOOP
DN THRO' GOODS UCJ @
UP THRO' GOODS
RR SDG 0.27
THROUGH 0.38
GOODS LINES
Upperby Holding Sdgs
Upperby Yard 0.11 (67.70)
Upperby (CL) (closed) DBS
Wagon Repr GF 0.16
On track machines sdg
THROUGH SDG
0.14 Cement Depot No. 1 (OC)
La Farge 0.34
Carlisle, St. Nicholas
Wash Shed
CARLISLE, UPPERBY
Carlisle, Petteril Bridge
Esso
Petteril Bridge Jn
All lines controlled by Carlisle PSB (CE)
Platforms
1 U16,D12
2 5
3 U13,D15
4 U17,D19
5, 6 8
7, 8 7
Carriage Sdgs
3 WALL
SDG 'A'
No1 ROAD
High Wapping Sdgs
69.07-10 Station Arches
0.13-16 English Damside Viaduct
Carlisle North Jn 0.19
'B' UP & DN GDS
'C' UP & DN GDS
Carlisle South Jn
NEC 2 [NW 9901] LNE : NE
Collier Lane Siding
CARLISLE 69.09/0.00
7 CGJ WCM 1 [NW 4001]
LMS : Cal
Carlisle Station area (South Jn to North Jn)
LMS : Citadel Station Committee (Cal & LNW Joint)
Miles from: Lancaster 69.09 Newcastle 60.18 Maryport 27.71 St. Pancras 308.04
0.00/59.49
London Road Jn
59.45 NEC 2 LNE : NE [NW 9901]
Carlisle, London Road Freight Sidings OOU (track mostly lifted)
Carlisle, London Road (ex J & W Watt) OOU
Carlisle, London Road (4 & 5 = DBS)
Origin of miles to Mossband Jn via Bog Jn Goods Lines (G)
@ [NW 4021] LMS : LNW
= NGD [NW 9911] LNE : NE
ø = Change of line directions
$ = ULR [NW 4023] LMS : LNW
OOU
307
59
306.52 (Durran Hill SB)
DN NEWCASTLE
UP NEWCASTLE
M6 58.10
58.00
LNW Carlisle PSB (CE)
LNE Corby Gates (CG)
[NW 9909] LNE : NE
NEC 2 Miles from Newcastle
LMS : Mid SAC [NW 9901]
M6 305.77
DOWN MIDLAND
UP MIDLAND
306 Miles from St. Pancras
34D : to Ribblehead & Settle
2 : 46A : to Newcastle
Caldew Jn 0.53
Caldew Viaduct
(Port Carlisle Branch Jn) 0.72
LMS : Cal [NW 4001] WCM 1
DOWN GOODS
UP GOODS
DOWN MAIN
UP MAIN
CALEDONIAN LINE
Eden Viaduct 1.23 1.26
a = BREAKDN TRAIN
Kingmoor Maintenance TMD (KD) Direct Rail Services
Kingmoor Jn 3.36(G)
UP PASSENGER LOOP
UP THROUGH SIDING
Etterby/Exchange Sidings (OOU)
Stainton Crossing 96.09
[NW 4027] ETC
Stainton Jn 95.67 0.02
[NW 4027] BSN
BRUNTHILL BRANCH SDG
Down Recess Sdgs
KMG 1
UP AVOIDING
WCM 1 [NW 4001] LMS : Cal
UP & DN BRUNTHILL BRANCH
29D : to Kingsmoor Yard
EDINBURGH to CARLISLE LINE (NB)
Miles from Edinburgh Waverley via Portobello Jn
LNE : NB ETC [NW 4027]
NR limit 95.05
95.00
Harker : Kingstown Burton Railfreight Group
D
Kronospan
Timber Loading Sdgs
Carlisle : B Group Sidings- (former Down Departure Sdgs) OOU
CARLISLE (KINGMOOR) YARD
[NW 4027] BSN BR
Brunthill Branch Jn 0.66
BRUNTHILL BRANCH SDG
DOWN ARRIVAL/DEPARTURE
4.04(G)
Down Recess Sidings
Up Departure Sdgs
'B' Group GF 4.48(G)
Virtual Quarry GF 4.47(G)
Virtual Quarry LOADING SDG
Rail Recovery Train
UNLOADING SDG
Used Ballast Stockpile (former Up Sorting Sdgs)
Up Reception Sdgs
4.43(G)
No. 2 DEPT LINE
No. 1 DEPT LINE
4(G)
UP AVOIDING
29C
DOWN DEPARTURE
UP AVOIDING/ARRIVAL
5.61(G)
1 KMG 2
Miles on Goods Lines (G) from Upperby Bridge Jn via former Bog Jn/Rome Street route to Mossband Jn.
Miles on Main Line from Carlisle Stn
6(G)
5
4.25
5.70(G)
4.31
CALEDONIAN LINE
WCM 1 [NW 4001] LMS : Cal
30A : to Gretna Junction

August 2013

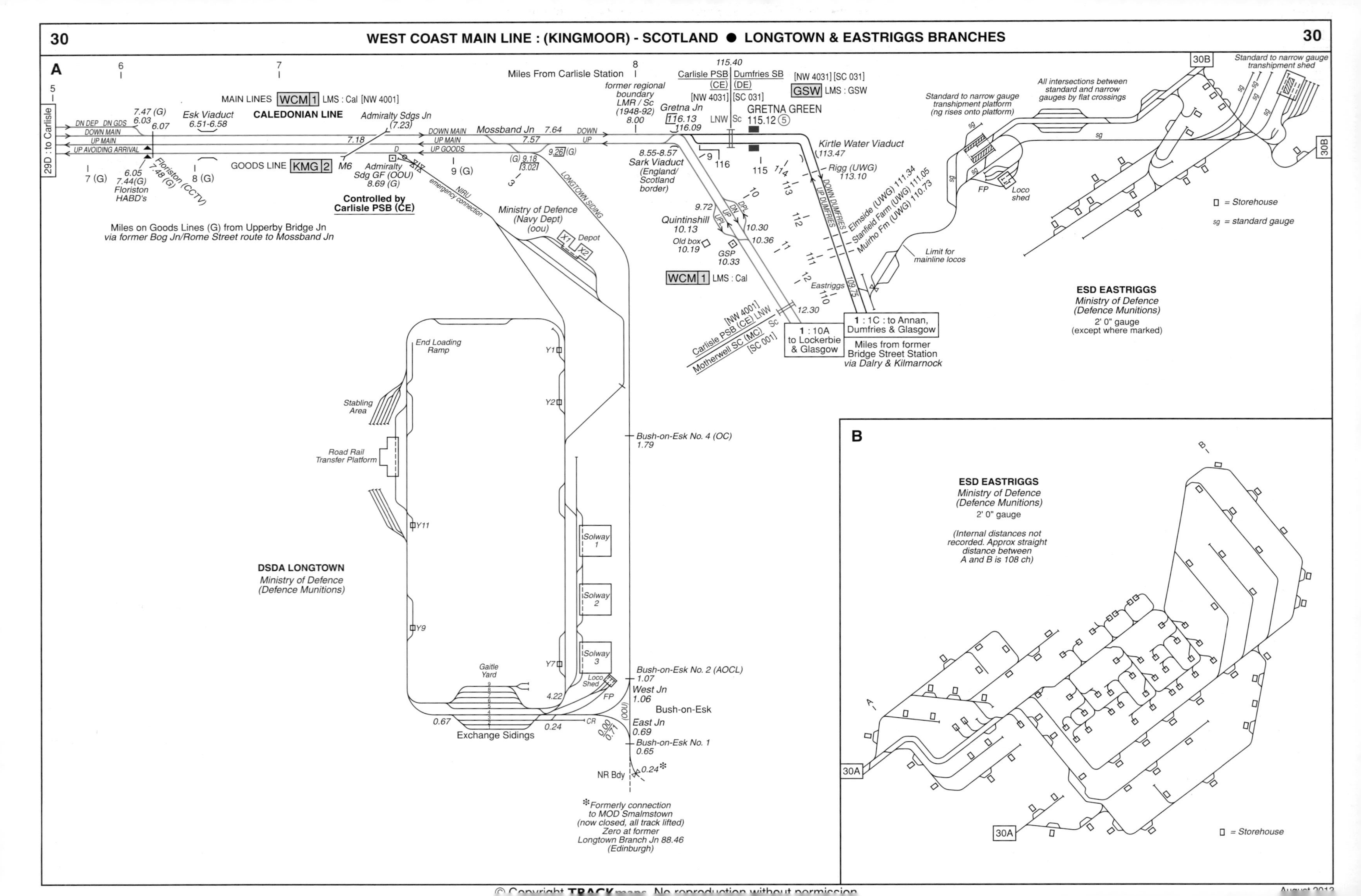
A
29D : to Carlisle
DN DEP DN GDS
DOWN MAIN
UP MAIN
UP AVOIDING ARRIVAL
7.47 (G)
6.03
6.07
Esk Viaduct
6.51-6.58
MAIN LINES WCM 1 LMS : Cal [NW 4001]
CALEDONIAN LINE
Admiralty Sdgs Jn
(7.23)
7.18
Miles From Carlisle Station
former regional boundary LMR / Sc (1948-92)
8.00
Mossband Jn 7.64
7.57
DOWN MAIN
UP MAIN
UP GOODS
DOWN
UP
9.26 (G)
(G) 9.18
3.02
7 (G)
6.05
7.44(G)
Floriston HABD's
Floriston (CCTV)
7.48 (G)
8 (G)
GOODS LINE KMG 2
M6
Admiralty Sdg GF (OOU)
8.69 (G)
9 (G)
Controlled by Carlisle PSB (CE)
NIRU emergency connection
Miles on Goods Lines (G) from Upperby Bridge Jn via former Bog Jn/Rome Street route to Mossband Jn
LONGTOWN SIDING
Ministry of Defence (Navy Dept) (oou)
Depot
X1
X2
115.40
Carlisle PSB (CE)
Dumfries SB (DE)
[NW 4031] [SC 031]
GSW LMS : GSW
Gretna Jn
116.13
116.09
LNW
Sc
GRETNA GREEN
115.12 (5)
8.55-8.57
Sark Viaduct (England/ Scotland border)
Kirtle Water Viaduct
(113.47
Rigg (UWG)
113.10
Elmside (UWG) 111.34
Stanfield Farm (UWG) 111.05
Muirho Fm (UWG) 110.73
DOWN DUMFRIES
UP DUMFRIES
Eastriggs
109.75
Quintinshill
10.13
9.72
DPL
DN
UP
UPL
10.30
10.36
Old box
10.19
GSP
10.33
WCM 1 LMS : Cal
12.30
[NW 4001]
Carlisle PSB (CE) LNW
Motherwell SC (MC) Sc
[SC 001]
1 : 10A to Lockerbie & Glasgow
1 : 1C : to Annan, Dumfries & Glasgow
Miles from former Bridge Street Station via Dalry & Kilmarnock
Limit for mainline locos
Standard to narrow gauge transhipment platform (ng rises onto platform)
All intersections between standard and narrow gauges by flat crossings
Standard to narrow gauge transhipment shed
30B
sg
FP
Loco shed
□ = Storehouse
sg = standard gauge
ESD EASTRIGGS
Ministry of Defence (Defence Munitions)
2' 0" gauge (except where marked)
End Loading Ramp
Stabling Area
Road Rail Transfer Platform
Y1
Y2
Y7
Y9
Y11
Solway 1
Solway 2
Solway 3
Gaitle Yard
Loco Shed
4.22
0.67
0.24
Exchange Sidings
CR
DSDA LONGTOWN
Ministry of Defence (Defence Munitions)
Bush-on-Esk No. 4 (OC)
1.79
Bush-on-Esk No. 2 (AOCL)
1.07
West Jn
1.06
Bush-on-Esk
(OOU)
East Jn
0.69
0.00
0.71
Bush-on-Esk No. 1
0.65
NR Bdy
0.24*
*Formerly connection to MOD Smalmstown (now closed, all track lifted) Zero at former Longtown Branch Jn 88.46 (Edinburgh)
B
ESD EASTRIGGS
Ministry of Defence (Defence Munitions)
2' 0" gauge
(Internal distances not recorded. Approx straight distance between A and B is 108 ch)
30A
□ = Storehouse

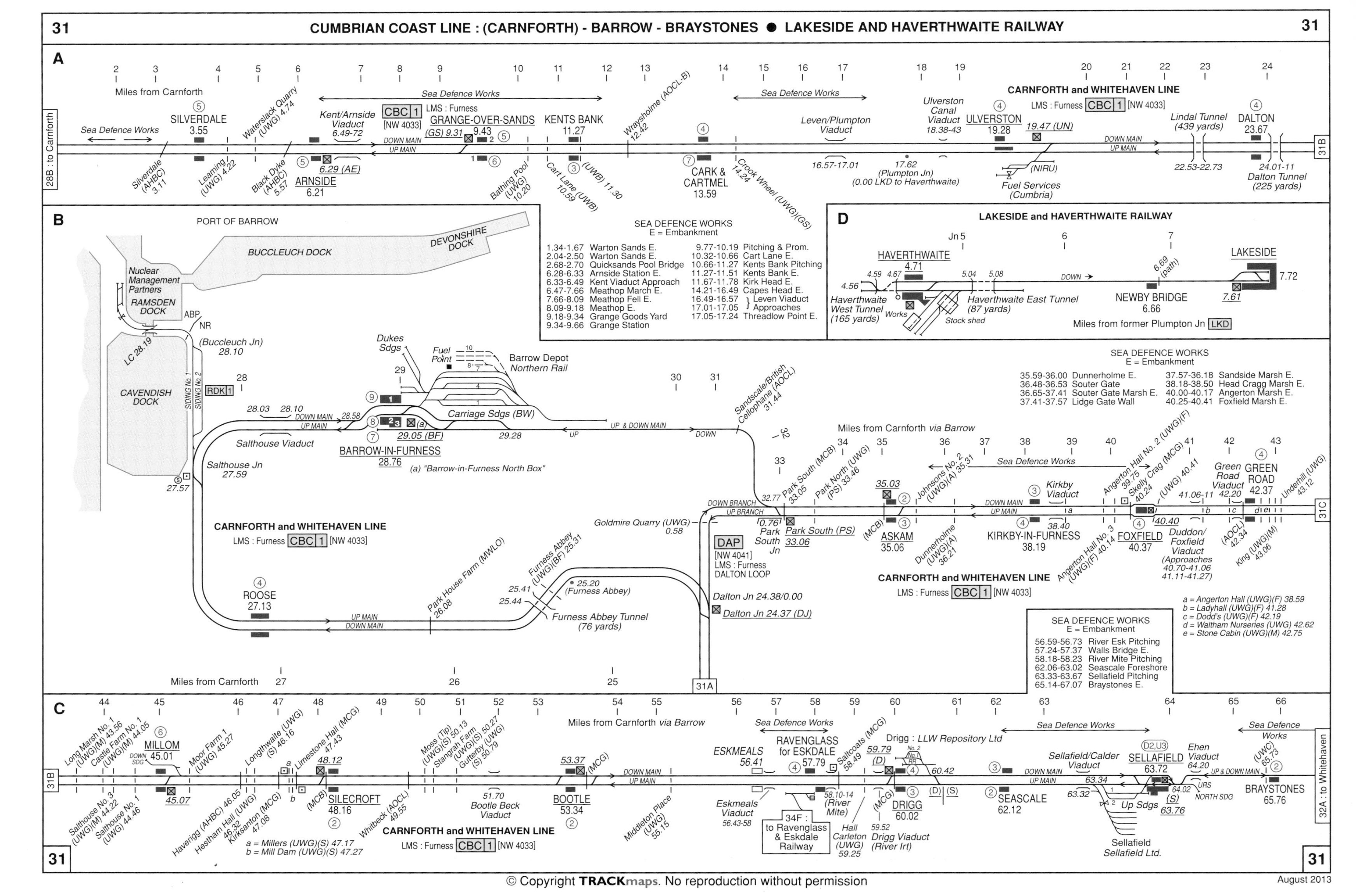
A
Miles from Carnforth
Sea Defence Works
28B : to Carnforth
SILVERDALE 3.55
Silverdale (AHBC) 3.11
Leaming (UWG) 4.22
Waterslack Quarry (UWG) 4.74
Black Dyke (AHBC) 5.57
Kent/Arnside Viaduct 6.49-72
6.29 (AE)
ARNSIDE 6.21
CBC 1 LMS : Furness [NW 4033]
GRANGE-OVER-SANDS 9.43
(GS) 9.31
DOWN MAIN
UP MAIN
Bathing Pool (UWG) 10.20
KENTS BANK 11.27
Cart Lane (UWB) 10.59
(UWB) 11.30
Wraysholme (AOCL-B) 12.42
CARK & CARTMEL 13.59
Crook Wheel (UWG)(GS) 14.24
Leven/Plumpton Viaduct
16.57-17.01
17.62 (Plumpton Jn) (0.00 LKD to Haverthwaite)
Ulverston Canal Viaduct 18.38-43
ULVERSTON 19.28
19.47 (UN)
(NIRU)
Fuel Services (Cumbria)
CARNFORTH and WHITEHAVEN LINE
LMS : Furness CBC 1 [NW 4033]
Lindal Tunnel (439 yards)
22.53-22.73
DALTON 23.67
24.01-11 Dalton Tunnel (225 yards)
31B
SEA DEFENCE WORKS
E = Embankment
1.34-1.67 Warton Sands E.
2.04-2.50 Warton Sands E.
2.68-2.70 Quicksands Pool Bridge
6.28-6.33 Arnside Station E.
6.33-6.49 Kent Viaduct Approach
6.47-7.66 Meathop March E.
7.66-8.09 Meathop Fell E.
8.09-9.18 Meathop E.
9.18-9.34 Grange Goods Yard
9.34-9.66 Grange Station
9.77-10.19 Pitching & Prom.
10.32-10.66 Cart Lane E.
10.66-11.27 Kents Bank Pitching
11.27-11.51 Kents Bank E.
11.67-11.78 Kirk Head E.
14.21-16.49 Capes Head E.
16.49-16.57 Leven Viaduct
17.01-17.05 Approaches
17.05-17.24 Threadlow Point E.
B
PORT OF BARROW
BUCCLEUCH DOCK
DEVONSHIRE DOCK
Nuclear Management Partners
RAMSDEN DOCK
CAVENDISH DOCK
ABP
NR
LC 28.19
(Buccleuch Jn) 28.10
SIDING No.1
SIDING No.2
RDK 1
28.03 28.10
Salthouse Viaduct
Salthouse Jn 27.59
27.57
Dukes Sdgs
Fuel Point
Barrow Depot Northern Rail
Carriage Sdgs (BW)
28.58
29.05 (BF)
29.28
BARROW-IN-FURNESS 28.76
(a) "Barrow-in-Furness North Box"
UP & DOWN MAIN
Sandscale/British Cellophane (AOCL) 31.44
CARNFORTH and WHITEHAVEN LINE
LMS : Furness CBC 1 [NW 4033]
ROOSE 27.13
Park House Farm (MWLO) 26.08
Furness Abbey (UWG)(BF) 25.31
25.41
25.44
25.20 (Furness Abbey)
Furness Abbey Tunnel (76 yards)
Goldmire Quarry (UWG) 0.58
DAP [NW 4041] LMS : Furness DALTON LOOP
Dalton Jn 24.38/0.00
Dalton Jn 24.37 (DJ)
Miles from Carnforth
31A
DOWN BRANCH
UP BRANCH
32.77
0.76 Park South Jn
Park South (PS) 33.06
Park South (MCB) 33.05
Park North (UWG) (PS) 33.46
35.03
ASKAM 35.06
(MCB)
Johnsons No. 2 (UWG)(A) 35.31
Dunnerholme (UWG)(A) 36.21
Miles from Carnforth via Barrow
Sea Defence Works
Kirkby Viaduct
38.40
KIRKBY-IN-FURNESS 38.19
Angerton Hall No. 3 (UWG)(F) 40.14
Angerton Hall No. 2 (UWG)(F) 39.75
Skelly Crag (MCG) 40.24
(UWG) 40.41
40.40
FOXFIELD 40.37
Duddon/Foxfield Viaduct (Approaches 40.70-41.06 41.11-41.27)
41.06-11
Green Road Viaduct 42.20
GREEN ROAD 42.37
(AOCL) 42.34
King (UWG)(M) 43.06
Underhill (UWG) 43.12
31C
CARNFORTH and WHITEHAVEN LINE
LMS : Furness CBC 1 [NW 4033]
SEA DEFENCE WORKS
E = Embankment
35.59-36.00 Dunnerholme E.
36.48-36.53 Souter Gate
36.65-37.41 Souter Gate Marsh E.
37.41-37.57 Lidge Gate Wall
37.57-36.18 Sandside Marsh E.
38.18-38.50 Head Cragg Marsh E.
40.00-40.17 Angerton Marsh E.
40.25-40.41 Foxfield Marsh E.
a = Angerton Hall (UWG)(F) 38.59
b = Ladyhall (UWG)(F) 41.28
c = Dodd's (UWG)(F) 42.19
d = Waltham Nurseries (UWG) 42.62
e = Stone Cabin (UWG)(M) 42.75
D
LAKESIDE and HAVERTHWAITE RAILWAY
Jn 5
HAVERTHWAITE 4.71
4.56 4.59 4.67
Haverthwaite West Tunnel (165 yards)
Works
Stock shed
5.04 5.08
Haverthwaite East Tunnel (87 yards)
DOWN →
6.69 (path)
NEWBY BRIDGE 6.66
LAKESIDE 7.72
7.61
Miles from former Plumpton Jn LKD
SEA DEFENCE WORKS
E = Embankment
56.59-56.73 River Esk Pitching
57.24-57.37 Walls Bridge E.
58.18-58.23 River Mite Pitching
62.06-63.02 Seascale Foreshore
63.33-63.67 Sellafield Pitching
65.14-67.07 Braystones E.
C
31B
Long Marsh No. 1 (UWG)(M) 43.56
Castle Farm No. 1 (UWG)(M) 44.05
Salthouse No. 3 (UWG)(M) 44.22
Salthouse No. 1 (UWG) 44.46
MILLOM 45.01
DOWN SDG
45.07
Moor Farm 1 (UWG) 45.27
Haverigg (AHBC) 46.05
Hestham Hall (UWG) 46.32
Kirksanton (MCG) 47.08
Longthwaite (UWG) (S) 46.16
Limestone Hall (MCG) 47.43
48.12
SILECROFT 48.16
(MCB)
a = Millers (UWG)(S) 47.17
b = Mill Dam (UWG)(S) 47.27
Whitbeck (AOCL) 49.55
Moss (Tip) (UWG)(S) 50.13
Stangrah Farm (UWG)(S) 50.27
Gutterby (UWG) (S) 50.79
51.70 Bootle Beck Viaduct
CARNFORTH and WHITEHAVEN LINE
LMS : Furness CBC 1 [NW 4033]
53.37
(MCG)
BOOTLE 53.34
Middleton Place (UWG) 55.15
Miles from Carnforth via Barrow
ESKMEALS 56.41
Eskmeals Viaduct 56.43-58
Sea Defence Works
RAVENGLASS for ESKDALE 57.79
58.10-14 (River Mite)
34F : to Ravenglass & Eskdale Railway
Saltcoats (MCG) 58.49
59.79 (D)
Hall Carleton (UWG) 59.25
59.52 Drigg Viaduct (River Irt)
Drigg : LLW Repository Ltd
60.42
(MCG)
DRIGG 60.02
(D) (S)
SEASCALE 62.12
Sea Defence Works
Sellafield/Calder Viaduct
63.34
63.32
Up Sdgs
SELLAFIELD 63.72
D2,U3
64.02
(S) 63.76
URS
NORTH SDG
Sellafield Sellafield Ltd.
Ehen Viaduct 64.20
UP & DOWN MAIN
(UWC) 65.73
BRAYSTONES 65.76
Sea Defence Works
32A : to Whitehaven
31

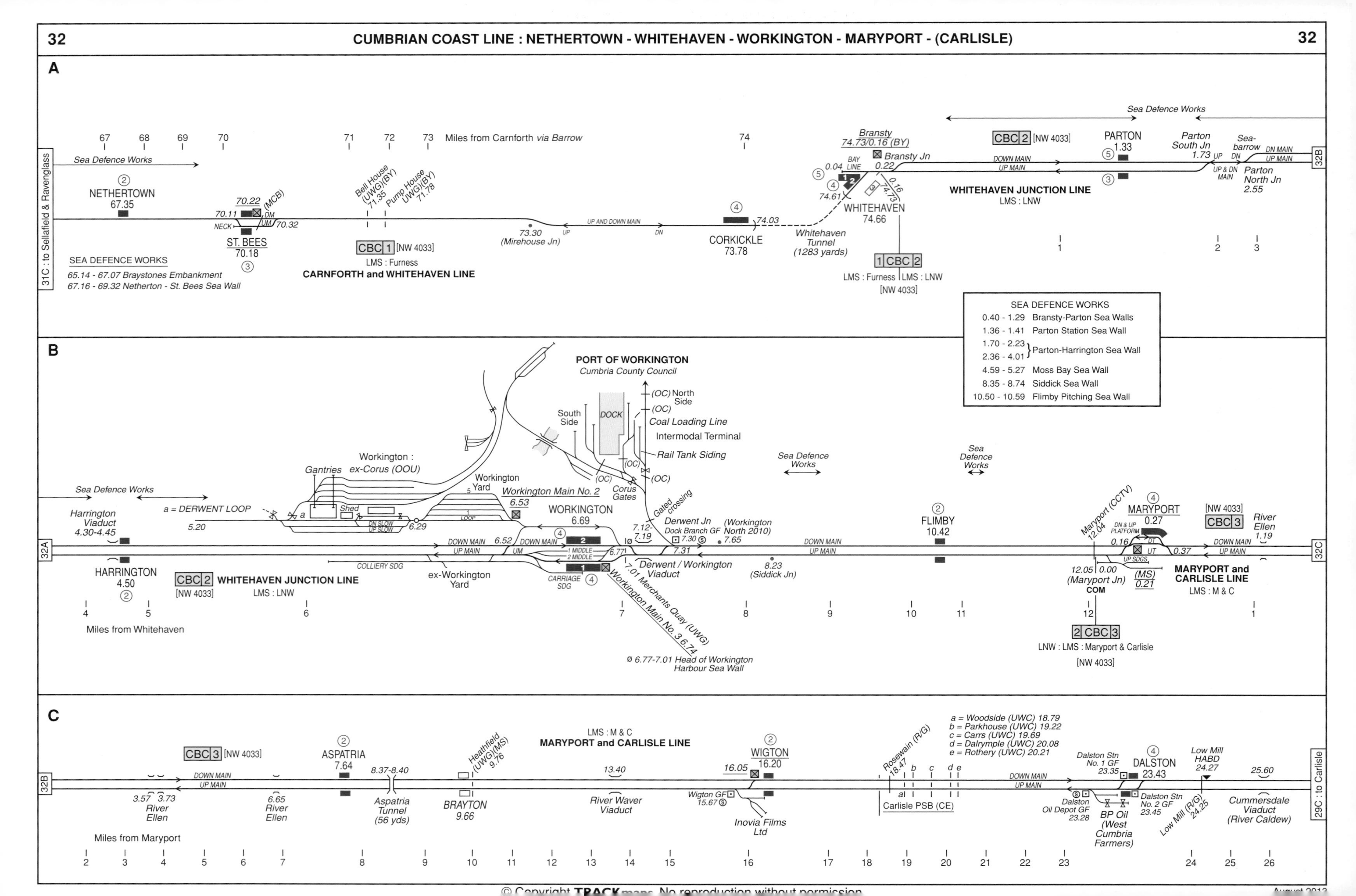
A
Miles from Carnforth via Barrow
Sea Defence Works
31C : to Sellafield & Ravenglass
NETHERTOWN
67.35
70.22
(MCB)
70.11
NECK
70.32
ST. BEES
70.18
SEA DEFENCE WORKS
65.14 - 67.07 Braystones Embankment
67.16 - 69.32 Netherton - St. Bees Sea Wall
Bell House (UWG)(BY) 71.35
Pump House (UWG)(BY) 71.78
CBC 1 [NW 4033]
LMS : Furness
CARNFORTH and WHITEHAVEN LINE
73.30
(Mirehouse Jn)
UP AND DOWN MAIN
CORKICKLE
73.78
74.03
Whitehaven Tunnel
(1283 yards)
Bransty
74.73/0.16 (BY)
Bransty Jn
0.22
BAY LINE
0.04
74.61
WHITEHAVEN
74.66
1 CBC 2
LMS : Furness LMS : LNW
[NW 4033]
CBC 2 [NW 4033]
DOWN MAIN
UP MAIN
WHITEHAVEN JUNCTION LINE
LMS : LNW
PARTON
1.33
Parton South Jn
1.73
Sea-barrow
Parton North Jn
2.55
32B
SEA DEFENCE WORKS
0.40 - 1.29 Bransty-Parton Sea Walls
1.36 - 1.41 Parton Station Sea Wall
1.70 - 2.23 / 2.36 - 4.01 Parton-Harrington Sea Wall
4.59 - 5.27 Moss Bay Sea Wall
8.35 - 8.74 Siddick Sea Wall
10.50 - 10.59 Flimby Pitching Sea Wall
B
PORT OF WORKINGTON
Cumbria County Council
DOCK
South Side
(OC) North Side
Coal Loading Line
Intermodal Terminal
Rail Tank Siding
Corus Gates
Gated crossing
Workington : ex-Corus (OOU)
Gantries
Shed
a = DERWENT LOOP
5.20
Harrington Viaduct
4.30-4.45
HARRINGTON
4.50
32A
CBC 2 WHITEHAVEN JUNCTION LINE
[NW 4033] LMS : LNW
Miles from Whitehaven
Workington Yard
6.29
COLLIERY SDG
ex-Workington Yard
Workington Main No. 2
6.53
WORKINGTON
6.69
6.52
1 MIDDLE
2 MIDDLE
CARRIAGE SDG
6.77
7.12-7.19
Derwent Jn
Dock Branch GF 7.30
(Workington North 2010) 7.65
7.31
Derwent / Workington Viaduct
7.01 Merchants Quay (UWG)
Workington Main No. 3 6.74
ø 6.77-7.01 Head of Workington Harbour Sea Wall
8.23
(Siddick Jn)
Sea Defence Works
FLIMBY
10.42
Maryport (CCTV)
12.04
MARYPORT
0.27
DN & UP PLATFORM
0.16
UP SDGS
0.37
12.05 0.00
(Maryport Jn)
COM
(MS)
0.21
2 CBC 3
LNW : LMS : Maryport & Carlisle
[NW 4033]
CBC 3 [NW 4033]
MARYPORT and CARLISLE LINE
LMS : M & C
River Ellen
1.19
32C
C
32B
CBC 3 [NW 4033]
3.57 3.73 River Ellen
6.65 River Ellen
Miles from Maryport
ASPATRIA
7.64
8.37-8.40
Aspatria Tunnel
(56 yds)
Heathfield (UWG)(MS) 9.76
BRAYTON
9.66
LMS : M & C
MARYPORT and CARLISLE LINE
13.40
River Waver Viaduct
16.05
WIGTON
16.20
Wigton GF 15.67
Inovia Films Ltd
Rosewain (R/G) 18.47
a = Woodside (UWC) 18.79
b = Parkhouse (UWC) 19.22
c = Carrs (UWC) 19.69
d = Dalrymple (UWC) 20.08
e = Rothery (UWC) 20.21
Carlisle PSB (CE)
Dalston Stn No. 1 GF 23.35
DALSTON
23.43
Dalston Oil Depot GF 23.28
BP Oil (West Cumbria Farmers)
Dalston Stn No. 2 GF 23.45
Low Mill HABD 24.27
Low Mill (R/G) 24.25
25.60
Cummersdale Viaduct (River Caldew)
29C : to Carlisle

August 2013

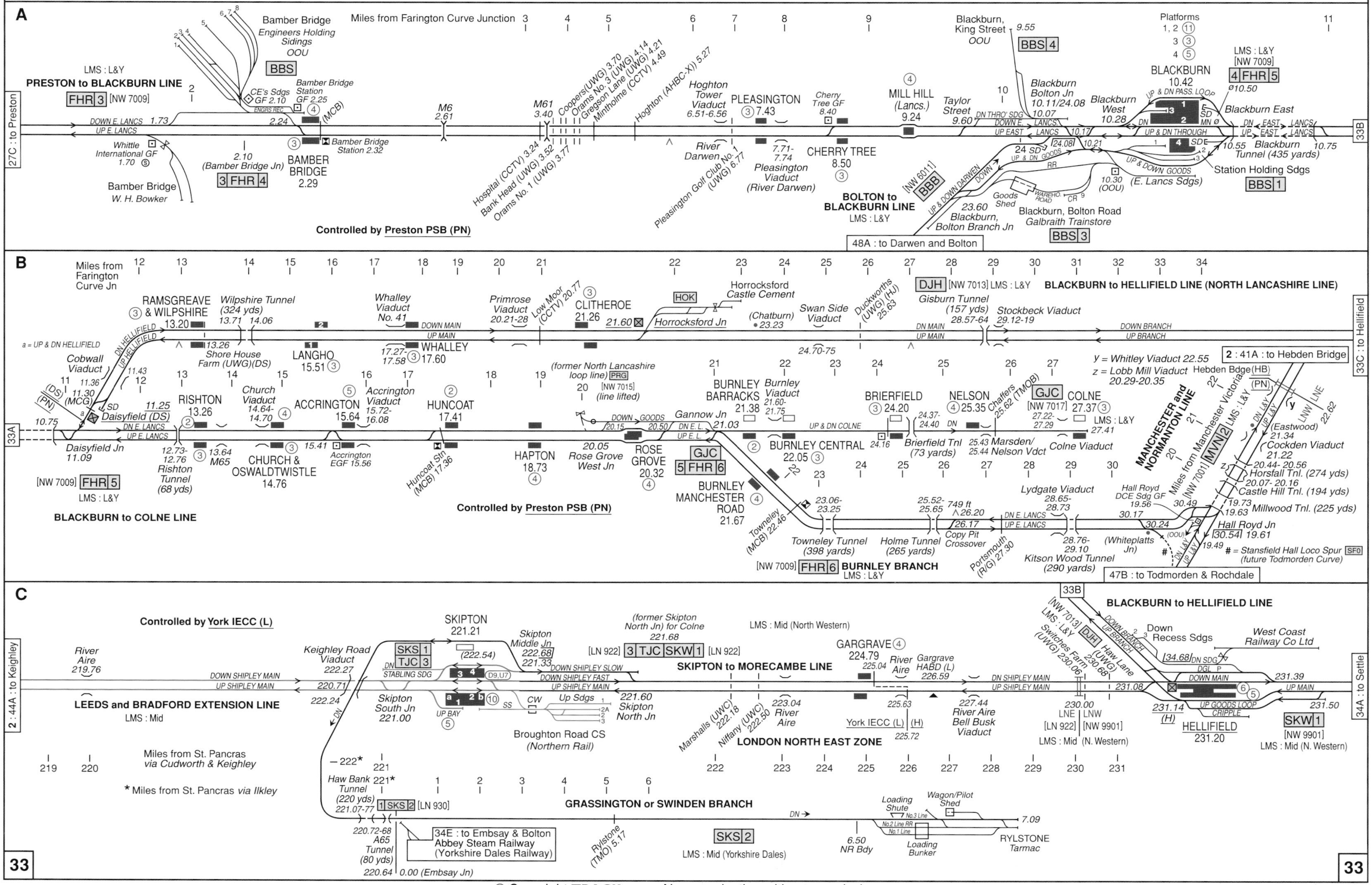

A

PRESTON to BLACKBURN LINE
LMS : L&Y
FHR 3 [NW 7009]

Miles from Farington Curve Junction 2 3 4 5 6 7 8 9 10 11

27C : to Preston
DOWN E. LANCS 1.73
UP E. LANCS
Whittle International GF 1.70 Ⓢ
Bamber Bridge W. H. Bowker
Bamber Bridge Engineers Holding Sidings OOU
BBS
CE's Sdgs GF 2.10
ENGRS REC
Bamber Bridge Station GF 2.25
2.24
(MCB) 4
Bamber Bridge Station 2.32
2.10 (Bamber Bridge Jn)
3 FHR 4
BAMBER BRIDGE 2.29 ③
M6 2.61
M61 3.40
Hospital (CCTV) 3.24
Bank Head (UWG) 3.52
Orams No. 1 (UWG) 3.77
Coopers(UWG) 3.70
Orams No. 3 (UWG) 4.14
Gregson Lane (UWG) 4.21
Minholme (CCTV) 4.49
Hoghton (AHBC-X) 5.27
Hoghton Tower Viaduct 6.51-6.56
River Darwen
Pleasington Golf Club No. 1 (UWG) 6.77
PLEASINGTON ③ 7.43
7.71-7.74 Pleasington Viaduct (River Darwen)
Cherry Tree GF 8.40
CHERRY TREE 8.50 ③
MILL HILL (Lans.) 9.24 ④
Taylor Street 9.60
BOLTON to BLACKBURN LINE
LMS : L&Y
BBB [NW 6011]
UP & DOWN DARWEN
DOWN
23.60 Blackburn, Bolton Branch Jn
48A : to Darwen and Bolton
Blackburn, King Street OOU 9.55
BBS 4
DN THRO' SDG
DOWN E. LANCS
UP EAST LANCS
Blackburn Bolton Jn 10.11/24.08
10.07
24.08
24 SD
UP & DN GOODS
RR
Goods Shed
WAREHO. ROAD
CR 9
Blackburn, Bolton Road Galbraith Trainstore
BBS 3
Blackburn West 10.28
10.17
10.21
10.30 (OOU)
(E. Lancs Sdgs)
UP & DOWN GOODS
Platforms 1, 2 ⑪ 3 ③ 4 ⑤
BLACKBURN 10.42
UP & DN PASS. LOOP
DN
UP & DN THROUGH
SD MN ø
SDE
LMS : L&Y [NW 7009]
4 FHR 5
ø10.50
Blackburn East
DN EAST LANCS
UP EAST LANCS
10.55 Blackburn Tunnel (435 yards) 10.75
Station Holding Sdgs
BBS 1
33B

Controlled by Preston PSB (PN)

B

Miles from Farington Curve Jn 12 13 14 15 16 17 18 19 20 21 22 23 24 25 26 27 28 29 30 31 32 33 34

BLACKBURN to HELLIFIELD LINE (NORTH LANCASHIRE LINE)
DJH [NW 7013] LMS : L&Y

a = UP & DN HELLIFIELD
33A
10.75
(PN) (DS) 11.30 (MCG) 11.36
11
Cobwall Viaduct
11.43
SD
Daisyfield (DS)
Daisyfield Jn 11.09
DN HELLIFIELD
UP HELLIFIELD
RAMSGREAVE & WILPSHIRE 13.20 ③
13.26
Wilpshire Tunnel (324 yds) 13.71 14.06
Shore House Farm (UWG)(DS)
LANGHO 15.51 ③
Whalley Viaduct No. 41
DOWN MAIN
UP MAIN
17.27-17.58 ③ WHALLEY 17.60
Primrose Viaduct 20.21-28
Low Moor (CCTV) 20.77
CLITHEROE 21.26 ③
21.60
HOK
Horrocksford Jn
Horrocksford Castle Cement
(Chatburn) 23.23
Swan Side Viaduct
24.70-75
Duckworths (UWG) (HJ) 25.63
DN MAIN
UP MAIN
Gisburn Tunnel (157 yds) 28.57-64
Stockbeck Viaduct 29.12-19
DOWN BRANCH
UP BRANCH
33C : to Hellifield

11.25
DN E. LANCS
UP E. LANCS
RISHTON 13.26 ②
12.73-12.76 Rishton Tunnel (68 yds)
13.64 M65 ③
Church Viaduct 14.64-14.70 ④
CHURCH & OSWALDTWISTLE 14.76 ③
ACCRINGTON 15.64 ⑤
15.41
Accrington EGF 15.56
Accrington Viaduct 15.72-16.08
HUNCOAT 17.41 ②
Huncoat Stn (MCB) 17.36
HAPTON 18.73 ④
(former North Lancashire loop line) PRG
20 [NW 7015] (line lifted)
DOWN GOODS
20.15 20.50
20.05 Rose Grove West Jn
ROSE GROVE 20.32 ④
Gannow Jn 21.03
DN E. L.
UP E. L.
GJC
5 FHR 6
BURNLEY BARRACKS 21.38
Burnley Viaduct 21.60-21.75
BURNLEY CENTRAL 22.05 ③ ②
BURNLEY MANCHESTER ROAD 21.67 ④
UP & DN COLNE
BRIERFIELD 24.20 ③
24.16
24.37-24.40
Brierfield Tnl (73 yards)
NELSON ④ 25.35
DN
Chaffers (TMOB) 25.62
25.43 Marsden/ 25.44 Nelson Vdct
GJC [NW 7017]
27.22-27.29
COLNE 27.37 ③
LMS : L&Y
27.41
Colne Viaduct
Towneley (MCB) 22.46
23.06-23.25
Towneley Tunnel (398 yards)
25.52-25.65
749 ft 26.20
26.17
Holme Tunnel (265 yards)
Copy Pit Crossover
Portsmouth (R/G) 27.30
DN E. LANCS
UP E. LANCS
Lydgate Viaduct 28.65-28.73
28.76-29.10
Kitson Wood Tunnel (290 yards)
Hall Royd DCE Sdg GF 19.56
30.17
30.24
30.49
(Whiteplatts Jn)
(OOU)
Hall Royd Jn 30.54 19.61
19.49
= Stansfield Hall Loco Spur SF0 (future Todmorden Curve)
47B : to Todmorden & Rochdale
MANCHESTER and NORMANTON LINE
Miles from Manchester Victoria
MVN 2 [NW 7001] LMS : L&Y
20 21 22
y = Whitley Viaduct 22.55
z = Lobb Mill Viaduct 20.29-20.35
2 : 41A : to Hebden Bridge
Hebden Bdge (HB)
(PN)
DN L&Y
UP L&Y
LNW LINE
22.62
(Eastwood) 21.34
Cockden Viaduct 21.22
20.44-20.56 Horsfall Tnl. (274 yds)
20.07-20.16 Castle Hill Tnl. (194 yds)
19.73 19.63 Millwood Tnl. (225 yds)

[NW 7009] FHR 5
LMS : L&Y
BLACKBURN to COLNE LINE

Controlled by Preston PSB (PN)

[NW 7009] FHR 6 BURNLEY BRANCH
LMS : L&Y

C

Controlled by York IECC (L)

2 : 44A : to Keighley
River Aire 219.76
DOWN SHIPLEY MAIN
UP SHIPLEY MAIN
LEEDS and BRADFORD EXTENSION LINE
LMS : Mid
219 220
Miles from St. Pancras via Cudworth & Keighley
* Miles from St. Pancras via Ilkley
Keighley Road Viaduct 222.27
220.71
222.24
DN
– 222*
221
Haw Bank 221* Tunnel (220 yds) 221.07-77
1 SKS 2 [LN 930]
220.72-68 A65 Tunnel (80 yds)
220.64 0.00 (Embsay Jn)
34E : to Embsay & Bolton Abbey Steam Railway (Yorkshire Dales Railway)
SKIPTON 221.21
SKS 1
TJC 3
DN STABLING SDG
(222.54)
3 4 (D9,U7)
a 1 2 b ⑩
UP BAY ⑤
SS
Skipton South Jn 221.00
Skipton Middle Jn 222.68 221.33
DOWN SHIPLEY SLOW
DOWN SHIPLEY FAST
UP SHIPLEY MAIN
CW
Up Sdgs 1 2A 2 3
Broughton Road CS (Northern Rail)
(former Skipton North Jn) for Colne 221.68
[LN 922] 3 TJC SKW 1 [LN 922]
SKIPTON to MORECAMBE LINE
221.60 Skipton North Jn
LMS : Mid (North Western)
Marshalls (UWC) 222.18
Niffany (UWC) 222.50
223.04 River Aire
LONDON NORTH EAST ZONE
GARGRAVE 224.79 ④
225.04
River Aire
Gargrave HABD (L) 226.59
225.63
York IECC (L) (H) 225.72
DN SHIPLEY MAIN
UP SHIPLEY MAIN
227.44 River Aire Bell Busk Viaduct
222 223 224 225 226 227 228 229 230 231
33B
BLACKBURN to HELLIFIELD LINE
[NW 7013] DJH LMS : L&Y
DOWN BRANCH
UP BRANCH
Switches Farm (UWG) 230.06
Haw Lane (UWG) 230.68
230.00
LNE | LNW
[LN 922] | [NW 9901]
LMS : Mid (N. Western)
231.08
Down Recess Sdgs
34.68 DN SDG
DGL P
DOWN MAIN
West Coast Railway Co Ltd
231.39
UP MAIN
UP GOODS LOOP
CRIPPLE
231.14 (H)
HELLIFIELD 231.20
⑥ ⑤
231.50
SKW 1 [NW 9901]
LMS : Mid (N. Western)
34A : to Settle

GRASSINGTON or SWINDEN BRANCH
1 2 3 4 5 6
DN →
Rylstone (TMO) 5.17
SKS 2
LMS : Mid (Yorkshire Dales)
6.50 NR Bdy
Loading Shute
No.3 Line
No.2 Line RR
No.1 Line
Loading Bunker
Wagon/Pilot Shed
7.09
RYLSTONE Tarmac

August 2013

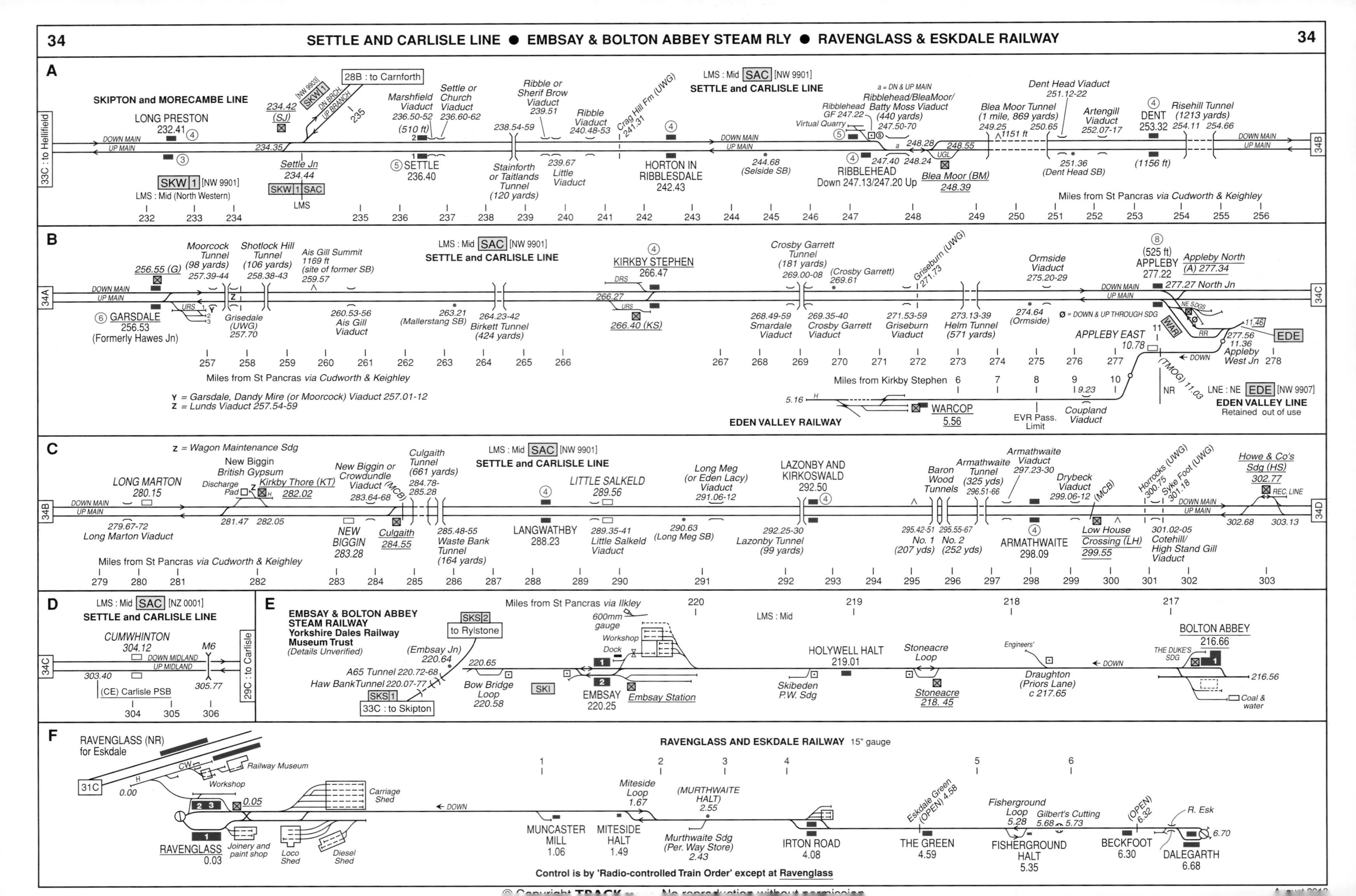
34
SETTLE AND CARLISLE LINE ● EMBSAY & BOLTON ABBEY STEAM RLY ● RAVENGLASS & ESKDALE RAILWAY
34
A
SKIPTON and MORECAMBE LINE
LONG PRESTON
232.41
33C : to Hellifield
SKW 1 [NW 9901]
LMS : Mid (North Western)
28B : to Carnforth
234.42
(SJ)
Settle Jn
234.44
SKW 1 SAC
LMS
Marshfield Viaduct 236.50-52
(510 ft)
Settle or Church Viaduct 236.60-62
SETTLE
236.40
Ribble or Sherif Brow Viaduct 239.51
Stainforth or Taitlands Tunnel (120 yards)
Little Viaduct 239.67
Ribble Viaduct 240.48-53
Crag Hill Fm (UWG) 241.31
HORTON IN RIBBLESDALE
242.43
LMS : Mid SAC [NW 9901]
SETTLE and CARLISLE LINE
244.68 (Selside SB)
a = DN & UP MAIN
Ribblehead/BleaMoor/ Batty Moss Viaduct (440 yards) 247.50-70
Ribblehead GF 247.22
Virtual Quarry
RIBBLEHEAD
Down 247.13/247.20 Up
Blea Moor (BM)
248.39
Blea Moor Tunnel (1 mile, 869 yards) 249.25 250.65
1151 ft
Dent Head Viaduct 251.12-22
251.36 (Dent Head SB)
Artengill Viaduct 252.07-17
DENT
253.32
(1156 ft)
Risehill Tunnel (1213 yards) 254.11 254.66
Miles from St Pancras via Cudworth & Keighley
34B
B
34A
256.55 (G)
GARSDALE
256.53
(Formerly Hawes Jn)
Moorcock Tunnel (98 yards) 257.39-44
Grisedale (UWG) 257.70
Shotlock Hill Tunnel (106 yards) 258.38-43
Ais Gill Summit 1169 ft (site of former SB) 259.57
Ais Gill Viaduct 260.53-56
263.21 (Mallerstang SB)
Birkett Tunnel 264.23-42 (424 yards)
LMS : Mid SAC [NW 9901]
SETTLE and CARLISLE LINE
KIRKBY STEPHEN
266.47
266.40 (KS)
Miles from St Pancras via Cudworth & Keighley
Y = Garsdale, Dandy Mire (or Moorcock) Viaduct 257.01-12
Z = Lunds Viaduct 257.54-59
Crosby Garrett Tunnel (181 yards) 269.00-08
(Crosby Garrett) 269.61
Smardale Viaduct 268.49-59
Crosby Garrett Viaduct 269.35-40
Griseburn (UWG) 271.73
Griseburn Viaduct 271.53-59
Helm Tunnel 273.13-39 (571 yards)
Ormside Viaduct 275.20-29
274.64 (Ormside)
Ø = DOWN & UP THROUGH SDG
APPLEBY
277.22
(525 ft)
Appleby North (A) 277.34
277.27 North Jn
APPLEBY EAST
10.78
Appleby West Jn
EDE
Miles from Kirkby Stephen
WARCOP
5.56
EVR Pass. Limit
Coupland Viaduct
EDEN VALLEY RAILWAY
LNE : NE EDE [NW 9907]
EDEN VALLEY LINE
Retained out of use
34C
C
z = Wagon Maintenance Sdg
LONG MARTON
280.15
Long Marton Viaduct
New Biggin British Gypsum
Kirkby Thore (KT) 282.02
Discharge Pad
NEW BIGGIN
283.28
New Biggin or Crowdundle Viaduct 283.64-68
Culgaith
284.55
Culgaith Tunnel (661 yards) 284.78-285.28
Waste Bank Tunnel 285.48-55 (164 yards)
LMS : Mid SAC [NW 9901]
SETTLE and CARLISLE LINE
LANGWATHBY
288.23
LITTLE SALKELD
289.56
Little Salkeld Viaduct 289.35-41
Long Meg (or Eden Lacy) Viaduct 291.06-12
290.63 (Long Meg SB)
LAZONBY AND KIRKOSWALD
292.50
Lazonby Tunnel 292.25-30 (99 yards)
Baron Wood Tunnels
No. 1 295.42-51 (207 yds)
No. 2 295.55-67 (252 yds)
Armathwaite Tunnel (325 yds) 296.51-66
Armathwaite Viaduct 297.23-30
ARMATHWAITE
298.09
Drybeck Viaduct 299.06-12
Low House Crossing (LH) 299.55
Horrocks (UWG) 300.75
Syke Foot (UWG) 301.18
Cotehill/ High Stand Gill Viaduct 301.02-05
Howe & Co's Sdg (HS) 302.77
Miles from St Pancras via Cudworth & Keighley
34D
D
LMS : Mid SAC [NZ 0001]
SETTLE and CARLISLE LINE
CUMWHINTON
304.12
(CE) Carlisle PSB
M6
305.77
29C : to Carlisle
E
EMBSAY & BOLTON ABBEY STEAM RAILWAY
Yorkshire Dales Railway Museum Trust
(Details Unverified)
Miles from St Pancras via Ilkley
SKS 2 to Rylstone
(Embsay Jn) 220.64
A65 Tunnel 220.72-68
Haw Bank Tunnel 220.07-77
SKS 1 33C : to Skipton
Bow Bridge Loop 220.58
SKI
600mm gauge
Workshop
Dock
EMBSAY
220.25
Embsay Station
LMS : Mid
HOLYWELL HALT
219.01
Skibeden P.W. Sdg
Stoneacre Loop
Stoneacre 218.45
Engineers'
Draughton (Priors Lane) c 217.65
BOLTON ABBEY
216.66
THE DUKE'S SDG
Coal & water
F
RAVENGLASS (NR) for Eskdale
31C
Railway Museum
Workshop
Carriage Shed
RAVENGLASS
0.03
Joinery and paint shop
Loco Shed
Diesel Shed
RAVENGLASS AND ESKDALE RAILWAY 15" gauge
MUNCASTER MILL
1.06
Miteside Loop 1.67
MITESIDE HALT
1.49
(MURTHWAITE HALT) 2.55
Murthwaite Sdg (Per. Way Store) 2.43
IRTON ROAD
4.08
Eskdale Green (OPEN) 4.58
THE GREEN
4.59
Fisherground Loop 5.28
Gilbert's Cutting 5.68 5.73
FISHERGROUND HALT
5.35
(OPEN) 6.32
BECKFOOT
6.30
R. Esk
DALEGARTH
6.68
Control is by 'Radio-controlled Train Order' except at Ravenglass

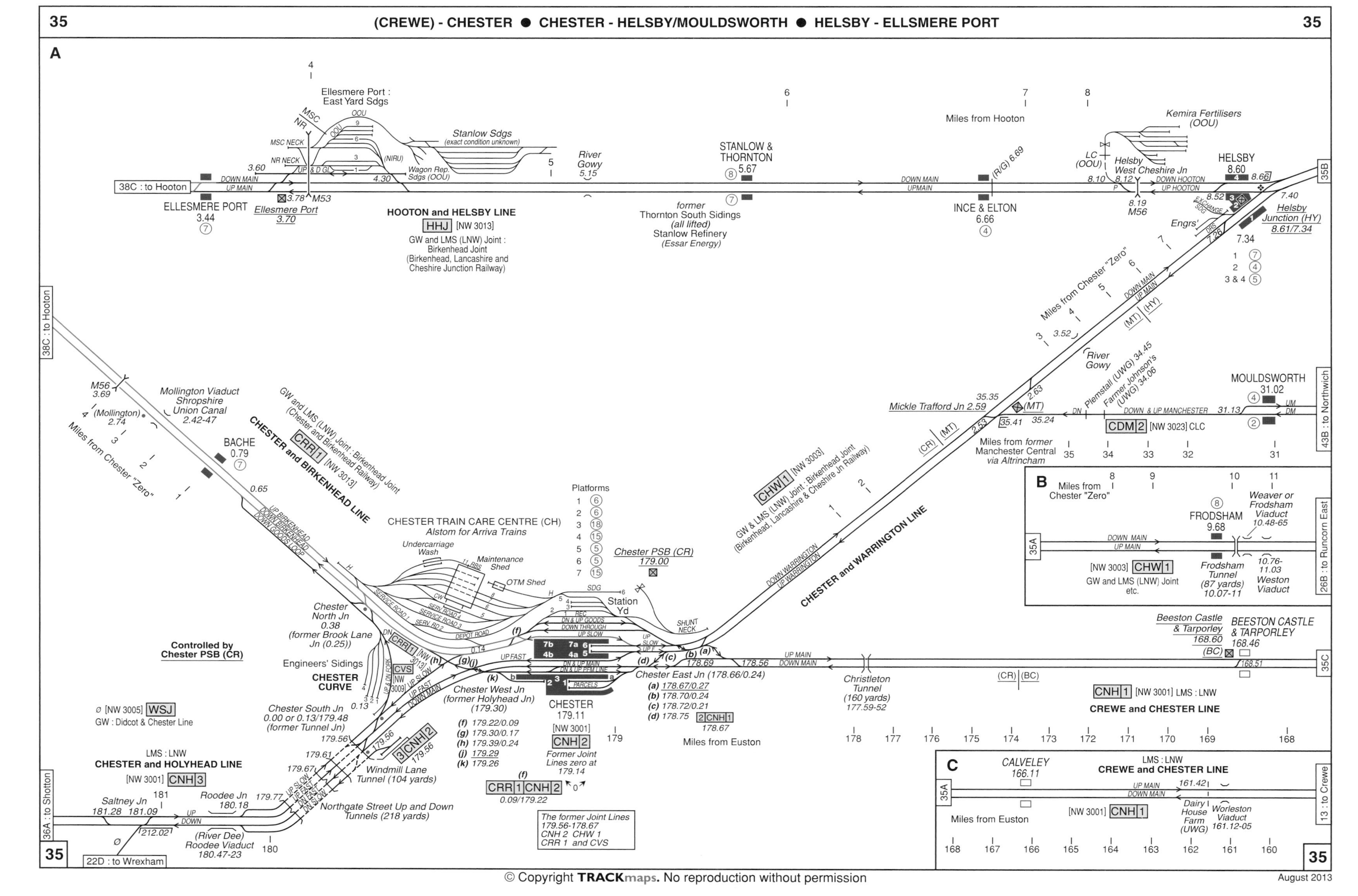
A
Ellesmere Port : East Yard Sdgs
Stanlow Sdgs (exact condition unknown)
Wagon Rep. Sdgs (OOU)
38C : to Hooton
ELLESMERE PORT 3.44
Ellesmere Port 3.70
3.78 M53
HOOTON and HELSBY LINE
HHJ [NW 3013]
GW and LMS (LNW) Joint : Birkenhead Joint (Birkenhead, Lancashire and Cheshire Junction Railway)
River Gowy 5.15
STANLOW & THORNTON 5.67
former Thornton South Sidings (all lifted)
Stanlow Refinery (Essar Energy)
Miles from Hooton
INCE & ELTON 6.66
(R/G) 6.69
Kemira Fertilisers (OOU)
LC (OOU)
Helsby West Cheshire Jn 8.12
8.19 M56
HELSBY 8.60
Helsby Junction (HY) 8.61/7.34
35B
Engrs'
Miles from Chester "Zero"
River Gowy
Plemstall (UWG) 34.45
Farmer Johnson's (UWG) 34.06
MOULDSWORTH 31.02
43B : to Northwich
DOWN & UP MANCHESTER
CDM 2 [NW 3023] CLC
Mickle Trafford Jn 2.59
Miles from former Manchester Central via Altrincham
CHW 1 [NW 3003]
GW & LMS (LNW) Joint : Birkenhead Joint (Birkenhead, Lancashire & Cheshire Jn Railway)
CHESTER and WARRINGTON LINE
B
Miles from Chester "Zero"
FRODSHAM 9.68
Weaver or Frodsham Viaduct 10.48-65
Frodsham Tunnel (87 yards) 10.07-11
10.76-11.03 Weston Viaduct
[NW 3003] CHW 1
GW and LMS (LNW) Joint etc.
26B : to Runcorn East
35A
Mollington Viaduct Shropshire Union Canal 2.42-47
M56 3.69
(Mollington) 2.74
BACHE 0.79
GW and LMS (LNW) Joint : Birkenhead Joint (Chester and Birkenhead Railway)
CRR 1 [NW 3013]
CHESTER and BIRKENHEAD LINE
UP BIRKENHEAD
DOWN BIRKENHEAD
DOWN GOODS LOOP
CHESTER TRAIN CARE CENTRE (CH)
Alstom for Arriva Trains
Undercarriage Wash
Maintenance Shed
OTM Shed
Platforms
1 (6)
2 (6)
3 (18)
4 (15)
5 (5)
6 (5)
7 (15)
Chester PSB (CR) 179.00
Station Yd
SHUNT NECK
Chester North Jn 0.38 (former Brook Lane Jn (0.25))
Controlled by Chester PSB (CR)
Engineers' Sidings
CHESTER CURVE
CVS [NW 3009]
Chester South Jn 0.00 or 0.13/179.48 (former Tunnel Jn)
Chester West Jn (former Holyhead Jn) (179.30)
CHESTER 179.11
[NW 3001] CNH 2
Former Joint Lines zero at 179.14
(f) 179.22/0.09
(g) 179.30/0.17
(h) 179.39/0.24
(j) 179.29
(k) 179.26
CRR 1 CNH 2 0.09/179.22
The former Joint Lines 179.56-178.67 CNH 2 CHW 1 CRR 1 and CVS
Chester East Jn (178.66/0.24)
(a) 178.67/0.27
(b) 178.70/0.24
(c) 178.72/0.21
(d) 178.75
2 CNH 1 178.67
Miles from Euston
Christleton Tunnel (160 yards) 177.59-52
Beeston Castle & Tarporley 168.60 (BC)
BEESTON CASTLE & TARPORLEY 168.46
35C
CNH 1 [NW 3001] LMS : LNW
CREWE and CHESTER LINE
ø [NW 3005] WSJ
GW : Didcot & Chester Line
LMS : LNW
CHESTER and HOLYHEAD LINE
[NW 3001] CNH 3
36A : to Shotton
Saltney Jn 181.28 181.09
Roodee Jn 180.18
(River Dee) Roodee Viaduct 180.47-23
22D : to Wrexham
Windmill Lane Tunnel (104 yards)
Northgate Street Up and Down Tunnels (218 yards)
3 CNH 2
C
CALVELEY 166.11
LMS : LNW
CREWE and CHESTER LINE
Miles from Euston
[NW 3001] CNH 1
Dairy House Farm (UWG)
161.42
Worleston Viaduct 161.12-05
13 : to Crewe

August 2013

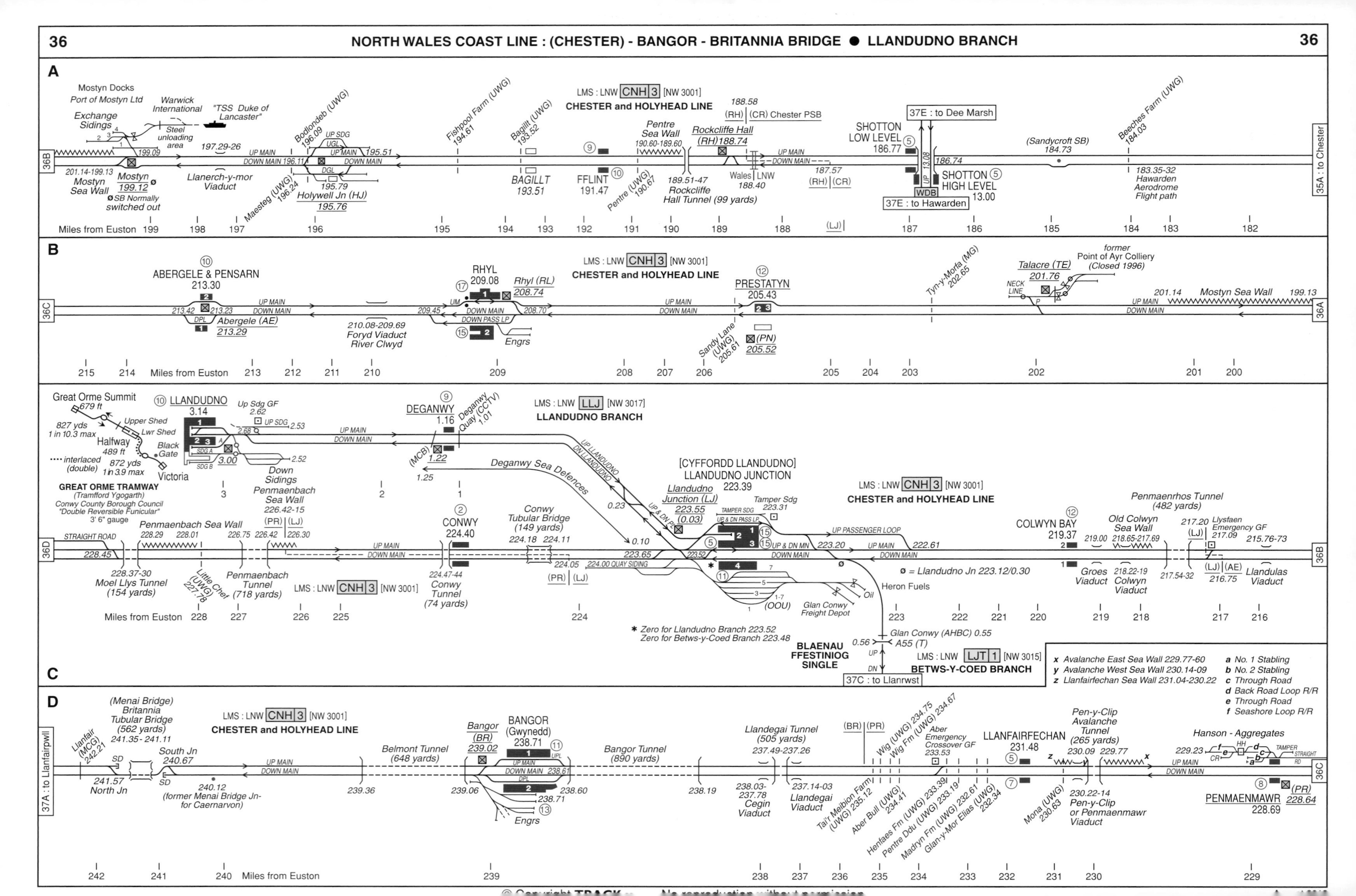
A
Mostyn Docks
Port of Mostyn Ltd
Exchange Sidings
Warwick International
"TSS Duke of Lancaster"
Steel unloading area
197.29-26
199.09
201.14-199.13
Mostyn Sea Wall
Mostyn 199.12
SB Normally switched out
Llanerch-y-mor Viaduct
Maesteg (UWG) 196.24
Bodlondeb (UWG) 196.09
UP SDG
UGL
DGL
UP MAIN
DOWN MAIN 196.11
195.51
195.79
Holywell Jn (HJ) 195.76
Fishpool Farm (UWG) 194.61
Bagillt (UWG) 193.52
BAGILLT 193.51
FFLINT 191.47
Pentre (UWG) 190.67
LMS : LNW CNH 3 [NW 3001]
CHESTER and HOLYHEAD LINE
Pentre Sea Wall 190.60-189.60
189.51-47 Rockcliffe Hall Tunnel (99 yards)
188.58
(RH) (CR) Chester PSB
Rockcliffe Hall (RH) 188.74
Wales LNW 188.40
187.57
(RH) (CR)
(LJ)
SHOTTON LOW LEVEL 186.77
37E : to Dee Marsh
UP 13.08
186.74
SHOTTON HIGH LEVEL 13.00
WDB
37E : to Hawarden
(Sandycroft SB) 184.73
Beeches Farm (UWG) 184.03
183.35-32 Hawarden Aerodrome Flight path
35A : to Chester
36B
Miles from Euston 199 198 197 196 195 194 193 192 191 190 189 188 187 186 185 184 183 182
B
36C
ABERGELE & PENSARN 213.30
213.42
213.23
DPL
Abergele (AE) 213.29
210.08-209.69 Foryd Viaduct River Clwyd
RHYL 209.08
209.45
UM
DOWN MAIN
DOWN PASS LP
Rhyl (RL) 208.74
208.70
Engrs
LMS : LNW CNH 3 [NW 3001]
CHESTER and HOLYHEAD LINE
PRESTATYN 205.43
Sandy Lane (UWG) 205.61
(PN) 205.52
Tyn-y-Morfa (MG) 202.65
Talacre (TE) 201.76
NECK LINE
former Point of Ayr Colliery (Closed 1996)
201.14
Mostyn Sea Wall
199.13
36A
Miles from Euston 215 214 213 212 211 210 209 208 207 206 205 204 203 202 201 200
C
Great Orme Summit 679 ft
827 yds 1 in 10.3 max
Upper Shed
Lwr Shed
Halfway 489 ft
Black Gate
872 yds 1 in 3.9 max
Victoria
interlaced (double)
GREAT ORME TRAMWAY
(Tramffordd Ygogarth)
Conwy County Borough Council
"Double Reversible Funicular"
3' 6" gauge
LLANDUDNO 3.14
Up Sdg GF 2.62
UP SDG 2.53
2.68
SDG A
SDG B
3.00
2.52
Down Sidings
DEGANWY 1.16
Deganwy Quay (CCTV) 1.01
(MCB) 1.22
1.25
LMS : LNW LLJ [NW 3017]
LLANDUDNO BRANCH
UP LLANDUDNO
DN LLANDUDNO
Deganwy Sea Defences
0.23
UP & DN PL
0.10
[CYFFORDD LLANDUDNO]
LLANDUDNO JUNCTION 223.39
Llandudno Junction (LJ) 223.55 (0.03)
Tamper Sdg 223.31
TAMPER SDG
UP & DN PASS LP
UP & DN MN
223.20
223.52
223.65
224.00 QUAY SIDING
(OOU)
Glan Conwy Freight Depot
Oil
Heron Fuels
ø = Llandudno Jn 223.12/0.30
* Zero for Llandudno Branch 223.52
Zero for Betws-y-Coed Branch 223.48
UP PASSENGER LOOP
222.61
LMS : LNW CNH 3 [NW 3001]
CHESTER and HOLYHEAD LINE
Penmaenbach Sea Wall 226.42-15
(PR) (LJ)
226.30
STRAIGHT ROAD
228.45
Penmaenbach Sea Wall 228.29 228.01
226.75 226.42
228.37-30 Moel Llys Tunnel (154 yards)
Little Chef (UWG) 227.78
Penmaenbach Tunnel (718 yards)
LMS : LNW CNH 3 [NW 3001]
CONWY 224.40
224.47-44 Conwy Tunnel (74 yards)
Conwy Tubular Bridge (149 yards) 224.18 224.11
224.05
(PR) (LJ)
COLWYN BAY 219.37
219.00
Old Colwyn Sea Wall 218.65-217.69
Groes Viaduct
218.22-19 Colwyn Viaduct
Penmaenrhos Tunnel (482 yards)
217.20 Llysfaen Emergency GF 217.09
(LJ)
217.54-32
(LJ) (AE) 216.75
215.76-73 Llandulas Viaduct
36D
36B
Miles from Euston 228 227 226 225 224 223 222 221 220 219 218 217 216
Glan Conwy (AHBC) 0.55
0.56
A55 (T)
BLAENAU FFESTINIOG SINGLE
LMS : LNW LJT 1 [NW 3015]
BETWS-Y-COED BRANCH
37C : to Llanrwst
x Avalanche East Sea Wall 229.77-60
y Avalanche West Sea Wall 230.14-09
z Llanfairfechan Sea Wall 231.04-230.22
a No. 1 Stabling
b No. 2 Stabling
c Through Road
d Back Road Loop R/R
e Through Road
f Seashore Loop R/R
D
37A : to Llanfairpwll
Llanfair (MCG) 242.21
SD
241.57 North Jn
(Menai Bridge) Britannia Tubular Bridge (562 yards) 241.35 - 241.11
South Jn 240.67
240.12 (former Menai Bridge Jn- for Caernarvon)
LMS : LNW CNH 3 [NW 3001]
CHESTER and HOLYHEAD LINE
239.36
Belmont Tunnel (648 yards)
Bangor (BR) 239.02
BANGOR (Gwynedd) 238.71
239.06
UPL
238.61
238.60
238.71
Engrs
Bangor Tunnel (890 yards)
238.19
Llandegai Tunnel (505 yards) 237.49-237.26
238.03-237.78 Cegin Viaduct
237.14-03 Llandegai Viaduct
(BR) (PR)
Tai'r Meibion Farm (UWG) 235.12
Wig (UWG) 234.75
Wig Fm (UWG) 234.67
Aber Bull (UWG) 234.41
Aber Emergency Crossover GF 233.53
Henfaes Fm (UWG) 233.39
Pentre Ddu (UWG) 233.19
Madryn Fm (UWG) 232.61
Glan-y-Mor Elias (UWG) 232.34
LLANFAIRFECHAN 231.48
Mona (UWG) 230.63
Pen-y-Clip Avalanche Tunnel (265 yards) 230.09 229.77
230.22-14 Pen-y-Clip or Penmaenmawr Viaduct
Hanson - Aggregates
229.23
CR
HH
TAMPER
STRAIGHT RD
PENMAENMAWR 228.69
(PR) 228.64
36C
Miles from Euston 242 241 240 239 238 237 236 235 234 233 232 231 230 229

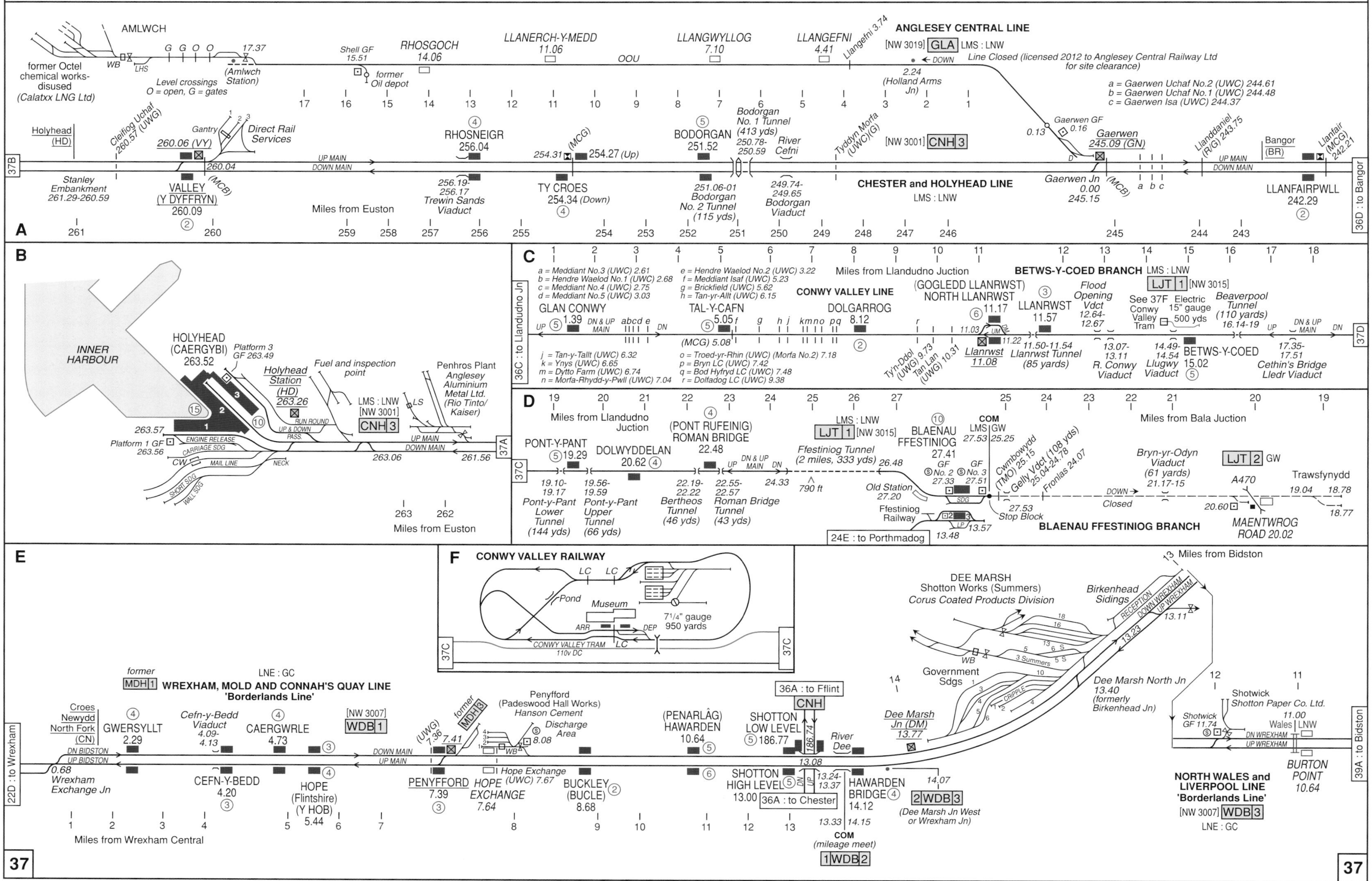

A

AMLWCH
former Octel chemical works-disused (Calatxx LNG Ltd)
WB LHS
G G O O 17.37 (Amlwch Station)
Level crossings O = open, G = gates
Shell GF 15.51
former Oil depot
RHOSGOCH 14.06
LLANERCH-Y-MEDD 11.06
OOU
LLANGWYLLOG 7.10
LLANGEFNI 4.41
Llangefni 3.74

ANGLESEY CENTRAL LINE
[NW 3019] GLA LMS : LNW
DOWN
Line Closed (licensed 2012 to Anglesey Central Railway Ltd for site clearance)
2.24 (Holland Arms Jn)
a = Gaerwen Uchaf No.2 (UWC) 244.61
b = Gaerwen Uchaf No.1 (UWC) 244.48
c = Gaerwen Isa (UWC) 244.37
17 16 15 14 13 12 11 10 9 8 7 6 5 4 3 2 1

Holyhead (HD)
Cleifiog Uchaf (UWG) 260.57
Gantry 1 2 3
260.06 (VY)
Direct Rail Services
260.04
Stanley Embankment 261.29-260.59
VALLEY (Y DYFFRYN) 260.09 (2) (MCB)
UP MAIN DOWN MAIN
Miles from Euston
(4) RHOSNEIGR 256.04
256.19-256.17 Trewin Sands Viaduct
254.31 (MCG) 254.27 (Up)
TY CROES 254.34 (Down) (4)
(5) BODORGAN 251.52
Bodorgan No. 1 Tunnel (413 yds) 250.78-250.59
River Cefni
251.06-01 Bodorgan No. 2 Tunnel (115 yds)
249.74-249.65 Bodorgan Viaduct
Tyddyn Morfa (UWC)(G)
[NW 3001] CNH 3
CHESTER and HOLYHEAD LINE
LMS : LNW
0.13 Gaerwen GF 0.16
Gaerwen 245.09 (GN)
D
Gaerwen Jn 0.00 245.15 (MCB)
a b c
Llanddaniel (R/G) 243.75
Bangor (BR)
Llanfair (MCG) 242.21
LLANFAIRPWLL 242.29 (2)
36D : to Bangor
37B
261 260 259 258 257 256 255 254 253 252 251 250 249 248 247 246 245 244 243

B

INNER HARBOUR
HOLYHEAD (CAERGYBI) 263.52
Platform 3 GF 263.49
Holyhead Station (HD) 263.26
(15) 1 2 3 (10)
263.57
Platform 1 GF 263.56
ENGINE RELEASE
CARRIAGE SDG
CW
MAIL LINE
SHORT SDG
WALL SDG
NECK
RUN ROUND
UP & DOWN PASS.
Fuel and inspection point
LMS : LNW [NW 3001] CNH 3
LS
Penhros Plant Anglesey Aluminium Metal Ltd. (Rio Tinto/ Kaiser)
UP MAIN DOWN MAIN
263.06
261.56
37A
263 262
Miles from Euston

C

1 2 3 4 5 6 7 8 9 10 11 12 13 14 15 16 17 18
a = Meddiant No.3 (UWC) 2.61
b = Hendre Waelod No.1 (UWC) 2.68
c = Meddiant No.4 (UWC) 2.75
d = Meddiant No.5 (UWC) 3.03
e = Hendre Waelod No.2 (UWC) 3.22
f = Meddiant Isaf (UWC) 5.23
g = Brickfield (UWC) 5.62
h = Tan-yr-Allt (UWC) 6.15
Miles from Llandudno Juction
CONWY VALLEY LINE
GLAN CONWY (5) 1.39
UP DN & UP MAIN abcd e DN
TAL-Y-CAFN (5) 5.05 f g h j k m n o p q
(MCG) 5.08
DOLGARROG 8.12 (2)
j = Tan-y-Tallt (UWC) 6.32
k = Ynys (UWC) 6.65
m = Dytto Farm (UWC) 6.74
n = Morfa-Rhydd-y-Pwll (UWC) 7.04
o = Troed-yr-Rhin (UWC) (Morfa No.2) 7.18
p = Bryn LC (UWC) 7.42
q = Bod Hyfryd LC (UWC) 7.48
r = Dolfadog LC (UWC) 9.38
r
Tyn-Ddol (UWG) 9.73
Tan Lan (UWG) 10.31
(GOGLEDD LLANRWST) NORTH LLANRWST (6) 11.17
11.03 UM DM 11.22
Llanrwst 11.08
(3) LLANRWST 11.57
11.50-11.54 Llanrwst Tunnel (85 yards)
BETWS-Y-COED BRANCH LMS : LNW
Flood Opening Vdct 12.64-12.67
13.07-13.11 R. Conwy Viaduct
LJT 1 [NW 3015]
See 37F Conwy Valley Tram
Electric 15" gauge 500 yds
14.49-14.54 Llugwy Viaduct
BETWS-Y-COED 15.02 (5)
Beaverpool Tunnel (110 yards) 16.14-19
UP DN & UP MAIN DN
17.35-17.51 Cethin's Bridge Lledr Viaduct
36C : to Llandudno Jn
37D

D

19 20 21 22 23 24 25 26 27 25 24 23 22 21 20 19
Miles from Llandudno Juction
PONT-Y-PANT (5) 19.29
19.10-19.17 Pont-y-Pant Lower Tunnel (144 yds)
19.56-19.59 Pont-y-Pant Upper Tunnel (66 yds)
DOLWYDDELAN 20.62 (4)
(4) (PONT RUFEINIG) ROMAN BRIDGE 22.48
22.19-22.22 Bertheos Tunnel (46 yds)
UP DN & UP MAIN DN
22.55-22.57 Roman Bridge Tunnel (43 yds)
24.33
LMS : LNW
LJT 1 [NW 3015]
Ffestiniog Tunnel (2 miles, 333 yds) 26.48
790 ft
(10) BLAENAU FFESTINIOG 27.41
GF (S) No. 2 27.33
GF (S) No. 3 27.51
COM LMS GW 27.53 25.25
Old Station 27.20
SDG
Ffestiniog Railway
LP 2 3
13.48 13.57
24E : to Porthmadog
27.53 Stop Block
Cwmbowydd (TMO) 25.15
Gelly Vdct (108 yds) 25.04-24.78
Fronlas 24.07
DOWN
Closed
BLAENAU FFESTINIOG BRANCH
Miles from Bala Juction
Bryn-yr-Odyn Viaduct (61 yards) 21.17-15
LJT 2 GW
A470
20.60
MAENTWROG ROAD 20.02
Trawsfynydd
19.04 18.78
18.77
37C

E

former MDH 1 **WREXHAM, MOLD AND CONNAH'S QUAY LINE**
'Borderlands Line'
LNE : GC
Croes Newydd North Fork (CN)
DN BIDSTON UP BIDSTON
0.68 Wrexham Exchange Jn
(4) GWERSYLLT 2.29
Cefn-y-Bedd Viaduct 4.09-4.13
CEFN-Y-BEDD 4.20 (3)
(4) CAERGWRLE 4.73
[NW 3007] WDB 1
(3)
(4) HOPE (Flintshire) (Y HOB) 5.44
DOWN MAIN UP MAIN
(UWG) 7.36
7.41
former MDH 3
PENYFFORD 7.39 (3)
Penyfford (Padeswood Hall Works) Hanson Cement
(S) 8.08
Discharge Area
WB
Hope Exchange (UWC) 7.67
HOPE EXCHANGE 7.64
BUCKLEY (BUCLE) 8.68 (2)
(PENARLÂG) HAWARDEN 10.64 (5)
(6)
36A : to Fflint
CNH
SHOTTON LOW LEVEL (5) 186.77
186.74
SHOTTON HIGH LEVEL (5) 13.00
DN UP
13.08
13.24-13.37
36A : to Chester
13.33 14.15
COM (mileage meet)
1 WDB 2
River Dee
HAWARDEN BRIDGE (4) 14.12
14.07
2 WDB 3
(Dee Marsh Jn West or Wrexham Jn)
Dee Marsh Jn (DM) 13.77
14
Government Sdgs
DEE MARSH
Shotton Works (Summers)
Corus Coated Products Division
18 16 13 6 S 5 S 5 3 Summers 10
WB
CRIPPLE 1 2 3 4 5 6
Birkenhead Sidings
RECEPTION DOWN WREXHAM UP WREXHAM
13.23
13.11
13 Miles from Bidston
Dee Marsh North Jn 13.40 (formerly Birkenhead Jn)
12 11
Shotwick GF 11.74
(S)
Shotwick
Shotton Paper Co. Ltd.
11.00
Wales LNW
DN WREXHAM UP WREXHAM
BURTON POINT 10.64
NORTH WALES and LIVERPOOL LINE
'Borderlands Line'
[NW 3007] WDB 3
LNE : GC
22D : to Wrexham
39A : to Bidston
1 2 3 4 5 6 7 8 9 10 11 12 13
Miles from Wrexham Central

F

CONWY VALLEY RAILWAY
LC LC
Pond
Museum
ARR DEP
7¼" gauge 950 yards
CONWY VALLEY TRAM 110v DC
LC
37C 37C

August 2013

A

TIMPERLEY and GARSTON LINE
LMS : LNW WJL 2 [MD 2001]

3 WJL 2

40 : to Garston & Liverpool Lime Street

186.72 (22.59)
186.57
(Speke) 186.21
Speke Jn (SE) | (DN) Ditton
185.58
UP DITTON FAST
DOWN DITTON FAST
UP DITTON SLOW
DN DITTON SLOW
Speke Jn GF 186.72 (22.59)
186.56
Garston Car Terminal Ford Motor Co.
Ramps
185.16 W. NECK
1 UP/DN REC
2 UP/DN R.
E. NECK
Halewood West Jn 185.16
Halewood East Jn 184.64
184.01 (Halebank)
* = 184.45
Exchange Sdgs
Halewood
Jaguar Land Rover
Car Ramps
187 186 185 184 Miles from Euston

2 WJL 1
SDJ 2

DITTON 182.79
Ditton East Jn
182.67 18.55
182.60
183.30
183.22
H
UP DITTON FAST
DOWN DITTON FAST
UP DITTON SLOW
DOWN DITTON SLOW
182.69
182.57 182.53
18.55
UP DITTON
DOWN DITTON
Ditton West Jn 183.22
CR
182.74
Reception Sdgs
Ditton (DN) 183.00
(DN) | (FF)
183
AHC Sdgs
Foundry Lane
UP LOW LEVEL
DOWN LOW LEVEL
O'CONNORS
SDG
Widnes Intermodal Rail Depot O'Connor
★ = Crane Pad
182
181.25
18
181.11
(DN) (RN)
182.10
17.60
17.50 (West Deviation Jn)
181.69
49 Spans
Ditton Viaduct
181.33
16 Spans
Runcorn Viaduct North (River Mersey: Spans 1-5)
3 Spans
180.77 Manchester Ship Canal
180.77
Runcorn Viaduct South
33 Spans
180.52 Bridgewater Canal
180.48
RUNCORN BRIDGE
River Mersey 915 yards
181 – The Queen Aethelfreda Viaduct
(RN) (DN)
0.25
A533(T)
(RN) 180.33
0.02
180.29
RUNCORN 180.40
Runcorn Jn 180.22
DN & UP FOLLY LANE
0.69 NR boundary

RDB
[MD 2003]
RUNCORN DOCK BRANCH FOLLY LANE SINGLE

FOLLY LANE
Ineos Chlor Chemicals
Loading facility
180

WIDNES LOOP
SDJ 2
[NW 2009]
LMS : LNW

WIDNES SOUTH 17.18
Viaduct 17.15 16.75
Controlled by Fiddlers Ferry (FF)
UP GOODS
DN GOODS
Carterhouse Jn (UWG) 16.27
D
38B
17 16 Miles from *former* Timperley Jn

RUNCORN BRANCH
[MD 2001] WJL 1 LMS : LNW

UP MAIN
DOWN MAIN
179.24
0.00
Halton Jn (HN) 179.20
DN CHESTER
26B : to Frodsham/Acton Bridge

B

FIDDLERS FERRY POWER STATION
Scottish & Southern Energy

TIMPERLEY and GARSTON LINE
[NW 2009] SDJ 2 LMS : LNW

HOPPER APPROACH TRACKS
(open)
WB
Control Building
Coal Track Hoppers
(open)
Gypsum (FGD) Loading Plant
A B C
RD 1
RD 2
CR
0.33
0.00
Fiddlers Ferry Power Station (FF) 14.46
Marsh House (CCTV) 14.09
Fiddlers Ferry (UWG) 13.63
Penketh Hall (UWG) 13.37
St Helens Canal
(MCB)
Litton's Mill LCF (MCG) 11.45
Monks Sdg 11.70
38A
UP GOODS
DOWN GOODS
26B : to Arpley Jn
15 14 13 12 Miles from *former* Timperley Jn

C

Controlled by Merseyrail (ML)
Located at Sandhills

CHESTER and BIRKENHEAD LINE
[NW 8013] CRR 2 GW & LMS (LNW) Joint : Birkenhead Joint
'Merseyrail Wirral Line'

39A : to Birkenhead
Rock Ferry South Jn 13.30
BEBINGTON 12.36 (6)
DOWN SDG
(6)
PORT SUNLIGHT 11.61
11.42
Merseyrail (ML)
SPITAL 11.16 (7)
BROMBOROUGH RAKE (6) 10.38
(6) 9.41
BROMBOROUGH 9.71
(ML) | (HN)
(6)
EASTHAM RAKE 8.68
8.53 M53
SIDING
RR
BAY
DOWN CHESTER
UP CHESTER
HOOTON 8.08
Hooton South Jn 0.02
(6) 1 2 (7)
3
8.17 Hooton North Jn (7)
7.68
Hooton (HN) ¶ 7.72

HHJ
2 CRR 1

[NW 3013] HHJ GW & LMS (LNW) Joint : (Birkenhead, Lancashire & Cheshire Jn Railway)
DOWN HELSBY
UP HELSBY
HOOTON and HELSBY LINE

UP BIRKENHEAD
DOWN BIRKENHEAD
CHESTER and BIRKENHEAD LINE
[NW 3011] CRR 1 GW & LMS (LNW) Joint : (Chester & Birkenhead Railway)

(HN) | (CR) Chester PSB
CAPENHURST 5.11 (7)
35A : to Chester

¶ = Due for closure Sept. 2013. Recontrol to Chester PSB (HN)

(Line ends before Nustar Eastham depot)
3 1/2 miles
3 1/2 miles
OOU
LITTLE SUTTON 1.47 (7)
OVERPOOL 2.28 (7)
Manisty Wharf (Coal Loading)
1 3/4 miles
LS (OOU)
Dock Rd
D
M53
Ellesmere Port Docks
Peel Ports Group
(1 mile) (Quality Freight Ltd)
MANCHESTER SHIP CANAL
Ellesmere Port : West End Sidings
(approx. distances from Ellesmere Port, NR)
Richard Lawson Transport
Ramps
MSC | NR
West End Sdgs
DOWN MAIN
UP MAIN
35A : to Helsby
3.37
ELLESMERE PORT 3.44 (7)

13 12 11 10 9 8 7 6 5 4 Miles from Chester

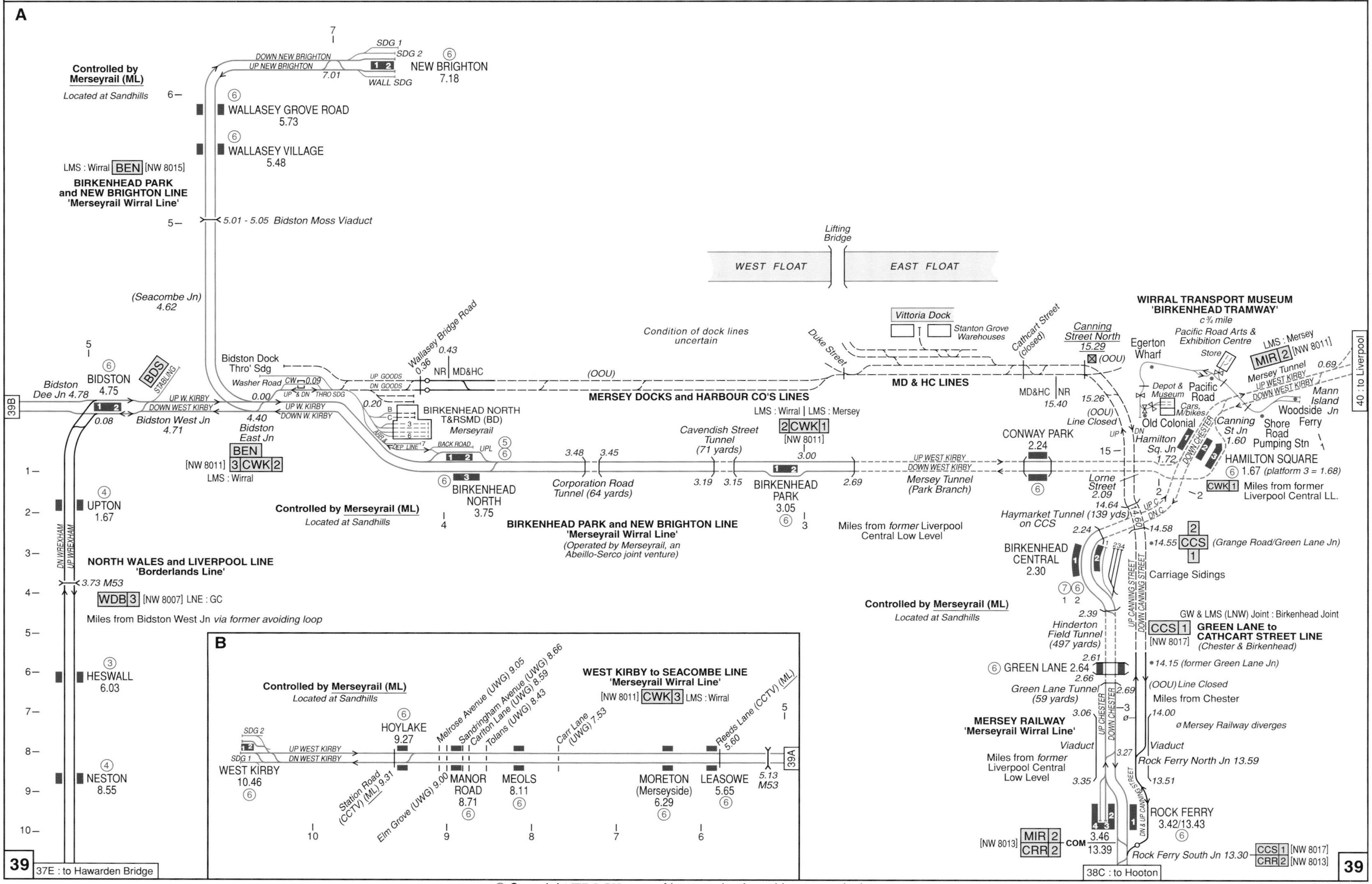
A
Controlled by Merseyrail (ML)
Located at Sandhills
LMS : Wirral BEN [NW 8015]
BIRKENHEAD PARK and NEW BRIGHTON LINE
'Merseyrail Wirral Line'
DOWN NEW BRIGHTON
UP NEW BRIGHTON
7.01
SDG 1
SDG 2
WALL SDG
NEW BRIGHTON
7.18
WALLASEY GROVE ROAD
5.73
WALLASEY VILLAGE
5.48
5.01 - 5.05 Bidston Moss Viaduct
(Seacombe Jn)
4.62
Bidston Dee Jn 4.78
BIDSTON
4.75
BDS
STABLING
UP W. KIRBY
DOWN WEST KIRBY
0.08
Bidston West Jn
4.71
Bidston Dock Thro' Sdg
Washer Road
0.00
4.40
Bidston East Jn
BEN
[NW 8011] 3 CWK 2
LMS : Wirral
Wallasey Bridge Road
0.36
0.43
NR
MD&HC
UP GOODS
DN GOODS
THRO SDG
0.20
BIRKENHEAD NORTH
T&RSMD (BD)
Merseyrail
BACK ROAD
DEP LINE
UPL
BIRKENHEAD NORTH
3.75
Controlled by Merseyrail (ML)
Located at Sandhills
(OOU)
MERSEY DOCKS and HARBOUR CO'S LINES
Condition of dock lines uncertain
Lifting Bridge
WEST FLOAT
EAST FLOAT
Duke Street
Vittoria Dock
Stanton Grove Warehouses
MD & HC LINES
Cathcart Street (closed)
Canning Street North
15.29
(OOU)
MD&HC
NR
15.40
15.26
(OOU) Line Closed
3.48
3.45
Corporation Road Tunnel (64 yards)
3.19
3.15
Cavendish Street Tunnel (71 yards)
LMS : Wirral | LMS : Mersey
2 CWK 1
[NW 8011]
3.00
BIRKENHEAD PARK
3.05
2.69
UP WEST KIRBY
DOWN WEST KIRBY
Mersey Tunnel (Park Branch)
Miles from former Liverpool Central Low Level
BIRKENHEAD PARK and NEW BRIGHTON LINE
'Merseyrail Wirral Line'
(Operated by Merseyrail, an Abeillo-Serco joint venture)
CONWAY PARK
2.24
WIRRAL TRANSPORT MUSEUM
'BIRKENHEAD TRAMWAY'
c¾ mile
Pacific Road Arts & Exhibition Centre
Store
Egerton Wharf
Depot & Museum
Pacific Road
Cars, M/bikes
Old Colonial
Hamilton Sq. Jn
1.72
DOWN CHESTER
Canning St Jn
1.60
Shore Road Pumping Stn
Woodside Ferry
Mann Island Jn
LMS : Mersey
MIR 2 [NW 8011]
Mersey Tunnel
UP WEST KIRBY
DOWN WEST KIRBY
0.69
40 : to Liverpool
HAMILTON SQUARE
1.67 (platform 3 = 1.68)
CWK 1 Miles from former Liverpool Central LL.
Lorne Street
2.09
14.64
Haymarket Tunnel (139 yds) on CCS
14.60
UP C
DN C
14.58
2 CCS 1
14.55 (Grange Road/Green Lane Jn)
Carriage Sidings
2.24
BIRKENHEAD CENTRAL
2.30
UP CANNING STREET
DOWN CANNING STREET
Controlled by Merseyrail (ML)
Located at Sandhills
2.39
Hinderton Field Tunnel (497 yards)
GW & LMS (LNW) Joint : Birkenhead Joint
CCS 1 [NW 8017]
GREEN LANE to CATHCART STREET LINE
(Chester & Birkenhead)
2.61
GREEN LANE 2.64
2.66
14.15 (former Green Lane Jn)
Green Lane Tunnel (59 yards)
2.69
(OOU) Line Closed
Miles from Chester
3.06
14.00
ø Mersey Railway diverges
MERSEY RAILWAY
'Merseyrail Wirral Line'
UP CHESTER
DOWN CHESTER
Viaduct
3.27
Rock Ferry North Jn 13.59
Miles from former Liverpool Central Low Level
3.35
13.51
DN & UP CANNING STREET
ROCK FERRY
3.42/13.43
[NW 8013] MIR 2 CRR 2
COM
3.46
13.39
Rock Ferry South Jn 13.30
CCS 1 [NW 8017]
CRR 2 [NW 8013]
38C : to Hooton
39B
UPTON
1.67
DN WREXHAM
UP WREXHAM
3.73 M53
NORTH WALES and LIVERPOOL LINE
'Borderlands Line'
WDB 3 [NW 8007] LNE : GC
Miles from Bidston West Jn via former avoiding loop
HESWALL
6.03
NESTON
8.55
37E : to Hawarden Bridge
B
Controlled by Merseyrail (ML)
Located at Sandhills
WEST KIRBY to SEACOMBE LINE
'Merseyrail Wirral Line'
[NW 8011] CWK 3 LMS : Wirral
SDG 2
SDG 1
UP WEST KIRBY
DN WEST KIRBY
WEST KIRBY
10.46
HOYLAKE
9.27
Station Road (CCTV) (ML) 9.31
Elm Grove (UWG) 9.00
Melrose Avenue (UWG) 9.05
Sandringham Avenue (UWG) 8.66
Carlton Lane (UWG) 8.59
Tolans (UWG) 8.43
MANOR ROAD
8.71
MEOLS
8.11
Carr Lane (UWG) 7.53
MORETON (Merseyside)
6.29
Reeds Lane (CCTV) (ML) 5.60
LEASOWE
5.65
5.13 M53
39A
39

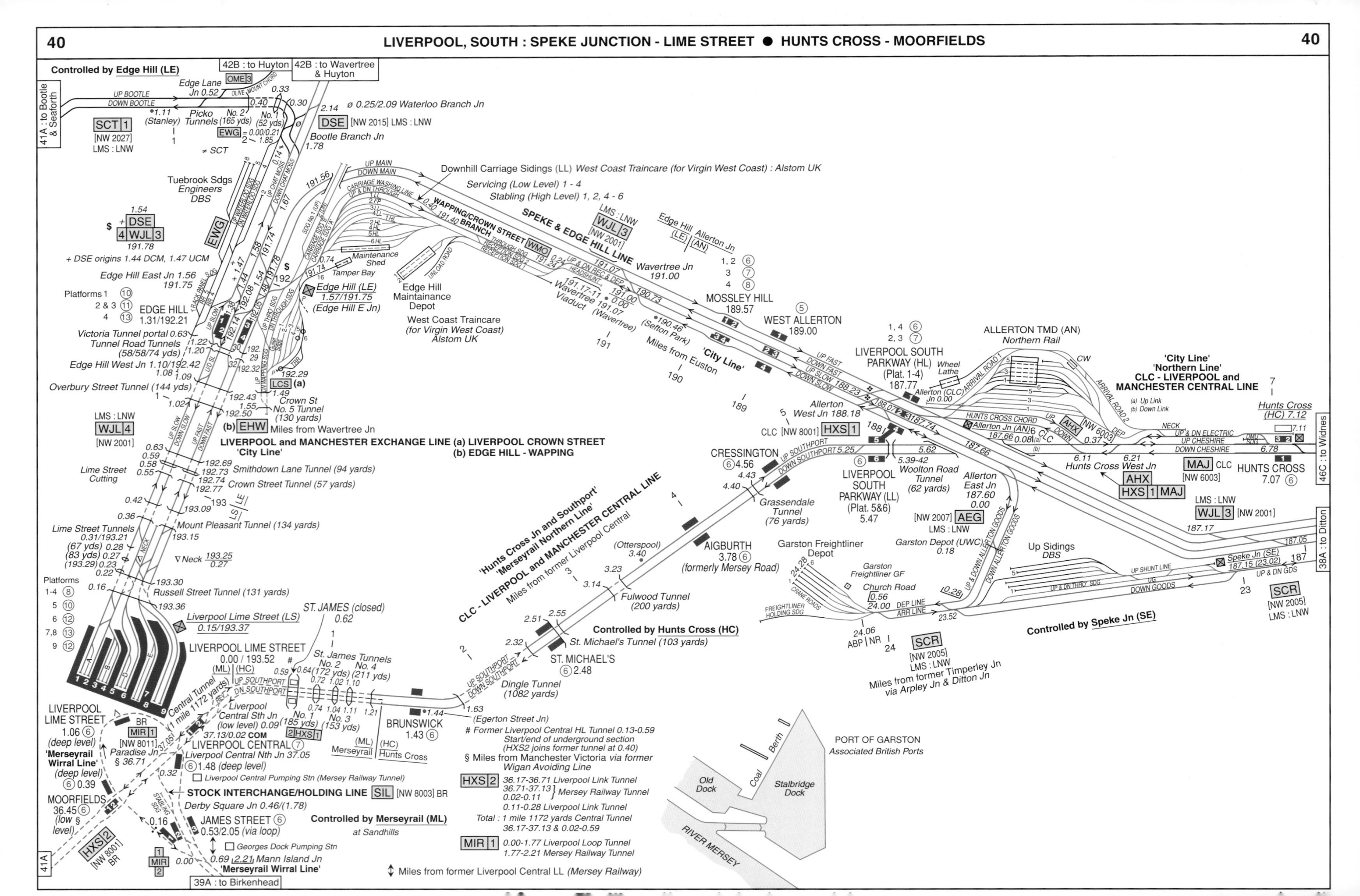

Controlled by Edge Hill (LE)
42B : to Huyton
42B : to Wavertree & Huyton
41A : to Bootle & Seaforth
UP BOOTLE
DOWN BOOTLE
Edge Lane Jn 0.52
OME 3
0.33
0.40
0.30
2.14
ø 0.25/2.09 Waterloo Branch Jn
•1.11 (Stanley)
Picko Tunnels
No. 2 (165 yds)
No. 1 (52 yds)
EWG = 0.00/0.21
2 — 1.85
DSE [NW 2015] LMS : LNW
Bootle Branch Jn 1.78
SCT 1 [NW 2027] LMS : LNW
≠ SCT
Tuebrook Sdgs Engineers DBS
EWG
1.54
$ + DSE
4 WJL 3
191.78
+ DSE origins 1.44 DCM, 1.47 UCM
Edge Hill East Jn 1.56 191.75
Platforms 1 (10)
2 & 3 (11)
4 (13)
EDGE HILL 1.31/192.21
Victoria Tunnel portal 0.63
Tunnel Road Tunnels (58/58/74 yds)
Edge Hill West Jn 1.10/192.42
Overbury Street Tunnel (144 yds)
UP MAIN
DOWN MAIN
191.56
Downhill Carriage Sidings (LL) West Coast Traincare (for Virgin West Coast) : Alstom UK
Servicing (Low Level) 1 - 4
Stabling (High Level) 1, 2, 4 - 6
WAPPING/CROWN STREET BRANCH
WMO
SPEKE & EDGE HILL LINE
LMS : LNW
WJL 3
[NW 2001]
Edge Hill (LE)
Allerton Jn (AN)
Wavertree Jn 191.00
1, 2 (6)
3 (7)
4 (8)
MOSSLEY HILL 189.57
(5)
WEST ALLERTON 189.00
Edge Hill (LE) 1.57/191.75 (Edge Hill E Jn)
Maintenance Shed
Tamper Bay
Edge Hill Maintainance Depot
West Coast Traincare (for Virgin West Coast) Alstom UK
191.17-11 Wavertree Viaduct
191.07 (Wavertree)
•190.46 (Sefton Park)
Miles from Euston
'City Line'
191
190
189
LCS (a)
192.29
1.49
Crown St No. 5 Tunnel (130 yards)
(b) EHW Miles from Wavertree Jn
LMS : LNW
WJL 4
[NW 2001]
LIVERPOOL and MANCHESTER EXCHANGE LINE (a) LIVERPOOL CROWN STREET
'City Line'
(b) EDGE HILL - WAPPING
Lime Street Cutting
192.69
192.73 Smithdown Lane Tunnel (94 yards)
192.74 Crown Street Tunnel (57 yards)
192.77
193.09
Mount Pleasant Tunnel (134 yards)
193.15
Lime Street Tunnels 0.31/193.21
(67 yds) 0.28
(83 yds) 0.27
(193.29) 0.23
∇ Neck 193.25 0.27
193.30
Russell Street Tunnel (131 yards)
193.36
Platforms
1-4 (8)
5 (10)
6 (12)
7,8 (13)
9 (12)
Liverpool Lime Street (LS) 0.15/193.37
LIVERPOOL LIME STREET 0.00 / 193.52
(ML) (HC)
ST. JAMES (closed) 0.62
St. James Tunnels
No. 2 (172 yds)
No. 4 (211 yds)
No. 1 (185 yds)
No. 3 (153 yds)
Central Tunnel (1 mile 1172 yards)
Liverpool Central Sth Jn (low level) 0.09
37.13/0.02 COM
2 HXS 1
LIVERPOOL CENTRAL (7)
Liverpool Central Nth Jn 37.05
(6) 1.48 (deep level)
Liverpool Central Pumping Stn (Mersey Railway Tunnel)
LIVERPOOL LIME STREET 1.06 (6) (deep level)
BR
MIR 1
[NW 8011]
Paradise Jn § 36.71
'Merseyrail Wirral Line' (deep level) (6) 0.39
MOORFIELDS 36.45 (6) (low § level)
HXS 2 [NW 8001] BR
41A
STOCK INTERCHANGE/HOLDING LINE SIL [NW 8003] BR
Derby Square Jn 0.46/(1.78)
JAMES STREET (6) 0.53/2.05 (via loop)
Georges Dock Pumping Stn
0.69 (2.21) Mann Island Jn
'Merseyrail Wirral Line'
39A : to Birkenhead
Controlled by Merseyrail (ML) at Sandhills
BRUNSWICK 1.43 (6)
•1.44
(ML) Merseyrail
(HC) Hunts Cross
1.63 (Egerton Street Jn)
Former Liverpool Central HL Tunnel 0.13-0.59 Start/end of underground section (HXS2 joins former tunnel at 0.40)
§ Miles from Manchester Victoria via former Wigan Avoiding Line
HXS 2 36.17-36.71 Liverpool Link Tunnel
36.71-37.13 } Mersey Railway Tunnel
0.02-0.11
0.11-0.28 Liverpool Link Tunnel
Total : 1 mile 1172 yards Central Tunnel 36.17-37.13 & 0.02-0.59
MIR 1 0.00-1.77 Liverpool Loop Tunnel
1.77-2.21 Mersey Railway Tunnel
Miles from former Liverpool Central LL (Mersey Railway)
Dingle Tunnel (1082 yards)
ST. MICHAEL'S (6) 2.48
St. Michael's Tunnel (103 yards)
Controlled by Hunts Cross (HC)
'Hunts Cross Jn and Southport'
'Merseyrail Northern Line'
CLC - LIVERPOOL and MANCHESTER CENTRAL LINE
Miles from former Liverpool Central
Fulwood Tunnel (200 yards)
(Otterspool) 3.40
AIGBURTH 3.78 (6) (formerly Mersey Road)
Grassendale Tunnel (76 yards)
CRESSINGTON (6) 4.56
UP SOUTHPORT
DOWN SOUTHPORT
CLC [NW 8001] HXS 1
Allerton West Jn 188.18
LIVERPOOL SOUTH PARKWAY (LL) (Plat. 5&6) 5.47
5.39-42 Woolton Road Tunnel (62 yards)
1, 4 (6)
2, 3 (7)
LIVERPOOL SOUTH PARKWAY (HL) (Plat. 1-4) 187.77
Wheel Lathe
Allerton (CLC) Jn 0.00
ALLERTON TMD (AN) Northern Rail
HUNTS CROSS CHORD
Allerton Jn (AN) 187.66
ARRIVAL ROAD 1
ARRIVAL ROAD 2
CW
AHX
NW 6003
'City Line'
'Northern Line'
CLC - LIVERPOOL and MANCHESTER CENTRAL LINE
(a) Up Link
(b) Down Link
Hunts Cross (HC) 7.12
UP & DN ELECTRIC
UP CHESHIRE
DOWN CHESHIRE
6.78
HUNTS CROSS 7.07 (6)
6.11
6.21
Hunts Cross West Jn
MAJ CLC [NW 6003]
AHX
HXS 1 MAJ
46C : to Widnes
Allerton East Jn 187.60 0.00
[NW 2007] AEG LMS : LNW
Garston Depot (UWC) 0.18
Up Sidings DBS
UP SHUNT LINE
DOWN GOODS
UP & DOWN ALLERTON GOODS
DOWN ALLERTON GOODS
LMS : LNW
WJL 3 [NW 2001]
187.17
187.05
Speke Jn (SE) 187.15 (23.02)
187
UP & DN GDS
38A : to Ditton
SCR [NW 2005] LMS : LNW
23
Controlled by Speke Jn (SE)
Garston Freightliner Depot
Garston Freightliner GF
Church Road 0.56
24.00
DEP LINE
ARR LINE
23.52
24.06
ABP | NR
24
SCR [NW 2005] LMS : LNW
Miles from former Timperley Jn via Arpley Jn & Ditton Jn
PORT OF GARSTON
Associated British Ports
Old Dock
Coal Berth
Stalbridge Dock
RIVER MERSEY

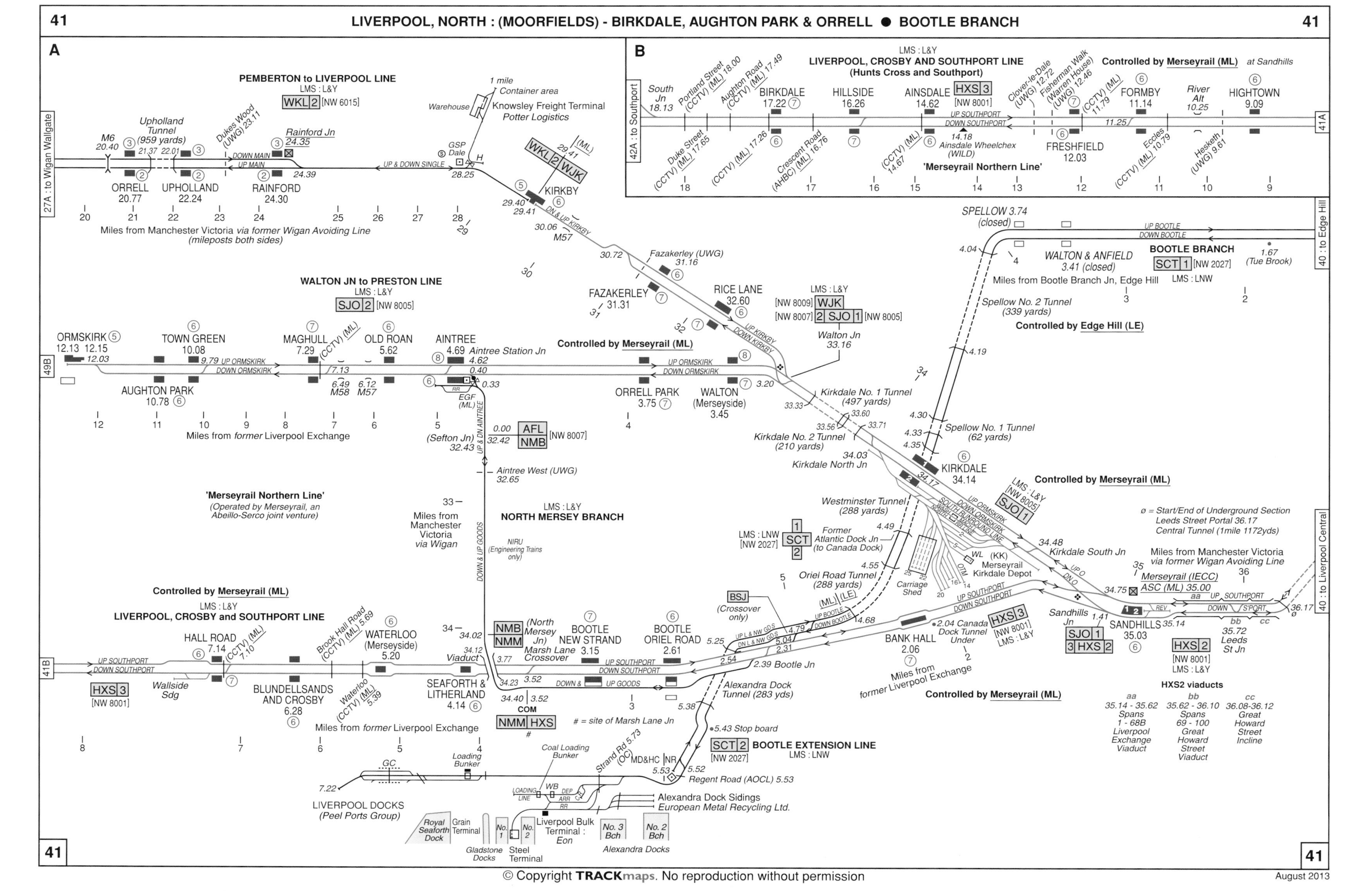
A
PEMBERTON to LIVERPOOL LINE
LMS : L&Y
WKL 2 [NW 6015]
27A : to Wigan Wallgate
M6 20.40
Upholland Tunnel (959 yards)
21.37 22.01
Dukes Wood (UWG) 23.11
Rainford Jn 24.35
DOWN MAIN
UP MAIN
24.39
UP & DOWN SINGLE
ORRELL 20.77
UPHOLLAND 22.24
RAINFORD 24.30
Miles from Manchester Victoria via former Wigan Avoiding Line (mileposts both sides)
1 mile Container area
Warehouse
Knowsley Freight Terminal
Potter Logistics
GSP Dale
28.25
WKL 2 WJK
29.41 (ML)
KIRKBY
29.40 29.41
DN & UP KIRKBY
30.06 M57
30.72
Fazakerley (UWG) 31.16
FAZAKERLEY 31.31
RICE LANE 32.60
UP KIRKBY
DOWN KIRKBY
LMS : L&Y
[NW 8009] WJK
[NW 8007] 2 SJO 1 [NW 8005]
Walton Jn 33.16
WALTON JN to PRESTON LINE
LMS : L&Y
SJO 2 [NW 8005]
49B
ORMSKIRK 12.13 12.15
12.03
TOWN GREEN 10.08
9.79 UP ORMSKIRK
DOWN ORMSKIRK
MAGHULL 7.29
(CCTV) (ML)
OLD ROAN 5.62
7.13
6.49 M58
6.12 M57
AINTREE 4.69
Aintree Station Jn 4.62
0.40
0.33
EGF (ML)
AUGHTON PARK 10.78
Miles from former Liverpool Exchange
Controlled by Merseyrail (ML)
ORRELL PARK 3.75
WALTON (Merseyside) 3.45
3.20
0.00 AFL NMB [NW 8007]
(Sefton Jn) 32.42 32.43
UP & DN AINTREE
Aintree West (UWG) 32.65
'Merseyrail Northern Line'
(Operated by Merseyrail, an Abeillo-Serco joint venture)
Miles from Manchester Victoria via Wigan
LMS : L&Y
NORTH MERSEY BRANCH
NIRU (Engineering Trains only)
DOWN & UP GOODS
Kirkdale No. 1 Tunnel (497 yards)
33.33
33.60
33.56
33.71
Kirkdale No. 2 Tunnel (210 yards)
34.03 Kirkdale North Jn
KIRKDALE 34.14
34.17
Controlled by Merseyrail (ML)
LMS : L&Y [NW 8005] SJO 1
UP ORMSKIRK
DOWN ORMSKIRK
SOUTH RUNROUND LINE
34.48 Kirkdale South Jn
WL (KK) Merseyrail Kirkdale Depot
Carriage Shed
Westminster Tunnel (288 yards)
4.49
LMS : LNW [NW 2027] 1 SCT 2
Former Atlantic Dock Jn (to Canada Dock)
4.55
Oriel Road Tunnel (288 yards)
(ML) (LE)
BSJ (Crossover only)
UP BOOTLE
DOWN BOOTLE
4.68
4.79
5.04
2.31
5.25
2.54
2.39 Bootle Jn
UP L & NW GDS
DN L & NW GDS
B
LMS : L&Y
LIVERPOOL, CROSBY AND SOUTHPORT LINE
(Hunts Cross and Southport)
Controlled by Merseyrail (ML) at Sandhills
42A : to Southport
South Jn 18.13
Portland Street (CCTV) (ML) 18.00
Aughton Road (CCTV) (ML) 17.49
BIRKDALE 17.22
HILLSIDE 16.26
AINSDALE 14.62
HXS 3 [NW 8001]
UP SOUTHPORT
DOWN SOUTHPORT
Clover-le-Dale (UWG) 12.72
Fisherman Walk (Warren House) (UWG) 12.46
(CCTV) (ML) 11.79
FORMBY 11.14
River Alt 10.25
HIGHTOWN 9.09
41A
11.25
Duke Street (CCTV) (ML) 17.65
(CCTV) (ML) 17.26
Crescent Road (AHBC) (ML) 16.76
(CCTV) (ML) 14.67
14.18 Ainsdale Wheelchex (WILD)
'Merseyrail Northern Line'
FRESHFIELD 12.03
Eccles (CCTV) (ML) 10.79
Hesketh (UWG) 9.61
SPELLOW 3.74 (closed)
UP BOOTLE
DOWN BOOTLE
40 : to Edge Hill
4.04
WALTON & ANFIELD 3.41 (closed)
BOOTLE BRANCH
SCT 1 [NW 2027]
LMS : LNW
1.67 (Tue Brook)
Miles from Bootle Branch Jn, Edge Hill
Spellow No. 2 Tunnel (339 yards)
Controlled by Edge Hill (LE)
4.19
4.30
4.33
4.35
Spellow No. 1 Tunnel (62 yards)
ø = Start/End of Underground Section
Leeds Street Portal 36.17
Central Tunnel (1mile 1172yds)
Miles from Manchester Victoria via former Wigan Avoiding Line
Merseyrail (IECC)
ASC (ML) 35.00
34.75
40 : to Liverpool Central
UP SOUTHPORT
DOWN S'PORT
REV
36.17
Sandhills Jn 1.41
SJO 1
3 HXS 2
SANDHILLS 35.03
35.14
35.72 Leeds St Jn
HXS 2 [NW 8001] LMS : L&Y
HXS2 viaducts
aa 35.14 - 35.62 Spans 1 - 68B Liverpool Exchange Viaduct
bb 35.62 - 36.10 Spans 69 - 100 Great Howard Street Viaduct
cc 36.08-36.12 Great Howard Street Incline
BANK HALL 2.06
2.04 Canada Dock Tunnel Under
HXS 3 [NW 8001] LMS : L&Y
Miles from former Liverpool Exchange
Controlled by Merseyrail (ML)
Controlled by Merseyrail (ML)
LMS : L&Y
LIVERPOOL, CROSBY and SOUTHPORT LINE
41B
UP SOUTHPORT
DOWN SOUTHPORT
HXS 3 [NW 8001]
HALL ROAD 7.14
(CCTV) (ML) 7.10
Wallside Sdg
Brook Hall Road (CCTV) (ML) 5.69
BLUNDELLSANDS AND CROSBY 6.28
WATERLOO (Merseyside) 5.20
Waterloo (CCTV) (ML) 5.39
Miles from former Liverpool Exchange
34.02
34.12 Viaduct
SEAFORTH & LITHERLAND 4.14
34.23
3.77
3.52
34.40 3.52
COM
NMM HXS
NMB NMM
(North Mersey Jn)
Marsh Lane Crossover
BOOTLE NEW STRAND 3.15
BOOTLE ORIEL ROAD 2.61
DOWN & UP GOODS
= site of Marsh Lane Jn
5.38
Alexandra Dock Tunnel (283 yds)
5.43 Stop board
SCT 2 [NW 2027]
BOOTLE EXTENSION LINE
LMS : LNW
Regent Road (AOCL) 5.53
5.52
5.53
MD&HC NR
Strand Rd 5.73 (OC)
Coal Loading Bunker
Loading Bunker
GC
7.22
LIVERPOOL DOCKS (Peel Ports Group)
LOADING LINE
WB
DEP
ARR
RR
Alexandra Dock Sidings
European Metal Recycling Ltd.
Royal Seaforth Dock
Grain Terminal
Gladstone Docks
No. 1
No. 2
Steel Terminal
Liverpool Bulk Terminal : Eon
No. 3 Bch
No. 2 Bch
Alexandra Docks

August 2013

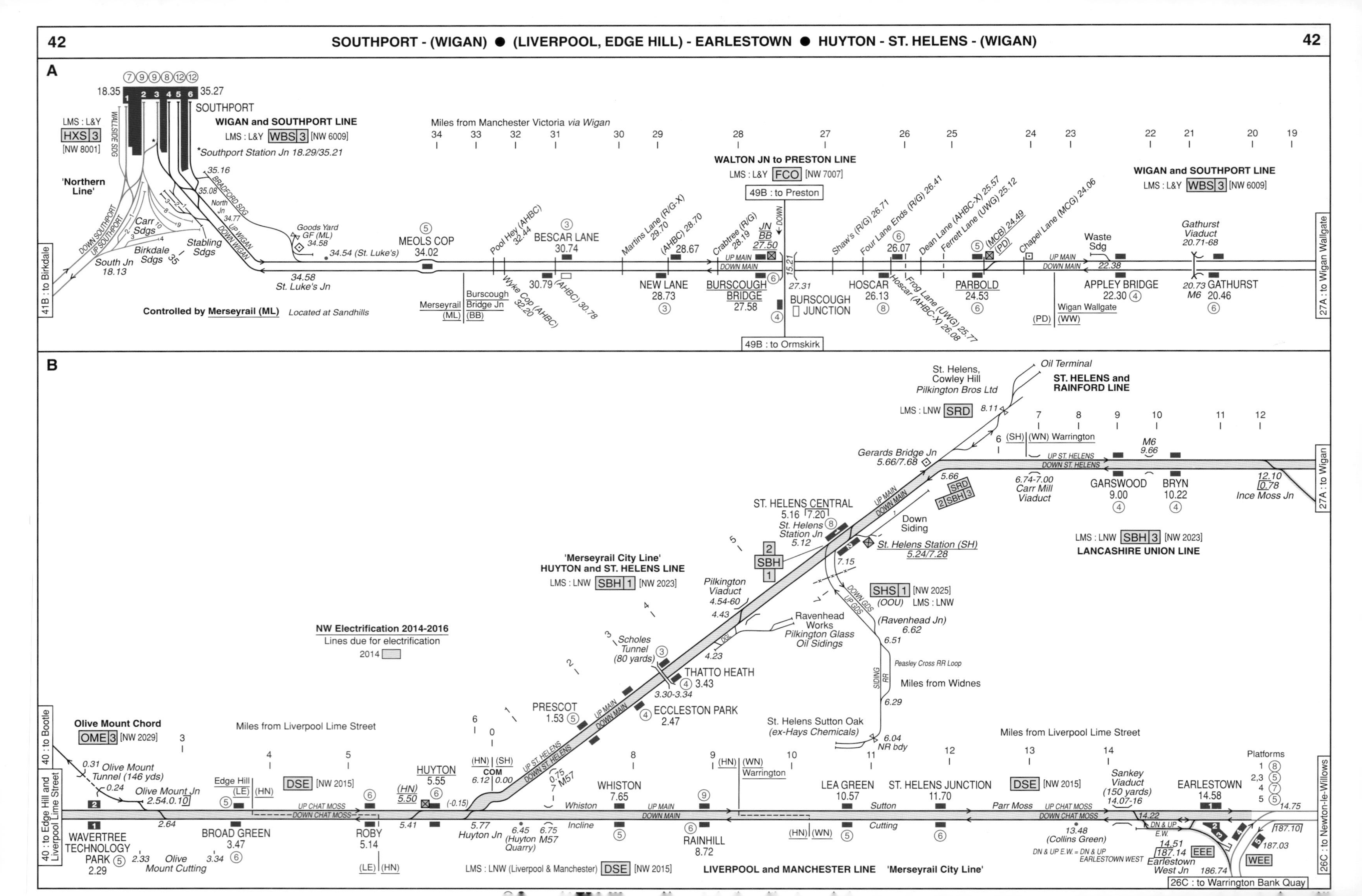
A
18.35
35.27
SOUTHPORT
LMS : L&Y
HXS 3
[NW 8001]
WALLSIDE SDG
WIGAN and SOUTHPORT LINE
LMS : L&Y WBS 3 [NW 6009]
*Southport Station Jn 18.29/35.21
'Northern Line'
35.16
BRADFORD SDG
35.08
North Jn
34.77
UP WIGAN
DOWN WIGAN
DOWN SOUTHPORT
UP SOUTHPORT
Carr Sdgs
Birkdale Sdgs
Stabling Sdgs
South Jn 18.13
Goods Yard GF (ML) 34.58
34.54 (St. Luke's)
34.58 St. Luke's Jn
Controlled by Merseyrail (ML)
Located at Sandhills
41B : to Birkdale
Miles from Manchester Victoria via Wigan
MEOLS COP 34.02
Merseyrail (ML)
Burscough Bridge Jn (BB)
Pool Hey (AHBC) 32.44
Wyke Cop (AHBC) 32.20
BESCAR LANE 30.74
30.79 (AHBC) 30.78
Martins Lane (R/G-X) 29.70
(AHBC) 28.70
28.67
NEW LANE 28.73
Crabtree (R/G) 28.19
JN BB 27.50
UP MAIN
DOWN MAIN
BURSCOUGH BRIDGE 27.58
WALTON JN to PRESTON LINE
LMS : L&Y FCO [NW 7007]
49B : to Preston
DOWN
15.21
27.31
BURSCOUGH JUNCTION
49B : to Ormskirk
Shaw's (R/G) 26.71
Four Lane Ends (R/G) 26.41
26.07
HOSCAR 26.13
Hoscar (AHBC-X) 26.08
Frog Lane (UWG) 25.77
Dean Lane (AHBC-X) 25.57
Ferrett Lane (UWG) 25.12
(MCB) 24.49
(PD)
PARBOLD 24.53
Chapel Lane (MCG) 24.06
Waste Sdg
22.38
APPLEY BRIDGE 22.30
Wigan Wallgate (WW)
(PD)
WIGAN and SOUTHPORT LINE
LMS : L&Y WBS 3 [NW 6009]
Gathurst Viaduct 20.71-68
20.73 M6
GATHURST 20.46
27A : to Wigan Wallgate
B
Oil Terminal
St. Helens, Cowley Hill Pilkington Bros Ltd
ST. HELENS and RAINFORD LINE
LMS : LNW SRD
8.11
(SH)
(WN) Warrington
Gerards Bridge Jn 5.66/7.68
UP ST. HELENS
DOWN ST. HELENS
M6 9.66
6.74-7.00 Carr Mill Viaduct
GARSWOOD 9.00
BRYN 10.22
12.10
0.78
Ince Moss Jn
27A : to Wigan
5.66
SRD
2 SBH 3
Down Siding
St. Helens Station (SH) 5.24/7.28
ST. HELENS CENTRAL 5.16 7.20
St. Helens Station Jn 5.12
SBH
LMS : LNW SBH 3 [NW 2023]
LANCASHIRE UNION LINE
'Merseyrail City Line'
HUYTON and ST. HELENS LINE
LMS : LNW SBH 1 [NW 2023]
7.15
SHS 1 [NW 2025]
(OOU) LMS : LNW
DOWN GDS
UP GDS
Pilkington Viaduct 4.54-60
4.43
4.23
Ravenhead Works Pilkington Glass Oil Sidings
(Ravenhead Jn) 6.62
6.51
Peasley Cross RR Loop
SIDING RR
Miles from Widnes
6.29
Scholes Tunnel (80 yards)
THATTO HEATH 3.43
3.30-3.34
ECCLESTON PARK 2.47
PRESCOT 1.53
St. Helens Sutton Oak (ex-Hays Chemicals)
6.04 NR bdy
NW Electrification 2014-2016
Lines due for electrification
2014
Olive Mount Chord
OME 3 [NW 2029]
Miles from Liverpool Lime Street
0.31 Olive Mount Tunnel (146 yds)
0.24
Olive Mount Jn 2.54.0.10
Edge Hill (LE) (HN)
DSE [NW 2015]
UP CHAT MOSS
DOWN CHAT MOSS
HUYTON 5.55
(HN) 5.50
(-0.15)
(HN) (SH)
COM
6.12 0.00
UP ST. HELENS
DOWN ST. HELENS
0.75 M57
WHISTON 7.65
Whiston
Incline
UP MAIN
DOWN MAIN
(HN) (WN) Warrington
LEA GREEN 10.57
ST. HELENS JUNCTION 11.70
Sutton
Cutting
DSE [NW 2015]
Parr Moss
Miles from Liverpool Lime Street
Sankey Viaduct (150 yards) 14.07-16
EARLESTOWN 14.58
Platforms
14.75
14.22
DN & UP E.W.
13.48 (Collins Green)
DN & UP E.W. = DN & UP EARLESTOWN WEST
14.51
187.14
EEE
Earlestown West Jn
186.74
187.10
187.03
WEE
26C : to Newton-le-Willows
26C : to Warrington Bank Quay
40 : to Bootle
40 : to Edge Hill and Liverpool Lime Street
WAVERTREE TECHNOLOGY PARK 2.29
2.64
2.33 Olive Mount Cutting 3.34
BROAD GREEN 3.47
ROBY 5.14
(LE) (HN)
5.41
5.77 Huyton Jn
6.45 (Huyton Quarry)
6.75 M57
RAINHILL 8.72
(HN) (WN)
LMS : LNW (Liverpool & Manchester) DSE [NW 2015]
LIVERPOOL and MANCHESTER LINE
'Merseyrail City Line'

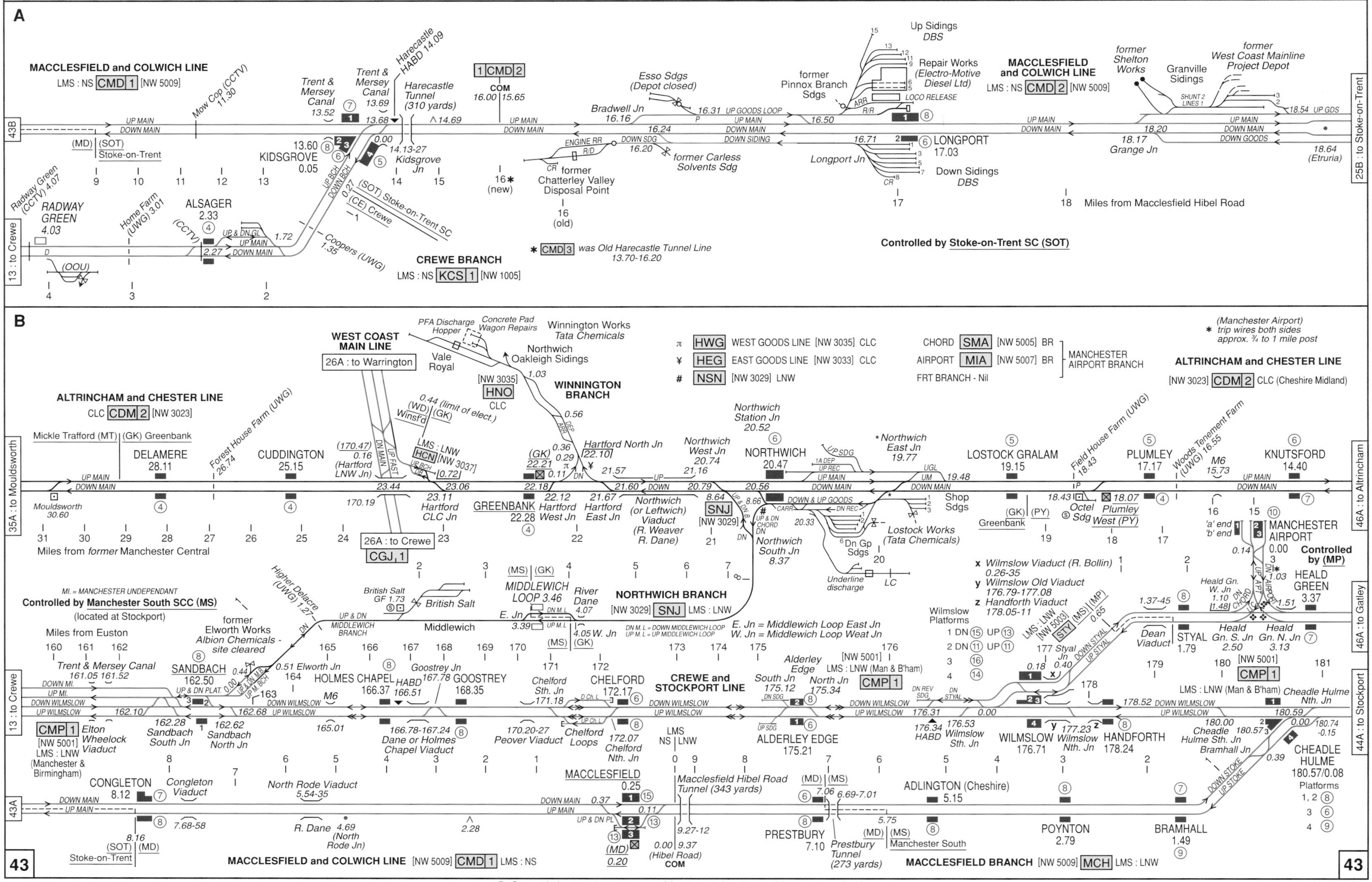

A

MACCLESFIELD and COLWICH LINE
LMS : NS CMD 1 [NW 5009]

MACCLESFIELD and COLWICH LINE
LMS : NS CMD 2 [NW 5009]

CREWE BRANCH
LMS : NS KCS 1 [NW 1005]

1 CMD 2 COM 16.00 | 15.65

* CMD 3 was Old Harecastle Tunnel Line 13.70-16.20

Controlled by Stoke-on-Trent SC (SOT)

43B | 13 : to Crewe | 25B : to Stoke-on-Trent

(MD) | (SOT) Stoke-on-Trent
Radway Green (CCTV) 4.07
RADWAY GREEN 4.03
(OOU)
Mow Cop (CCTV) 11.30
Home Farm (UWG) 3.01
ALSAGER 2.33 (CCTV) 2.27
Trent & Mersey Canal 13.52
Trent & Mersey Canal 13.69
KIDSGROVE 13.60 0.05
13.68 0.00 0.27 1.72
Harecastle HABD 14.09
Harecastle Tunnel (310 yards) ^14.69
14.13-27 Kidsgrove Jn
(SOT) Stoke-on-Trent SC
(CE) Crewe
Coopers (UWG) 1.35
former Chatterley Valley Disposal Point
16 (old) 16* (new)
Esso Sdgs (Depot closed)
Bradwell Jn 16.16 16.24 16.31 16.20
former Carless Solvents Sdg
former Pinnox Branch Sdgs 16.50
Up Sidings DBS
Repair Works (Electro-Motive Diesel Ltd)
LOCO RELEASE
Longport Jn 16.71
LONGPORT 17.03
Down Sidings DBS
former Shelton Works
Granville Sidings
former West Coast Mainline Project Depot
18.17 Grange Jn 18.20 18.54 18.64 (Etruria)

Miles from Macclesfield Hibel Road: 4 3 2 9 10 11 12 13 14 15 16 17 18

B

WEST COAST MAIN LINE
26A : to Warrington
26A : to Crewe CGJ 1

ALTRINCHAM and CHESTER LINE
CLC CDM 2 [NW 3023]

ALTRINCHAM and CHESTER LINE
[NW 3023] CDM 2 CLC (Cheshire Midland)

WINNINGTON BRANCH
[NW 3035] HNO CLC

π	HWG	WEST GOODS LINE [NW 3035]	CLC
¥	HEG	EAST GOODS LINE [NW 3033]	CLC
#	NSN	[NW 3029]	LNW

CHORD	SMA	[NW 5005]	BR
AIRPORT	MIA	[NW 5007]	BR
FRT BRANCH - Nil			

MANCHESTER AIRPORT BRANCH

* (Manchester Airport) trip wires both sides approx. ¾ to 1 mile post

35A : to Mouldsworth | 46A : to Altrincham | 46A : to Gatley | 44A : to Stockport | 13 : to Crewe | 43A

Mickle Trafford (MT) | (GK) Greenbank
Mouldsworth 30.60
DELAMERE 28.11
Forest House Farm (UWG) 26.74
CUDDINGTON 25.15
(170.47) 0.16 (Hartford LNW Jn) 170.19 23.44
LMS : LNW HCN [NW 3037] 0.72
0.44 (limit of elect.) (WD) (GK) Winsf'd
23.06 23.11 Hartford CLC Jn
PFA Discharge Hopper; Concrete Pad Wagon Repairs; Vale Royal
Winnington Works Tata Chemicals
Northwich Oakleigh Sidings 1.03 0.56
GREENBANK 22.28 22.18 (GK) 22.21 0.36 0.29 0.11
22.12 Hartford West Jn
Hartford North Jn 22.10
21.67 Hartford East Jn 21.57 21.60
Northwich West Jn 20.74 21.16 20.79
Northwich (or Leftwich) Viaduct (R. Weaver R. Dane)
8.64 SNJ [NW 3029] 8.66
Northwich Station Jn 20.52
NORTHWICH 20.47 20.56
Northwich South Jn 8.37
20.33
6 Dn Gp Sdgs
Underline discharge LC
Lostock Works (Tata Chemicals)
*Northwich East Jn 19.77
Shop Sdgs 19.48
LOSTOCK GRALAM 19.15
(GK) | (PY) Greenbank
Field House Farm (UWG) 18.43
18.43 Octel Sdg 18.07 Plumley West (PY)
PLUMLEY 17.17
Woods Tenement Farm (UWG) 16.55
M6 15.73
KNUTSFORD 14.40
Miles from former Manchester Central: 31 30 29 28 27 26 25 24 23 22 21 20 19 18 17 16 15

MI. = MANCHESTER UNDEPENDANT
Controlled by Manchester South SCC (MS) (located at Stockport)

Miles from Euston 160 161 162 ... 181

NORTHWICH BRANCH
[NW 3029] SNJ LMS : LNW

DN M.L = DOWN MIDDLEWICH LOOP
UP M.L = UP MIDDLEWICH LOOP

E. Jn = Middlewich Loop East Jn
W. Jn = Middlewich Loop Weat Jn

Higher Delacre (UWG) 1.27
British Salt GF 1.73 British Salt
MIDDLEWICH BRANCH
Middlewich
(MS) | (GK) MIDDLEWICH LOOP 3.46
E. Jn 3.39 River Dane 4.07 4.05 W. Jn (MS) | (GK)

former Elworth Works Albion Chemicals - site cleared
Trent & Mersey Canal 161.05 161.52
SANDBACH 162.50 0.44 0.00 0.51 Elworth Jn
162.10 162.28 Sandbach South Jn 162.62 Sandbach North Jn 162.68 163
HOLMES CHAPEL 166.37 HABD 166.51 165.01
166.78-167.24 Dane or Holmes Chapel Viaduct
Goostrey Jn 167.78 GOOSTREY 168.35
170.20-27 Peover Viaduct
Chelford Sth. Jn 171.18
CHELFORD 172.17
Chelford Loops 172.07 Chelford Nth. Jn

CREWE and STOCKPORT LINE
CMP 1 [NW 5001] LMS : LNW (Manchester & Birmingham)
LMS : LNW (Man & B'ham) [NW 5001] CMP 1
LMS NS | LNW

Alderley Edge South Jn 175.12 North Jn 175.34
ALDERLEY EDGE 175.21
176.31 176.34 HABD 176.53 Wilmslow Sth. Jn
0.00
WILMSLOW 176.71
177 Styal Jn 0.18 0.40
LMS : LNW [NW 5003] STY (MS) | (MP) 0.65
177.23 Wilmslow Nth. Jn
HANDFORTH 178.24
178.52
Dean Viaduct 1.37-45
STYAL 1.79
Heald Gn. W. Jn 1.10 1.48
Heald Gn. S. Jn 2.50
Heald Gn. N. Jn 3.13
HEALD GREEN 3.37 1.51
MANCHESTER AIRPORT 0.00 0.14 1.03
'a' end 'b' end
Controlled by (MP)
180.00 Cheadle Hulme Sth. Jn 180.57
Bramhall Jn 0.39
Cheadle Hulme Nth. Jn 180.59 0.00 180.74 -0.15
CHEADLE HULME 180.57/0.08

x Wilmslow Viaduct (R. Bollin) 0.26-35
y Wilmslow Old Viaduct 176.79-177.08
z Handforth Viaduct 178.05-11

Wilmslow Platforms
1 DN (15) UP (13)
2 DN (11) UP (11)
3 (16)
4 (14)

Cheadle Hulme Platforms
1, 2 (8)
3 (6)
4 (9)

CONGLETON 8.12
Elton Wheelock Viaduct
Congleton Viaduct 7.68-58
8.16 (SOT) | (MD) Stoke-on-Trent
North Rode Viaduct 5.54-35
R. Dane 4.69 (North Rode Jn)
2.28
MACCLESFIELD 0.25 0.37 0.11
(MD) 0.20
0.00 9.37 (Hibel Road) COM
Macclesfield Hibel Road Tunnel (343 yards) 9.27-12
PRESTBURY 7.10
(MD) | (MS) 7.06 6.69-7.01
Prestbury Tunnel (273 yards)
5.75 (MD) | (MS) Manchester South
ADLINGTON (Cheshire) 5.15
POYNTON 2.79
BRAMHALL 1.49

MACCLESFIELD and COLWICH LINE [NW 5009] CMD 1 LMS : NS

MACCLESFIELD BRANCH [NW 5009] MCH LMS : LNW

August 2013

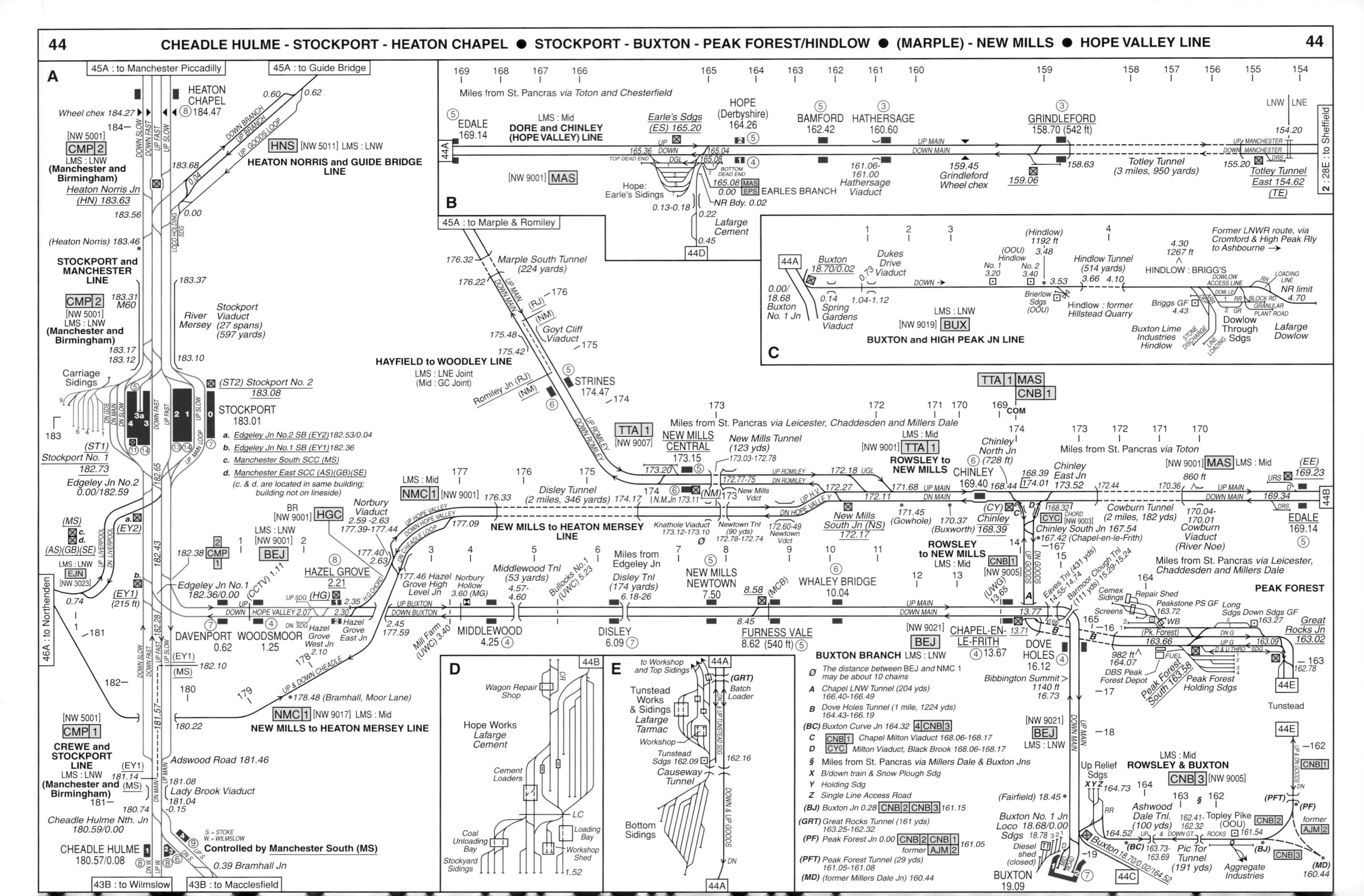
44
CHEADLE HULME - STOCKPORT - HEATON CHAPEL ● STOCKPORT - BUXTON - PEAK FOREST/HINDLOW ● (MARPLE) - NEW MILLS ● HOPE VALLEY LINE
44
A
45A : to Manchester Piccadilly
45A : to Guide Bridge
HEATON CHAPEL 184.47
Wheel chex 184.27
[NW 5001] CMP 2 LMS : LNW (Manchester and Birmingham)
Heaton Norris Jn (HN) 183.63
HNS [NW 5011] LMS : LNW
HEATON NORRIS and GUIDE BRIDGE LINE
(Heaton Norris) 183.46
STOCKPORT and MANCHESTER LINE
CMP 2 [NW 5001] LMS : LNW (Manchester and Birmingham)
183.31 M60
River Mersey
Stockport Viaduct (27 spans) (597 yards)
Carriage Sidings
(ST2) Stockport No. 2 183.08
STOCKPORT 183.01
(ST1) Stockport No. 1 182.73
Edgeley Jn No.2 0.00/182.59
a. Edgeley Jn No.2 SB (EY2)182.53/0.04
b. Edgeley Jn No.1 SB (EY1)182.36
c. Manchester South SCC (MS)
d. Manchester East SCC (AS)(GB)(SE)
(c. & d. are located in same building; building not on lineside)
LMS : LNW EJN [NW 3023]
46A : to Northenden
Edgeley Jn No.1 182.36/0.00
DAVENPORT 0.62
WOODSMOOR 1.25
HAZEL GROVE 2.21
Hazel Grove West Jn
Hazel Grove East Jn
BR [NW 9001] HGC
LMS : LNW [NW 9001] BEJ
Norbury Viaduct 2.59 -2.63 177.39-177.44
177.46 Hazel Grove High Level Jn
Norbury Hollow 3.60 (MG)
Mill Farm (UWC) 3.40
MIDDLEWOOD 4.25
Middlewood Tnl (53 yards) 4.57-4.60
Bullocks No.1 (UWC) 5.23
Miles from Edgeley Jn
Disley Tnl (174 yards) 6.18-26
DISLEY 6.09
NEW MILLS NEWTOWN 7.50
FURNESS VALE 8.62 (540 ft)
WHALEY BRIDGE 10.04
CHAPEL-EN-LE-FRITH 13.67
DOVE HOLES 16.12
Bibbington Summit 1140 ft 16.73
BUXTON 19.09
NMC 1 [NW 9017] LMS : Mid
NEW MILLS to HEATON MERSEY LINE
178.48 (Bramhall, Moor Lane)
[NW 5001] CMP 1
CREWE and STOCKPORT LINE LMS : LNW (Manchester and Birmingham)
Adswood Road 181.46
Lady Brook Viaduct
Cheadle Hulme Nth. Jn 180.59/0.00
CHEADLE HULME 180.57/0.08
Controlled by Manchester South (MS)
0.39 Bramhall Jn
43B : to Wilmslow
43B : to Macclesfield
B
Miles from St. Pancras via Toton and Chesterfield
EDALE 169.14
LMS : Mid DORE and CHINLEY (HOPE VALLEY) LINE
[NW 9001] MAS
Earle's Sdgs (ES) 165.20
Hope: Earle's Sidings
HOPE (Derbyshire) 164.26
EARLES BRANCH
NR Bdy. 0.02
Lafarge Cement
BAMFORD 162.42
HATHERSAGE 160.60
Hathersage Viaduct
159.45 Grindleford Wheel chex
GRINDLEFORD 158.70 (542 ft)
Totley Tunnel (3 miles, 950 yards)
Totley Tunnel East 154.62 (TE)
2 : 28E : to Sheffield
45A : to Marple & Romiley
Marple South Tunnel (224 yards)
Goyt Cliff Viaduct
Romiley Jn (RJ)
HAYFIELD to WOODLEY LINE LMS : LNE Joint (Mid : GC Joint)
STRINES 174.47
C
Buxton 18.70/0.02
Buxton No. 1 Jn
Spring Gardens Viaduct
Dukes Drive Viaduct
LMS : LNW [NW 9019] BUX
BUXTON and HIGH PEAK JN LINE
Hindlow Tunnel (514 yards)
Hindlow : former Hillstead Quarry
HINDLOW : BRIGG'S
Briggs GF 4.43
Buxton Lime Industries Hindlow
Dowlow Through Sdgs
Lafarge Dowlow
NR limit 4.70
Former LNWR route, via Cromford & High Peak Rly to Ashbourne →
TTA 1 MAS CNB 1
Miles from St. Pancras via Leicester, Chaddesden and Millers Dale
TTA 1 [NW 9007]
NEW MILLS CENTRAL 173.15
New Mills Tunnel (123 yds)
[NW 9001] TTA 1 LMS : Mid ROWSLEY to NEW MILLS
CHINLEY 169.40
Chinley North Jn (728 ft)
Chinley East Jn 173.52
Miles from St. Pancras via Toton
[NW 9001] MAS LMS : Mid
EDALE 169.14
Disley Tunnel (2 miles, 346 yards)
NEW MILLS to HEATON MERSEY LINE
Knathole Viaduct
Newtown Tnl (90 yds)
New Mills South Jn (NS) 172.17
171.45 (Gowhole)
170.37 (Buxworth)
Chinley 168.39
Chinley South Jn 167.54
167.42 (Chapel-en-le-Frith)
Cowburn Tunnel (2 miles, 182 yds)
Cowburn Viaduct (River Noe)
ROWSLEY to NEW MILLS LMS : Mid
CNB 1 [NW 9005]
Eaves Tnl (431 yds)
Barmoor Clough Tnl (111 yds)
Miles from St. Pancras via Leicester, Chaddesden and Millers Dale
PEAK FOREST
Cemex Sidings
Repair Shed
Peakstone PS GF
Long Sdgs Down Sdgs GF
Great Rocks Jn 163.02
DBS Peak Forest Depot
Peak Forest South 163.58
Peak Forest Holding Sdgs
Tunstead
BUXTON BRANCH LMS : LNW
Ø The distance between BEJ and NMC 1 may be about 10 chains
A Chapel LNW Tunnel (204 yds) 166.40-166.49
B Dove Holes Tunnel (1 mile, 1224 yds) 164.43-166.19
(BC) Buxton Curve Jn 164.32 4 CNB 3
C CNB 1 Chapel Milton Viaduct 168.06-168.17
D CYC Milton Viaduct, Black Brook 168.06-168.17
§ Miles from St. Pancras via Millers Dale & Buxton Jns
X B/down train & Snow Plough Sdg
Y Holding Sdg
Z Single Line Access Road
(BJ) Buxton Jn 0.28 CNB 2 CNB 3 161.15
(GRT) Great Rocks Tunnel (161 yds) 163.25-162.32
(PF) Peak Forest Jn 0.00 CNB 2 CNB 1 former AJM 2 161.05
(PFT) Peak Forest Tunnel (29 yds) 161.05-161.08
(MD) (former Millers Dale Jn) 160.44
[NW 9021] BEJ LMS : LNW
(Fairfield) 18.45
Buxton No. 1 Jn Loco 18.68/0.00 Sdgs
Diesel shed (closed)
Up Relief Sdgs
LMS : Mid ROWSLEY & BUXTON CNB 3 [NW 9005]
Ashwood Dale Tnl. (100 yds)
Topley Pike (OOU) 161.54
Pic Tor Tunnel (191 yds)
Aggregate Industries
D
Wagon Repair Shop
Hope Works Lafarge Cement
Cement Loaders
Coal Unloading Bay
Stockyard Sidings
Loading Bay
Workshop Shed
E
to Workshop and Top Sidings
(GRT) Batch Loader
Tunstead Works & Sidings Lafarge Tarmac
Tunstead Sdgs 162.09
Causeway Tunnel
Bottom Sidings

A

46A

M. P. West Jn 188.72

Centre Pfms 13 & 14 188.61

188.68

COL [NW 6001] LMS : MSJ&A

Vdct & arches 190.15-188.56

Manchester Piccadilly (MP)

188.70 (in station building)

GF 188.67

MANCHESTER Ø PICCADILLY 188.70 -0.05

188.56

188.54

Manchester Piccadilly East Jn 188.48

In/Out Gantry 188.41

Out Gantry 188.33

Out Gantry 188.27

(0.18) (0.25) (0.39)

Ø formerly 'London Road' LNWR/GC Terminus (188.64)

✱ At 188.56 Span 119 on CMP 2 links to Span 1A on COL

Piccadilly platforms

Platforms	
1-4	12
5	17
6, 7	14
8	17
9	9
10	9
11, 12	5
13, 14	13

ARDWICK TMD Siemens for First Transpennine Express

Controlled by Manchester North (MN)

LMS : L&Y PPA 1 [NW 7025] 2.07

Ardwick Jn 188.12 188.08

Viaduct

0.53 # 0.58

188.02

ARDWICK 0.64

(MP) (AS) MANCHESTER and SHEFFIELD LINE HAJ [NW 5015] LNE : GC

a = ARDWICK RECEPTION LINE
b = ASHBURYS RECEPTION LINE
c = TRAIN WASH BYPASS
d = SOUTH TRAINWASH ROAD
e = NORTH TRAINWASH ROAD

Fuel Point · Ardwick East Jn 0.76 · Triple Point

CMP 2 [NW 5001] LMS : LNW

Viaduct arches 0-200 187.59-88.70

187.61

Arch 0 187.59

Longsight Depot Jn or Longsight North Jn 187.54

Up Freight Sdgs 2-13

Depot Jn 187.44

Manchester International Depot (oou)

187.17 · 187.12

187 — Miles from Euston via Crewe

186.56 · 9.44

186.46 Slade Lane Jn

186.39 · 186.36

STY [NW 5003] LMS : LNW

186.77 Longsight South Jn

Electric Loco Shed · Triple Point

Longsight Depot GF · Y = NEW WASHER RD

Electric T&RSMD (LG) ALSTOM UK Manchester Traincare Centre

ELR'S Longsight LMD

1	187.10-49	MD & CC Shed
2	187.26-47	Up Freight Sdgs
3	187.27-46	TMD North Shed
4	187.11-27	South Shed
5	187.20-55	Hyde Road Sdgs
6	187.10-53	CW Line
7	187.07-24	Elec. TD
8	187.48-55	North End Arr & Dep

STOCKPORT and MANCHESTER LINE CMP 2 [NW 5001] LMS : LNW (Manchester & Birmingham)

LEVENSHULME 186.01

(MP) (HN) Heaton Norris

MAULDETH ROAD 8.07

186 — 185 — 8 —

46A : to Burnage · 44A : to Stockport

LONGSIGHT TRACTION MAINTENANCE DEPOT

a Carriage Maintenance Depot (MA) ALSTOM UK Manchester Traincare Centre

b Diesel TMD (LO) former North or 'X' Shed (13x-20x) South Shed (13-18)

x North Shed Sdgs (13x-25)

y Offloading apron (21)

z Breakdown train (24)

47A : to Miles Platting

(MN) (BF) 1.76

PARK 2.18

Baguley Fold Jn (BF) 2.39

2.28

2.13 COM (Park Street Jn)

PPP PARKS FORK

[NW 7027] 2 LMS : L&Y

0.19 Philips Park South Jn

(MN) (AS) MESCC 2.43

Viaduct 2.43-2.47

ARDWICK BRANCH 1 LMS : L&Y PPA [NW 7025] 2 LMS : Mid

3.12 0.57 (Old Midland Jn)

0.43 Ancoats Vdct. 0.47-0.20

0.13 (Ancoats Jn) Ashburys W Jn 0.00

‡ PPA 3

1.30 · 1.36 · 1.56

46.24 ASHBURYS 1.42

Ashburys East Jn 1.56 · Stockport Canal

REDDISH BRANCH [NW 9007] TTA 2 LNE (GC) & LMS (Mid) Joint

BELLE VUE 45.30

RYDER BROW 45.00

REDDISH NORTH 44.09

REDDISH SOUTH 1.50

HEATON NORRIS and GUIDE BRIDGE LINE [NW 5011] HNS LMS : LNW

0.62 · 0.60

44A : to Heaton Norris Jn & Stockport

Clayton Bridge Viaduct 3.34-39

Clayton Bridge (CCTV) 3.22

ASHTON BRANCH [NW 7021] MVL 1 LMS : L&Y (Miles Platting to Stalybridge)

NW Electrification 2014-2016 Lines due for electrification 2016

Controlled by Manchester East (AS)(GB)(SE) Located at Stockport

AYS Ashburys Lafarge

GORTON 2.54 · 2.49 · 2.50

FAIRFIELD 3.52

OLDHAM, ASHTON and GUIDE BRIDGE LINE DJO 1 [NW 5013] LMS : LNW

(Crowthorne Jn) COM 0.53 5.28

— 46 Miles from Liverpool Central (CLC) via Cheadle & Stockport Tiviot Dale

Jaum Field Farm (UWG) 5.27

Moss Lane (UWG) 5.17

5.41

Ashton Moss North Jn 5.52

0.40 · 0.30 · 5.31 M60

ASHTON MOSS CURVE 0.00/1.19 COM

Miles from Guide Bridge Stn Jn

M60 4.29 · 4.59 · 4.39 · 4.49

DJO 2 · 1

Miles from Heaton Norris Jn · 3.32 · 3.10 · 3.06 M60

DENTON 3.39 · M67

Denton Jn (DJ) 4.13

4.10

(Oldham, Ashton & Guide Bridge Jn) 6.03

ASHTON-UNDER-LYNE 6.33

[NW 7021] MVL 1 LMS : L&Y

LNE : GC AMJ (Ashton Moss Stn Jn) DJO 2

GC & LNW Joint [NW 5013]

(Dukinfield Jn) Tame Vdct. 0.51 0.48

Brookside Sidings Engrs'

Tamper Shed

GBS 1

GUIDE BRIDGE 4.76 · 4.73 · NECK

4.70 Guide Bridge Stn Jn

HNS [NW 5011] LMS : LNW

Guide Bridge West Jn 5.10/0.04

5.19-23 River Tame Viaduct

SAJ [NW 5021] LNE : GC

ballast stockpile

Avenue Sidings Engrs' GBS 2

0.23 (Guide Bridge North Jn)

East Curve Viaduct (River Tame) 0.43

0.00 Guide Bridge East Jn 5.32 (former Dewsnap Sdgs) 5.61

6.07 · 6.16 Hyde Jn

HYDE NORTH 6.33

HYDE BRANCH RYH 2 [NW 9011] LNE (GC) & LMS (Mid) Joint 7.11

HYDE CENTRAL 7.27

M67 Hyde Viaducts 7.16-7.29

(GB) MESCC (RJ)

FLOWERY FIELD 6.56

NEWTON for Hyde 7.27

(GB) MESCC (DG) Dinting

GODLEY 7.72

Newton Vdct 7.32-37 · M67 7.39

Godley Arches 7.77

Miles from former Manchester London Road via Guide Bridge

8.20 GODLEY EAST

HATTERSLEY 8.58

HAJ [NW 5015] LNE : GC

45D

Katherine Street Tunnel (92 yards) (MESCC) (SE)

6.55 · 6.60 · 0.60-65 · 0.67-72 · 0.79-1.10 · 1.13-21

ASHTON BRANCH

LMS : L&Y 1 MVL 2 7.46

STALYBRIDGE 7.63

Stalybridge Jn 7.46 · 7.40

Stalybridge Viaduct

LNE : GC 2 MVL 3 [NW 7021] LMS : LNW 7.74 (Staley & Millbrook Jn)

Miles from Manchester Victoria

H = HUDDERSFIELD

8.10 Stalybridge Old Tunnel · 7.58 · 45B

8.08 Stalybridge Tunnel Jn

Dukinfield West Vdct. (Peak Forest Canal)

Dukinfield East Vdct.

No. 1 Ashton Vdcts. No. 2

1.74 ATO Chemicals 2.08

STALYBRIDGE BRANCH LINE [NW 5021] SAJ LNE : GC

a = 7.66-73 Gds Yard Arches 1-17
b = 7.74-76 Coal Drop Arches 1-4
c = 7.77-8.09 Stalybridge Vdct. Spans 1-21

B HUDDERSFIELD and MANCHESTER LINE

8.41 · 9.79-10.08

Stalybridge Old Tunnel (668 yards)

Scout Tunnel (202 yards)

MOSSLEY 10.39 (Greater Manchester) [NW 7021] MVL 3 LMS : LNW

GREENFIELD 12.54

45A · 45C

C

(SE) (DE) 13.50-64

Diggle Jn (DE) 14.59 · 14.61 · 15.05 · 15.11 · 14.67

Standedge Tnl. (3m. 66 yards) 15 650 ft

Uppermill Vdct. (Saddleworth) (SE) (DE)

[NW 7021] MVL 3 LMS : LNW

LNW | LNE

2 : 41A : to Huddersfield

REDDISH JN to ROMILEY JN LINE

2 TTA 1 [NW 9007]

Reddish Vdct 43 · 181 · 42.77 · 181.00

2.30 · 43.40 · 43.05-18 COM (Reddish Jn)

BRINNINGTON 180.45 · M60 180.23

40 Miles from Liverpool Central (CLC)

GMC

Bredbury Gtr. Manchester Waste plc

Peak Forest Canal

Bredbury Tarmac · 39.31 · 39.58 · 39.64

GF 79.41

GLAZEBROOK and GODLEY LINE

U = Unloading chute

BREDBURY 179.34

CLC Vdct. · WJP 1 [NW 9013]

40.14 · 40.29-36

Bredbury High Level Tunnel (160 yards) 178.70-78

Romiley Jn (RJ) 178.31 · 178.33

ROMILEY 178.27

[NW 9007] TTA 1 LNE (GC) & LMS (Mid) Joint

RYH 1 [NW 9011]

HAYFIELD to WOODLEY LINE

COM 2 RYH 1

8.45 Apethorne Jn

8.74 · 179.44 · Woodley Jn 40.53

WOODLEY 8.72 (Manchester London Road) (40.56 Liverpool Central) (179.47 St. Pancras)

177 Miles from St. Pancras and Millers Dale

177.21-34 Marple Viaduct (River Goyt) 11.02

177.23 Marple Wharf Jn

Marple North Tunnel (99 yards) 176.74-78

MARPLE 176.57

MACCLESFIELD, BOLLINGTON and MARPLE LINE LNE (GE) & LMS (Mid) Joint

Miles from Macclesfield 10 · MRH [NW 9009]

ROSE HILL MARPLE 10.04 · 10.56 · 9.78

44A : to New Mills

D

§ = Mottram Arches 9.72-10.02
¥ = Mottram Viaduct 10.07-15

Miles from former Manchester London Road

MANCHESTER and SHEFFIELD LINE LNE : GC

45A

BROADBOTTOM 9.60

A626

MOTTRAM STAFF HALT 10.71

11.42-62 · HAJ [NW 5015]

Dinting Vale Viaduct

Dinting West Jn · 11.62 · 1.05

DINTING 11.72 · Dinting East Jn 0.78 · 12.00

DSD [NW 5017] · GDW [NW 5019]

0.72 Dinting South Jn

Dinting Lane (UWB) 0.61

GDW [NW 5019]

GLOSSOP 0.01

HADFIELD 12.61

HAJ [NW 5015]

August 2013

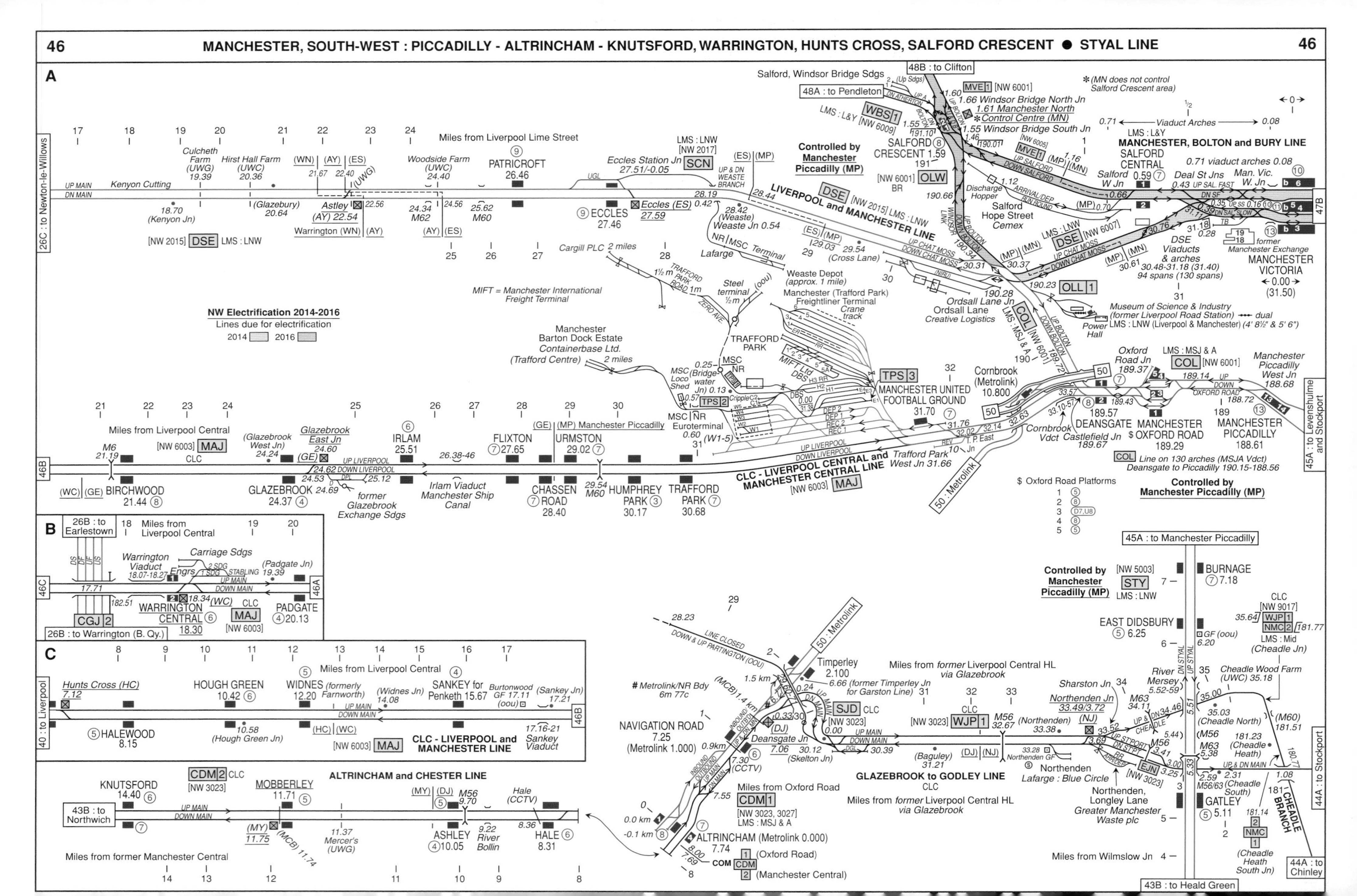
A
48B : to Clifton
48A : to Pendleton
Salford, Windsor Bridge Sdgs
26C : to Newton-le-Willows
Miles from Liverpool Lime Street
Kenyon Cutting
Culcheth Farm (UWG) 19.39
Hirst Hall Farm (UWC) 20.36
18.70 (Kenyon Jn)
(Glazebury) 20.64
Astley 22.56
(AY) 22.54
Warrington (WN)
Woodside Farm (UWC) 24.40
24.34 M62
25.62 M60
PATRICROFT 26.46
[NW 2015] DSE LMS : LNW
Eccles Station Jn 27.51/-0.05
LMS : LNW [NW 2017] SCN
ECCLES 27.46
Eccles (ES) 27.59
UP & DN WEASTE BRANCH
(Weaste) 28.42
Weaste Jn 0.54
Lafarge
NR MSC Terminal
Cargill PLC 2 miles
LIVERPOOL and MANCHESTER LINE
[NW 2015] LMS : LNW
Controlled by Manchester Piccadilly (MP)
WBS 1 LMS : L&Y [NW 6009]
SALFORD CRESCENT 1.59
[NW 6001] BR OLW
MVE 1 [NW 6001]
1.66 Windsor Bridge North Jn
1.61 Manchester North
*Control Centre (MN)
1.55 Windsor Bridge South Jn
*(MN does not control Salford Crescent area)
Viaduct Arches
LMS : L&Y
MANCHESTER, BOLTON and BURY LINE
SALFORD CENTRAL
Salford W Jn 0.59
0.71 viaduct arches 0.08
Deal St Jns
Man. Vic. W. Jn
Discharge Hopper
Salford Hope Street Cemex
DSE Viaducts & arches 30.48-31.18 (31.40) 94 spans (130 spans)
former Manchester Exchange
MANCHESTER VICTORIA 0.00 (31.50)
47B
Weaste Depot (approx. 1 mile)
Manchester (Trafford Park) Freightliner Terminal
Crane track
Steel terminal
TRAFFORD PARK
MIFT Ltd DBS
MIFT = Manchester International Freight Terminal
Ordsall Lane Jn 190.28
Ordsall Lane Creative Logistics
OLL 1
Museum of Science & Industry (former Liverpool Road Station)
LMS : LNW (Liverpool & Manchester) (4' 8½" & 5' 6")
Power Hall
COL [NW 6001] LMS : MSJ & A
NW Electrification 2014-2016
Lines due for electrification
2014 2016
Manchester Barton Dock Estate Containerbase Ltd. (Trafford Centre) 2 miles
MSC Loco Shed
TPS 2
TPS 3
MANCHESTER UNITED FOOTBALL GROUND 31.70
Cornbrook (Metrolink) 10.800
Oxford Road Jn 189.37
Manchester Piccadilly West Jn 188.68
DEANSGATE 189.57
Cornbrook Vdct
Castlefield Jn 189.67
MANCHESTER OXFORD ROAD 189.29
MANCHESTER PICCADILLY 188.61
45A : to Levenshulme and Stockport
COL Line on 130 arches (MSJA Vdct)
Deansgate to Piccadilly 190.15-188.56
$ Oxford Road Platforms
Controlled by Manchester Piccadilly (MP)
Miles from Liverpool Central
46B
M6 21.19
BIRCHWOOD 21.44
[NW 6003] MAJ CLC
Glazebrook West Jn 24.24
Glazebrook East Jn 24.60
GLAZEBROOK 24.37
former Glazebrook Exchange Sdgs
IRLAM 25.51
Irlam Viaduct Manchester Ship Canal
FLIXTON 27.65
CHASSEN ROAD 28.40
URMSTON 29.02
M60 29.54
HUMPHREY PARK 30.17
TRAFFORD PARK 30.68
MSC NR Euroterminal 0.60 (W1-5)
Trafford Park West Jn 31.66
CLC - LIVERPOOL CENTRAL and MANCHESTER CENTRAL LINE
[NW 6003] MAJ
50 : Metrolink
B
26B : to Earlestown
Miles from Liverpool Central
Warrington Viaduct 18.07-18.27
Carriage Sdgs
(Padgate Jn) 19.39
46C
WARRINGTON CENTRAL 18.30
CGJ 2
CLC MAJ [NW 6003]
PADGATE 20.13
46A
26B : to Warrington (B. Qy.)
C
Miles from Liverpool Central
40 : to Liverpool
Hunts Cross (HC) 7.12
HALEWOOD 8.15
HOUGH GREEN 10.42
10.58 (Hough Green Jn)
WIDNES (formerly Farnworth) 12.20
(Widnes Jn) 14.08
SANKEY for Penketh 15.67
Burtonwood GF 17.11 (oou)
(Sankey Jn) 17.21
17.16-21 Sankey Viaduct
[NW 6003] MAJ
CLC - LIVERPOOL and MANCHESTER LINE
ALTRINCHAM and CHESTER LINE
CDM 2 CLC [NW 3023]
KNUTSFORD 14.40
43B : to Northwich
MOBBERLEY 11.71
(MY) 11.75
(MCB) 11.74
11.37 Mercer's (UWG)
M56 9.70
ASHLEY 10.05
9.22 River Bollin
Hale (CCTV)
HALE 8.31
Miles from former Manchester Central
28.23
LINE CLOSED
DOWN & UP PARTINGTON (OOU)
Metrolink/NR Bdy 6m 77c
NAVIGATION ROAD 7.25 (Metrolink 1.000)
Timperley 2.100
6.66 (former Timperley Jn for Garston Line)
SJD CLC [NW 3023]
Deansgate Jn 7.06
30.12 (Skelton Jn)
7.30 (CCTV)
Miles from Oxford Road
CDM 1
[NW 3023, 3027] LMS : MSJ & A
ALTRINCHAM (Metrolink 0.000) 7.74
COM CDM
(Oxford Road)
(Manchester Central)
Miles from former Liverpool Central HL via Glazebrook
WJP 1
M56 32.67
(Northenden) 33.38
(Baguley) 31.21
GLAZEBROOK to GODLEY LINE
CLC
Northenden Lafarge : Blue Circle
Sharston Jn
Northenden Jn 33.49/3.72
M63 34.11
River Mersey 5.52-59
EJN [NW 3023]
Northenden, Longley Lane Greater Manchester Waste plc
Miles from Wilmslow Jn
Controlled by Manchester Piccadilly (MP)
[NW 5003] STY LMS : LNW
45A : to Manchester Piccadilly
BURNAGE 7.18
EAST DIDSBURY 6.25
GF (oou) 6.20
CLC [NW 9017] WJP 1 NMC 2
LMS : Mid (Cheadle Jn)
Cheadle Wood Farm (UWC) 35.18
35.03 (Cheadle North)
(M60) 181.51
181.23 (Cheadle Heath)
CHEADLE BRANCH
2.31 (Cheadle South)
GATLEY 5.11
NMC
(Cheadle Heath South Jn)
44A : to Stockport
44A : to Chinley
43B : to Heald Green

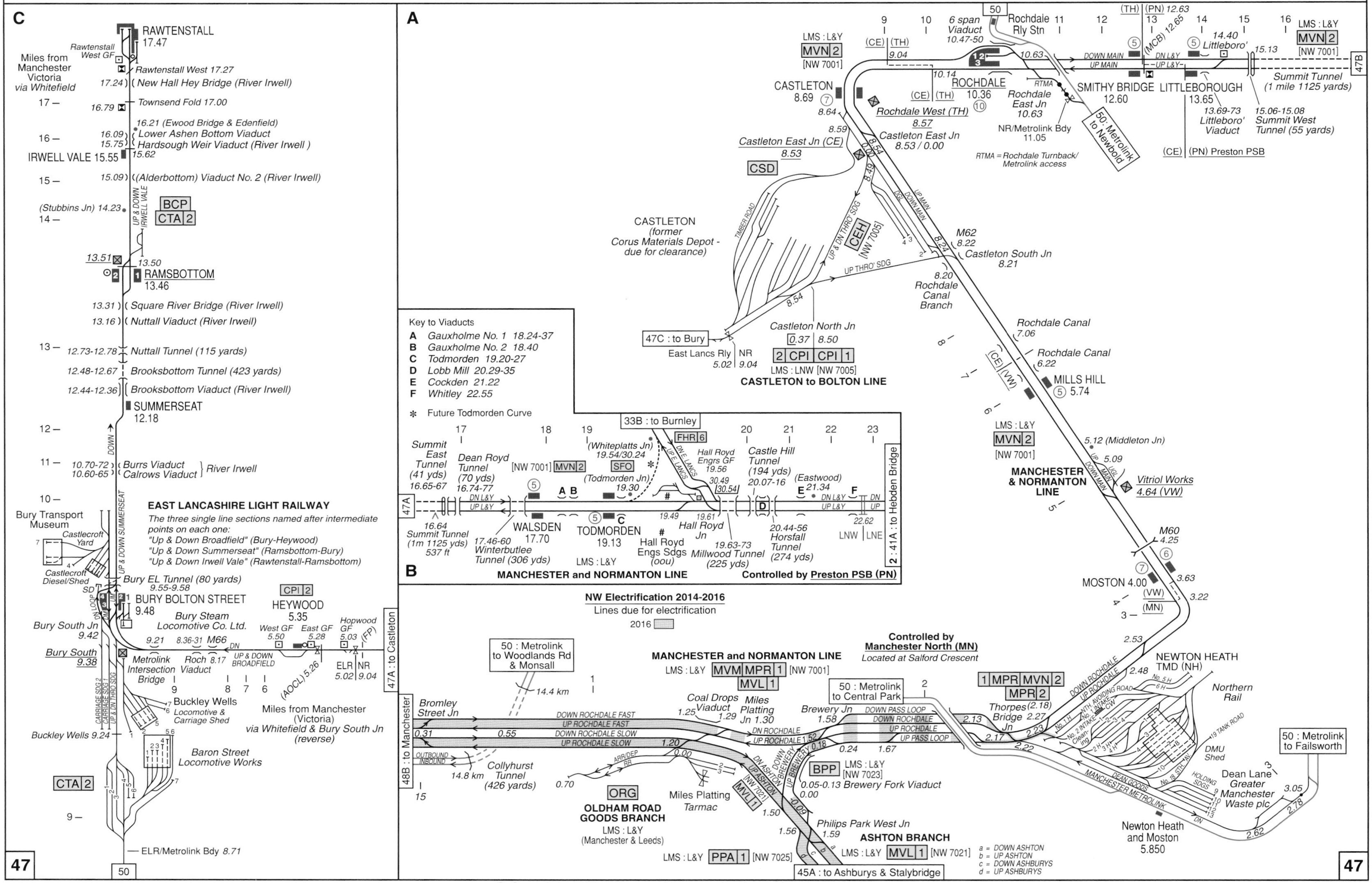

C

Miles from Manchester Victoria via Whitefield

RAWTENSTALL 17.47
Rawtenstall West GF
Rawtenstall West 17.27
17.24 (New Hall Hey Bridge (River Irwell)
16.79 Townsend Fold 17.00
16.21 (Ewood Bridge & Edenfield)
16.09 Lower Ashen Bottom Viaduct
15.75 Hardsough Weir Viaduct (River Irwell)
IRWELL VALE 15.55 15.62
15.09 ((Alderbottom) Viaduct No. 2 (River Irwell)
(Stubbins Jn) 14.23
UP & DOWN IRWELL VALE
BCP
CTA 2
13.51 13.50
RAMSBOTTOM 13.46
13.31 (Square River Bridge (River Irwell)
13.16 (Nuttall Viaduct (River Irwell)
12.73-12.78 Nuttall Tunnel (115 yards)
12.48-12.67 Brooksbottom Tunnel (423 yards)
12.44-12.36 Brooksbottom Viaduct (River Irwell)
SUMMERSEAT 12.18
DOWN
10.70-72 Burrs Viaduct
10.60-65 Calrows Viaduct } River Irwell
UP & DOWN SUMMERSEAT

EAST LANCASHIRE LIGHT RAILWAY

The three single line sections named after intermediate points on each one:
"Up & Down Broadfield" (Bury-Heywood)
"Up & Down Summerseat" (Ramsbottom-Bury)
"Up & Down Irwell Vale" (Rawtenstall-Ramsbottom)

Bury Transport Museum
Castlecroft Yard
Castlecroft Diesel/Shed
SD
Bury EL Tunnel (80 yards) 9.55-9.58
BURY BOLTON STREET 9.48
Bury Steam Locomotive Co. Ltd.
Bury South Jn 9.42
Bury South 9.38
9.21 8.36-31 M66
Metrolink Intersection Bridge
Roch 8.17 Viaduct
UP & DOWN BROADFIELD
CPI 2
HEYWOOD 5.35
West GF 5.50
East GF 5.28
Hopwood GF 5.03
(FP)
(AOCL) 5.26
ELR | NR 5.02 | 9.04
Miles from Manchester (Victoria) via Whitefield & Bury South Jn (reverse)
CARRIAGE SDG 2
CARRIAGE SDG 1
UP & DN THRO SDG
Buckley Wells Locomotive & Carriage Shed
Buckley Wells 9.24
Baron Street Locomotive Works
CTA 2
ELR/Metrolink Bdy 8.71
50
47A : to Castleton

A

CASTLETON 8.69 ⑦
LMS : L&Y MVN 2 [NW 7001]
(CE) (TH) 9.04
6 span Viaduct 10.47-50
50
Rochdale Rly Stn
10.63
10.14
ROCHDALE (CE) (TH) 10.36 ⑩
RTMA
Rochdale East Jn 10.63
NR/Metrolink Bdy 11.05
RTMA = Rochdale Turnback/ Metrolink access
50: Metrolink to Newbold
(TH) (PN) 12.63
(MCB) 12.65
DOWN MAIN
UP MAIN
DN L&Y
UP L&Y
SMITHY BRIDGE 12.60
LITTLEBOROUGH 13.65
⑤ Littleboro' 14.40
15.13
13.69-73 Littleboro' Viaduct
15.06-15.08 Summit West Tunnel (55 yards)
Summit Tunnel (1 mile 1125 yards)
LMS : L&Y MVN 2 [NW 7001]
47B
(CE) | (PN) Preston PSB
8.64
8.59
Rochdale West (TH) 8.57
Castleton East Jn 8.53 / 0.00
Castleton East Jn (CE) 8.53
CSD
8.54
0.00
8.49
TIMBER ROAD
UP & DN THRO' SDG
CEH [NW 7005]
DGL
UP MAIN
DOWN MAIN
M62 8.22
8.24
Castleton South Jn 8.21
8.20 Rochdale Canal Branch
UP THRO' SDG
CASTLETON (former Corus Materials Depot - due for clearance)
47C : to Bury
East Lancs Rly 5.02 | NR 9.04
8.54
Castleton North Jn 0.37 8.50
2 CPI CPI 1
LMS : LNW [NW 7005]
CASTLETON to BOLTON LINE
Rochdale Canal 7.06
Rochdale Canal 6.22
(CE) (VW)
MILLS HILL ⑤ 5.74
LMS : L&Y MVN 2 [NW 7001]
5.12 (Middleton Jn)
UP 5.09
UGL
MAIN
DOWN MAIN
MANCHESTER & NORMANTON LINE
Vitriol Works 4.64 (VW)
M60 4.25
⑥ 3.63
MOSTON 4.00 ⑦
(VW)
(MN)
3.22
2.53

Key to Viaducts
- A Gauxholme No. 1 18.24-37
- B Gauxholme No. 2 18.40
- C Todmorden 19.20-27
- D Lobb Mill 20.29-35
- E Cockden 21.22
- F Whitley 22.55

* Future Todmorden Curve

B

33B : to Burnley
FHR 6
Summit East Tunnel (41 yds) 16.65-67
Dean Royd Tunnel (70 yds) 16.74-77
[NW 7001] MVN 2
(Whiteplatts Jn) 19.54/30.24
SFO
(Todmorden Jn) 19.30
DN E. LANCS
UP E. LANCS
Hall Royd Engrs GF 19.56
30.49 30.54
Castle Hill Tunnel (194 yds) 20.07-16
(Eastwood) 21.34
47A
DN L&Y
UP L&Y
16.64 Summit Tunnel (1m 1125 yds) 537 ft
17.46-60 Winterbutlee Tunnel (306 yds)
WALSDEN 17.70
⑤ TODMORDEN 19.13
LMS : L&Y
19.49 19.61
Hall Royd Engs Sdgs (oou)
Hall Royd Jn
19.63-73 Millwood Tunnel (225 yds)
20.44-56 Horsfall Tunnel (274 yds)
22.62
LNW | LNE
2 : 41A : to Hebden Bridge
MANCHESTER and NORMANTON LINE
Controlled by Preston PSB (PN)

NW Electrification 2014-2016
Lines due for electrification
2016

50 : Metrolink to Woodlands Rd & Monsall
14.4 km
14.8 km
48B : to Manchester
Bromley Street Jn
0.31
0.55
DOWN ROCHDALE FAST
UP ROCHDALE FAST
DOWN ROCHDALE SLOW
UP ROCHDALE SLOW
OUTBOUND
INBOUND
Collyhurst Tunnel (426 yards)
0.70
ARR/DEP
RR
ORG
OLDHAM ROAD GOODS BRANCH
LMS : L&Y (Manchester & Leeds)
1.20
0.00
Miles Platting Tarmac
MANCHESTER and NORMANTON LINE
LMS : L&Y MVM MPR 1 [NW 7001]
MVL 1
Coal Drops Viaduct 1.25 1.29
Miles Platting Jn 1.30
DN ROCHDALE
UP ROCHDALE
DN ASHTON
UP ASHTON [NW 7021]
MVL 1
1.50
1.56
PPA 1 [NW 7025]
LMS : L&Y
DOWN BREWERY
UP BREWERY
0.18
1.52
-0.09
Philips Park West Jn 1.59
ASHTON BRANCH
LMS : L&Y MVL 1 [NW 7021]
45A : to Ashburys & Stalybridge
a = DOWN ASHTON
b = UP ASHTON
c = DOWN ASHBURYS
d = UP ASHBURYS
50 : Metrolink to Central Park
Brewery Jn 1.58
DOWN PASS LOOP
DOWN ROCHDALE
UP ROCHDALE
UP PASS LOOP
0.24
1.67
BPP
LMS : L&Y [NW 7023]
0.05-0.13 Brewery Fork Viaduct
0.00
Controlled by Manchester North (MN)
Located at Salford Crescent
1 MPR MVN 2
MPR 2
Thorpes (2.18) Bridge 2.27 Jn
2.13
2.17
2.23
2.22
DOWN ROCHDALE
UP ROCHDALE
2.48
NEWTON HEATH TMD (NH)
Northern Rail
NTH. AVOIDING ROAD
No. 2 INTAKE
No. 1 INTAKE
CW
Clean-ing
No. 5 H
6 H
19 TANK ROAD
DMU Shed
HOLDING SDGS
No. 18 STH
Dean Lane Greater Manchester Waste plc
DEAN GOODS
MANCHESTER METROLINK
DN
Newton Heath and Moston 5.850
3.05
2.78
2.62
50 : Metrolink to Failsworth

August 2013

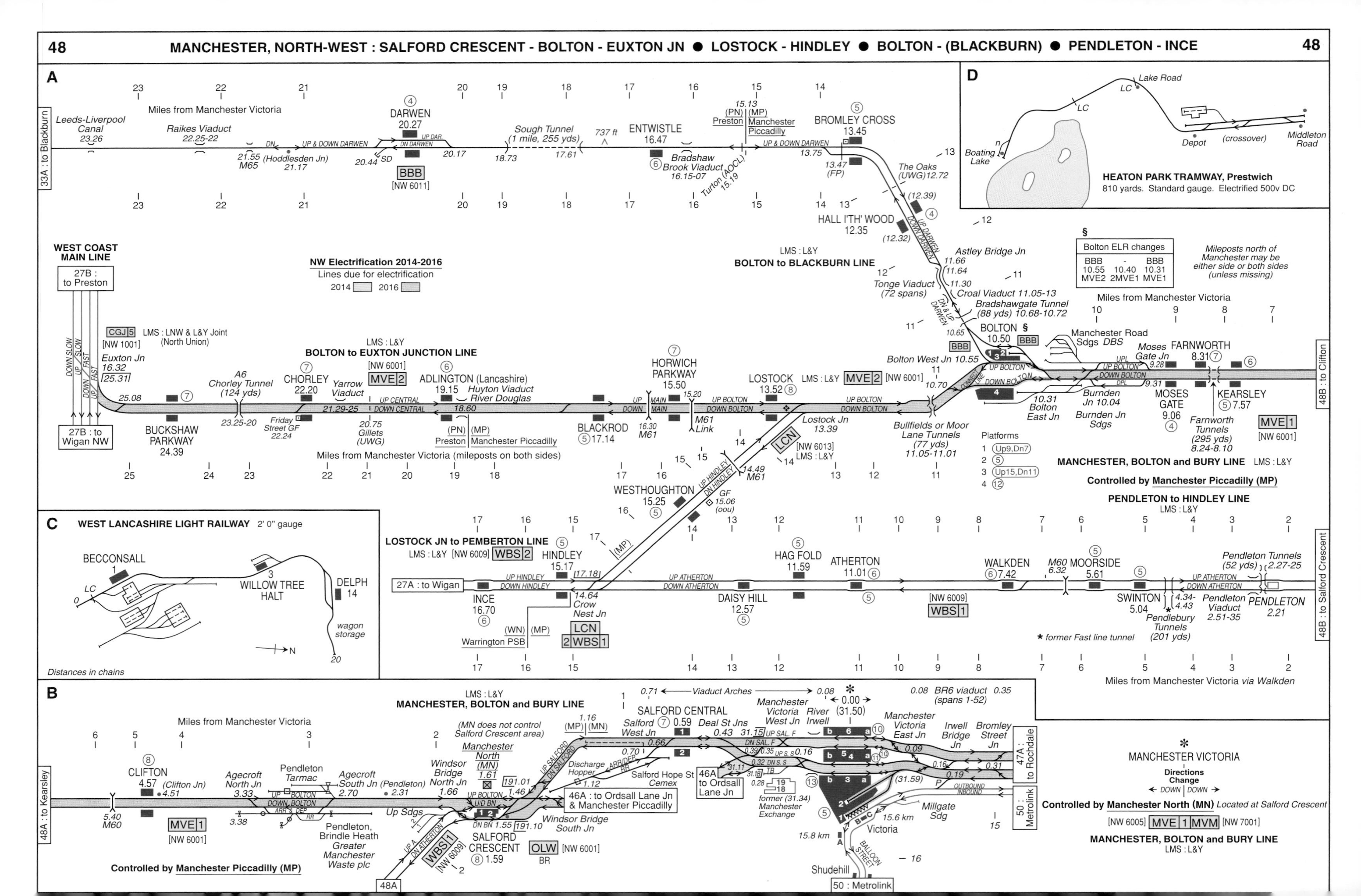
A
33A : to Blackburn
Miles from Manchester Victoria
Leeds-Liverpool Canal 23.26
Raikes Viaduct 22.25-22
21.55 M65
(Hoddlesden Jn) 21.17
DARWEN 20.27
BBB [NW 6011]
20.44 SD
20.17
Sough Tunnel (1 mile, 255 yds)
18.73
17.61
737 ft
ENTWISTLE 16.47
Bradshaw Brook Viaduct 16.15-07
Turton (AOCL) 15.19
15.13 (PN) Preston (MP) Manchester Piccadilly
UP & DOWN DARWEN
BROMLEY CROSS 13.45
13.75
13.47 (FP)
The Oaks (UWG) 12.72
(12.39)
HALL I'TH' WOOD 12.35
(12.32)
UP DARWEN
DOWN DARWEN
LMS : L&Y
BOLTON to BLACKBURN LINE
Astley Bridge Jn 11.66
11.64
11.30
Tonge Viaduct (72 spans)
Croal Viaduct 11.05-13
Bradshawgate Tunnel (88 yds) 10.68-10.72
DN & UP DARWEN
10.65
BOLTON § 10.50
BBB
Bolton West Jn 10.55
10.70
Manchester Road Sdgs DBS
Moses Gate Jn 9.28
FARNWORTH 8.31
9.31
Burnden Jn 10.04
10.31 Bolton East Jn
Burnden Jn Sdgs
MOSES GATE 9.06
KEARSLEY 7.57
Farnworth Tunnels (295 yds) 8.24-8.10
MVE1 [NW 6001]
48B : to Clifton
Platforms
1 Up9,Dn7
2 5
3 Up15,Dn11
4 12
§ Bolton ELR changes
BBB 10.55 MVE2
- 10.40 2MVE1
BBB 10.31 MVE1
Mileposts north of Manchester may be either side or both sides (unless missing)
Miles from Manchester Victoria
MANCHESTER, BOLTON and BURY LINE LMS : L&Y
Controlled by Manchester Piccadilly (MP)
WEST COAST MAIN LINE
27B : to Preston
27B : to Wigan NW
DOWN SLOW
UP SLOW
DOWN FAST
UP FAST
CGJ5 [NW 1001]
LMS : LNW & L&Y Joint (North Union)
Euxton Jn 16.32
25.31
25.08
NW Electrification 2014-2016
Lines due for electrification
2014 2016
LMS : L&Y
BOLTON to EUXTON JUNCTION LINE
[NW 6001] MVE2
BUCKSHAW PARKWAY 24.39
A6 Chorley Tunnel (124 yds)
23.25-20
CHORLEY 22.20
Friday Street GF 22.24
Yarrow Viaduct
21.29-25
20.75 Gillets (UWG)
UP CENTRAL
DOWN CENTRAL
ADLINGTON (Lancashire) 19.15
Huyton Viaduct River Douglas
18.60
(PN) Preston (MP) Manchester Piccadilly
Miles from Manchester Victoria (mileposts on both sides)
BLACKROD 17.14
16.30 M61
HORWICH PARKWAY 15.50
15.20
M61 Link
LOSTOCK 13.52
LMS : L&Y MVE2 [NW 6001]
UP BOLTON
DOWN BOLTON
Lostock Jn 13.39
LCN [NW 6013] LMS : L&Y
Bullfields or Moor Lane Tunnels (77 yds) 11.05-11.01
14.49 M61
WESTHOUGHTON 15.25
GF 15.06 (oou)
UP HINDLEY
DN HINDLEY
(MP)
D
Lake Road
LC
Boating Lake
Depot
(crossover)
Middleton Road
HEATON PARK TRAMWAY, Prestwich
810 yards. Standard gauge. Electrified 500v DC
C
WEST LANCASHIRE LIGHT RAILWAY 2' 0" gauge
BECCONSALL
LC
WILLOW TREE HALT
DELPH 14
wagon storage
N
Distances in chains
LOSTOCK JN to PEMBERTON LINE
LMS : L&Y [NW 6009] WBS2
27A : to Wigan
INCE 16.70
HINDLEY 15.17
17.18
14.64 Crow Nest Jn
(WN) Warrington PSB
(MP)
LCN 2WBS1
PENDLETON to HINDLEY LINE
LMS : L&Y
UP ATHERTON
DOWN ATHERTON
DAISY HILL 12.57
HAG FOLD 11.59
ATHERTON 11.01
[NW 6009] WBS1
WALKDEN 7.42
M60 6.32
MOORSIDE 5.61
SWINTON 5.04
4.34-4.43 Pendlebury Tunnels (201 yds)
Pendleton Viaduct 2.51-35
Pendleton Tunnels (52 yds) 2.27-25
PENDLETON 2.21
48B : to Salford Crescent
* former Fast line tunnel
Miles from Manchester Victoria via Walkden
B
48A : to Kearsley
Miles from Manchester Victoria
5.40 M60
CLIFTON 4.57 (Clifton Jn) 4.51
MVE1 [NW 6001]
Agecroft North Jn 3.33
3.38
Pendleton Tarmac
Agecroft South Jn 2.70
(Pendleton) 2.31
Pendleton, Brindle Heath Greater Manchester Waste plc
Up Sdgs
Controlled by Manchester Piccadilly (MP)
LMS : L&Y
MANCHESTER, BOLTON and BURY LINE
(MN does not control Salford Crescent area)
Manchester North (MN)
Windsor Bridge North Jn 1.66
1.61
1.16 (MP) (MN)
191.01
1.46
DN BN 1.55
191.10
Windsor Bridge South Jn
SALFORD CRESCENT 1.59
OLW [NW 6001] BR
WBS1 [NW 6009]
48A
UP SALFORD
DN SALFORD
Discharge Hopper 1.12
46A : to Ordsall Lane Jn & Manchester Piccadilly
Salford Hope St Cemex
0.70
0.66
SALFORD CENTRAL 0.59
Salford West Jn
Deal St Jns 0.43
31.15
0.71 Viaduct Arches 0.08
46A to Ordsall Lane Jn
31.11
31.18
0.39
0.35
0.32
0.28
0.16
19 18
former (31.34) Manchester Exchange
Manchester Victoria West Jn
River Irwell
* 0.00 (31.50)
0.08 BR6 viaduct 0.35 (spans 1-52)
Manchester Victoria East Jn
Irwell Bridge Jn
Bromley Street Jn
0.09
0.16
0.19
0.31
(31.59)
47A : to Rochdale
50 : Metrolink
OUTBOUND
INBOUND
Millgate Sdg
15.6 km
15.8 km
Victoria
Shudehill
BALLOON STREET
50 : Metrolink
* MANCHESTER VICTORIA
Directions Change
DOWN | DOWN
Controlled by Manchester North (MN) Located at Salford Crescent
[NW 6005] MVE1 MVM [NW 7001]
MANCHESTER, BOLTON and BURY LINE
LMS : L&Y

E

Mileage	Stop
17.965	Fleetwood Ferry
17.780/18.255	
17.625	Victoria Street
17.280	London Street
16.760	Fisherman's Walk
16.355	Stanley Road
15.770	Lindel Road
15.305	Heathfield Road
14.555	Broadwater
14.075	Rossall Square
13.600	Rossall School
12.565	Rossall Beach
12.090	Thornton Gate
11.745	West Drive
11.435	Cleveleys
10.655	Anchorsholme Lane
9.950 ★	Little Bispham
8.995	Norbreck
8.535	Sandhurst Avenue
8.155	Bispham
7.840	Cavendish Road
7.325	Lowther Avenue
6.795 ★	Cabin
6.555	Cliffs Hotel
6.310	Glyn Square
5.640	Wilton Parade
5.350	Pleasant Street
4.720	North Pier (N. Bound)
	(former route towards Blackpool North)
★ 4.360	North Pier (S. Bound)
4.140	Tower
3.840	Central Pier
3.420	Manchester Square
2.800	St Chad's Road
2.405	Waterloo Road
2.065	South Pier
1.805	Pleasure Beach
★	★ Heritage Tram Stops (no platform)
1.095	Burlington Road

RIGBY ROAD DEPOT (Heritage trains only) — 17 Roads

49F

A

18.08 Oil Sdgs GF 17.73 — former Thornton Power Station — 18

No. 4 17.61, Hillhouse GFs, No. 5 17.45, No. 3 17.44 — LOOP, DOWN GDS

BURN NAZE 17.40 — open LC — DOWN & UP BURN NAZE GOODS — OOU — 17

[NW 4009] WPS — LMS : LNW & L&Y Joint (Preston & Wyre Joint)

Hilly Laid (TMOG) 16.43 — THORNTON CLEVELEYS 16.20 — Thornton (TMOB) 16.10 — Tarn Gate (UWG) 15.58 — 16 — 14.71 — UG — DG — 14.47

Poulton (No. 3) (PT) 14.44 — Poulton-le-Fylde Jn 14.40 — POULTON-LE-FYLDE (5) 14.31

Blackpool Carriage Sidings — (BP) BCR — ENGINE LOOP — Blackpool North PGF 16.70

LAYTON 16.32 (5) (MCB) 15 — 16.69 (7) — Carleton Crossing 15.44 — (BN2) (C)

Blackpool North No. 2 (BN2) 17.30 — 17.27 — 17.33 — 17.30 — 17.46 (9) — (10) — (11)

BLACKPOOL NORTH (10) 17.49 *(Platforms 2 & 3)* — Platforms 1 2 3 4 5 6 7 8

[NW 4005] PBN — **POULTON to BLACKPOOL LINE** — LMS : LNW & L&Y Joint (Preston & Wyre Joint)

NW Electrification 2014-2016 — Lines due for electrification 2016

LMS : LNW & L&Y Joint (Preston & Wyre Joint) — PBN [NW 4005] — UP MAIN — DOWN MAIN — (PT) (KM) — M55 10.38

Miles from Preston Station: 17, 16, 15, 14, 13, 12, 11, 10, 9, 8, 7, 6, 5, 4, 3, 2, 1

Kirkham & Wesham Tip Engineers — 9.60 — 9.40 — 9.20 KIRKHAM TIP SDG — KBS 2 — 8.63 — 8.44 — 8.36 — 8.28 — 49D — Engineers

Kirkham North Jn (KM) 8.29 — 8.42 — UP FAST — DOWN FAST — UP & DN SLOW — DOWN SLOW — KIRKHAM AND WESHAM 7.67 (4) — 7.35 — Kirkham South Jn

LMS : LNW & L&Y Joint (Preston & Wyre Joint) — **PRESTON and FLEETWOOD LINE** — PBN [NW 4005] — Salwick (SK) 5.03 — UP MAIN — DOWN MAIN — SALWICK (4) 5.17 — (KM) (SK) — DGL — 4.78 (S) Dn Sdgs GF — 4.41 — UP MAIN (FYLDE) — DOWN MAIN (FYLDE) — 1.03-0.74 — Tulketh Viaduct — (SK) Preston PSB (PN) — 27C : to Preston

B

Miles from *former* Liverpool Exchange: 13, 14, 15, 16, 17, 18

41A — (ML) (RD) — ORMSKIRK (4) 12.13 12.15 — 12.27 — DOWN & UP ORMSKIRK

BURSCOUGH JUNCTION (4) 14.61 — 42A : to Southport — 27.31 — 15.21 — DN — UP — WBS 3 [NW 6009] — 42A : to Wigan LMS : L&Y

RUFFORD 17.49 (RD) (3) — 17.51 — 17.40 — 17.58 — (4) (MCB) — River Douglas Viaduct 17.59-61 — 49C

WALTON JN to PRESTON LINE
LMS : L&Y
Controlled by Merseyrail (ML) at Sandhills
FCO [NW 7007]

C

Mileposts: 19, 20, 21, 22, 23, 24, 25

49B — 18.67 High Lane (UWG) — 19.13 Finney Lane (UWG) — 19.68 Club Lane (UWG) — CROSTON (4) 20.18 — DOWN & UP ORMSKIRK — FCO [NW 7007] — 22.38 Pages (UWG) — Midge Hall (MH) 22.78 — (MCB) — (MIDGE HALL) 23.03 — 23.28 Sod Hall (UWG) — 27C : to Preston

WALTON JN to PRESTON LINE LMS : L&Y

D

Mileposts: 20, 19, 18; 17, 16, 15, 14, 13

BLACKPOOL SOUTH (4) 20.00

(5) BLACKPOOL PLEASURE BEACH 19.18

(5) SQUIRES GATE 18.34

ST. ANNES-ON-THE-SEA 16.51 (7)

(2) ANSDELL & FAIRHAVEN 14.75

LYTHAM 13.56 (5)

DN — DN & UP MAIN — **SOUTH FYLDE LINE**

KIRKHAM to BLACKPOOL SOUTH LINE
Controlled by Kirkham North Jn (KM)

Moss Side (ABCL) 11.09 — MOSS SIDE 11.14 (4) — KBS 1 [NW 4007]

LMS : LNW & L&Y Joint (Preston & Wyre Joint) — 9, 10, 11, 12 — Tarnbrick (UWG) 8.54 — 49A

F

49E — 0.560 — Harrow Place

BLACKPOOL ELECTRIC TRAMWAY
Operated by Blackpool Transport Services Ltd., 1435mm gauge
600V DC overhead
All stops raised platform

Starr Gate 0.000 — CW — STARR GATE DEPOT — Maintenance Workshop (pit roads) 1 2 3 — Stabling Sdgs 4 6 8 10

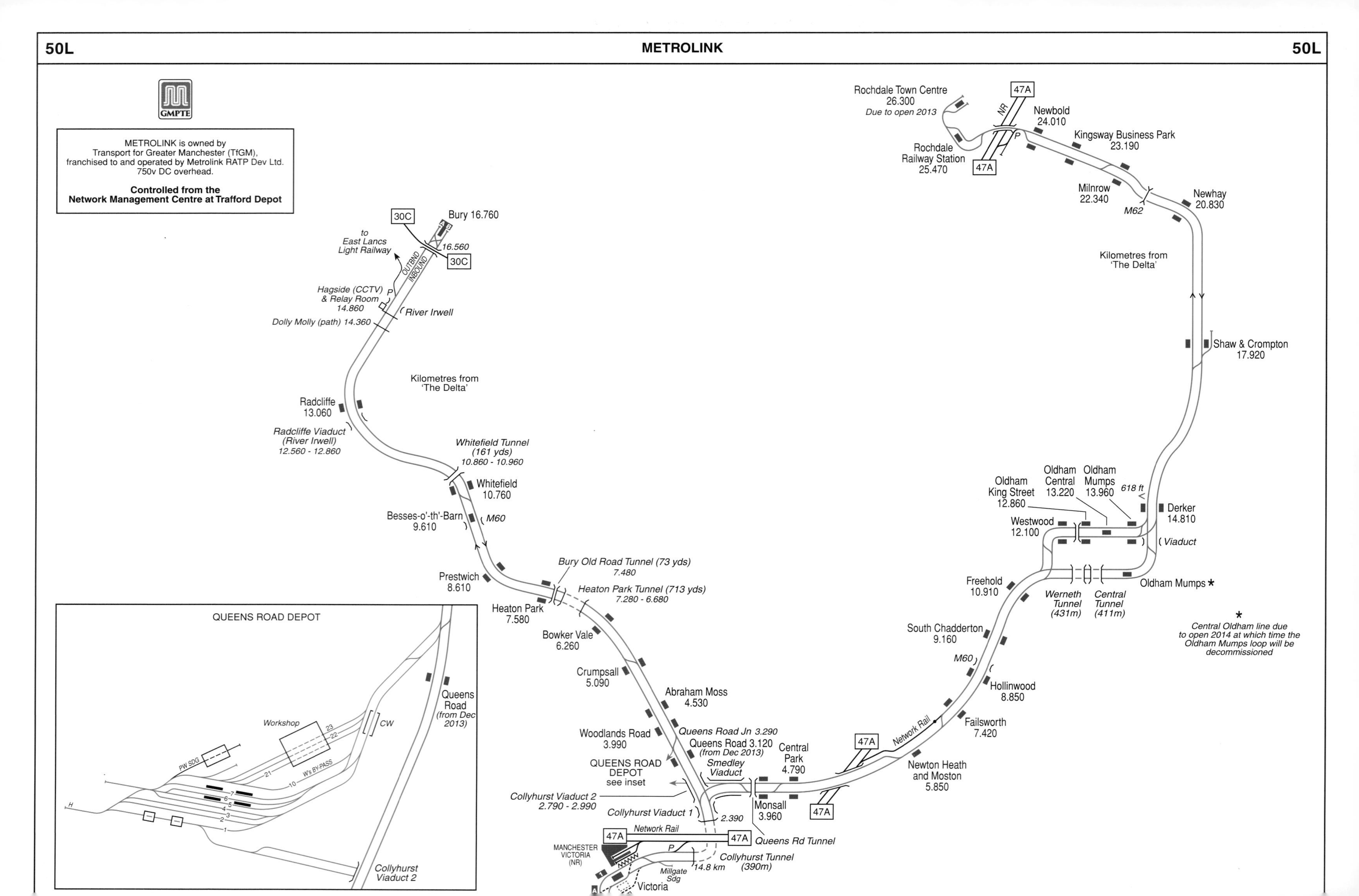
GMPTE
METROLINK is owned by
Transport for Greater Manchester (TfGM),
franchised to and operated by Metrolink RATP Dev Ltd.
750v DC overhead.
Controlled from the
Network Management Centre at Trafford Depot
Rochdale Town Centre 26.300
Due to open 2013
Rochdale Railway Station 25.470
NR
47A
P
Newbold 24.010
Kingsway Business Park 23.190
Milnrow 22.340
M62
Newhay 20.830
Kilometres from 'The Delta'
Shaw & Crompton 17.920
Derker 14.810
Viaduct
618 ft
Oldham Mumps 13.960
Oldham Central 13.220
Oldham King Street 12.860
Westwood 12.100
Werneth Tunnel (431m)
Central Tunnel (411m)
Oldham Mumps *
* Central Oldham line due to open 2014 at which time the Oldham Mumps loop will be decommissioned
Freehold 10.910
South Chadderton 9.160
M60
Hollinwood 8.850
Failsworth 7.420
Network Rail
Newton Heath and Moston 5.850
Central Park 4.790
Monsall 3.960
Queens Rd Tunnel
Collyhurst Tunnel (390m)
14.8 km
Millgate Sdg
Victoria
MANCHESTER VICTORIA (NR)
2.390
Smedley Viaduct
Queens Road Jn 3.290
Queens Road 3.120 (from Dec 2013)
Abraham Moss 4.530
Woodlands Road 3.990
QUEENS ROAD DEPOT see inset
Collyhurst Viaduct 1
Collyhurst Viaduct 2 2.790 - 2.990
Crumpsall 5.090
Bowker Vale 6.260
Heaton Park Tunnel (713 yds) 7.280 - 6.680
Bury Old Road Tunnel (73 yds) 7.480
Heaton Park 7.580
Prestwich 8.610
Besses-o'-th'-Barn 9.610
Whitefield 10.760
Whitefield Tunnel (161 yds) 10.860 - 10.960
Radcliffe 13.060
Radcliffe Viaduct (River Irwell) 12.560 - 12.860
Dolly Molly (path) 14.360
Hagside (CCTV) & Relay Room 14.860
River Irwell
to East Lancs Light Railway
OUTBND
INBOUND
30C
16.560
Bury 16.760
QUEENS ROAD DEPOT
Workshop
23
22
CW
PW SDG
21
10
W's BY-PASS
7
6
5
4
3
2
1
H
Queens Road (from Dec 2013)
Collyhurst Viaduct 2

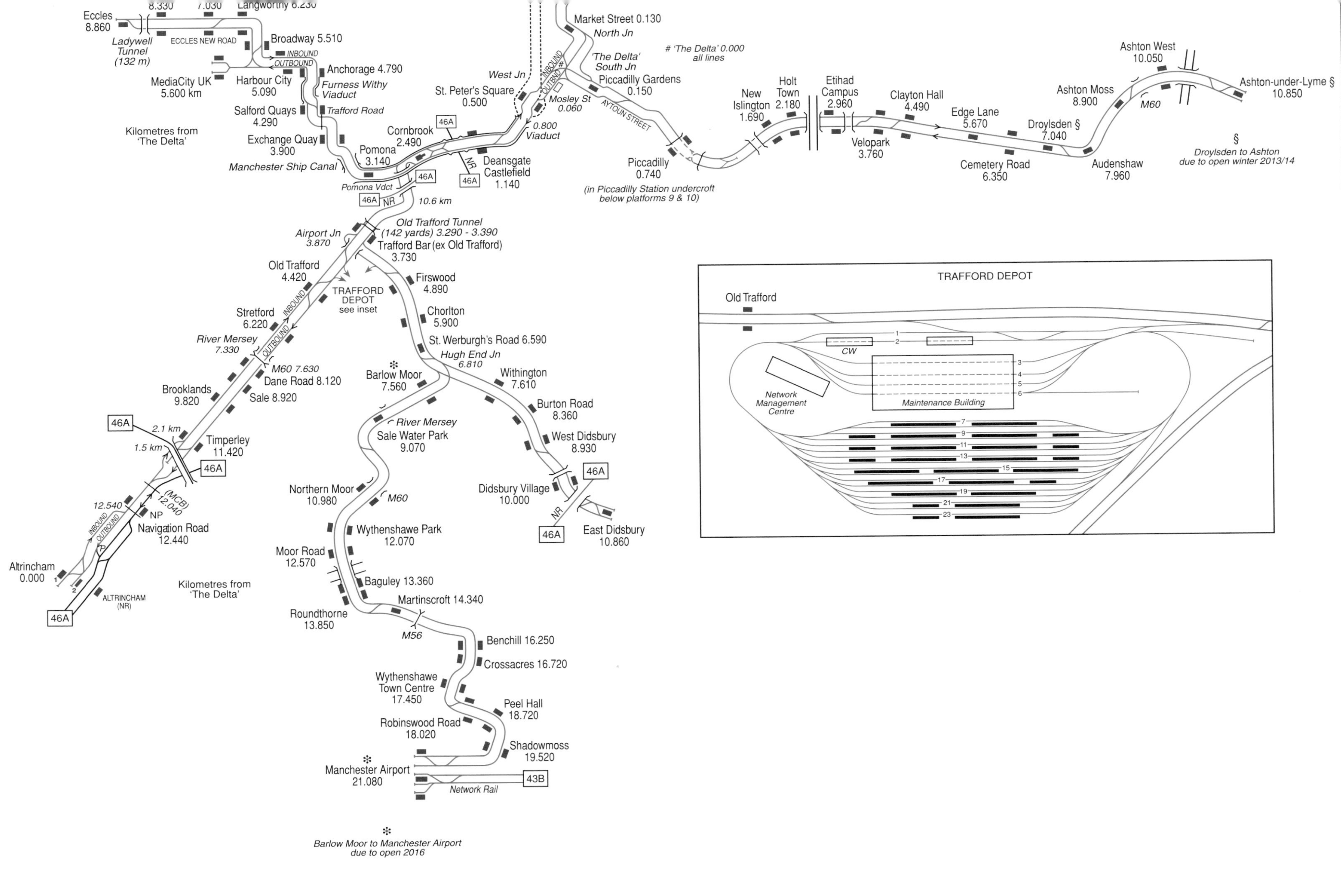
Eccles
8.860
Ladywell
Tunnel
(132 m)
8.330
7.030
Langworthy 6.230
ECCLES NEW ROAD
Broadway 5.510
INBOUND
OUTBOUND
MediaCity UK
5.600 km
Harbour City
5.090
Anchorage 4.790
Furness Withy
Viaduct
Salford Quays
4.290
Trafford Road
Kilometres from
'The Delta'
Exchange Quay
3.900
Manchester Ship Canal
Pomona
3.140
Cornbrook
2.490
46A
Pomona Vdct
NR
10.6 km
St. Peter's Square
0.500
West Jn
Deansgate
Castlefield
1.140
0.800
Viaduct
Mosley St
0.060
Market Street 0.130
North Jn
'The Delta'
South Jn
Piccadilly Gardens
0.150
AYTOUN STREET
'The Delta' 0.000
all lines
Piccadilly
0.740
(in Piccadilly Station undercroft
below platforms 9 & 10)
New
Islington
1.690
Holt
Town
2.180
Etihad
Campus
2.960
Velopark
3.760
Clayton Hall
4.490
Edge Lane
5.670
Cemetery Road
6.350
Droylsden §
7.040
Audenshaw
7.960
Ashton Moss
8.900
M60
Ashton West
10.050
Ashton-under-Lyme §
10.850
§
Droylsden to Ashton
due to open winter 2013/14
Airport Jn
3.870
Old Trafford Tunnel
(142 yards) 3.290 - 3.390
Trafford Bar (ex Old Trafford)
3.730
Old Trafford
4.420
TRAFFORD
DEPOT
see inset
Firswood
4.890
Chorlton
5.900
St. Werburgh's Road 6.590
Hugh End Jn
6.810
Stretford
6.220
River Mersey
7.330
M60 7.630
Dane Road 8.120
Sale 8.920
Brooklands
9.820
2.1 km
1.5 km
Timperley
11.420
(MCB)
12.040
NP
Navigation Road
12.440
12.540
Altrincham
0.000
ALTRINCHAM
(NR)
Kilometres from
'The Delta'
Barlow Moor
7.560
River Mersey
Sale Water Park
9.070
Withington
7.610
Burton Road
8.360
West Didsbury
8.930
Didsbury Village
10.000
East Didsbury
10.860
Northern Moor
10.980
M60
Wythenshawe Park
12.070
Moor Road
12.570
Baguley 13.360
Roundthorne
13.850
Martinscroft 14.340
M56
Benchill 16.250
Crossacres 16.720
Wythenshawe
Town Centre
17.450
Peel Hall
18.720
Robinswood Road
18.020
Shadowmoss
19.520
Manchester Airport
21.080
43B
Network Rail
Barlow Moor to Manchester Airport
due to open 2016
TRAFFORD DEPOT
Old Trafford
CW
Network
Management
Centre
Maintenance Building

August 2013

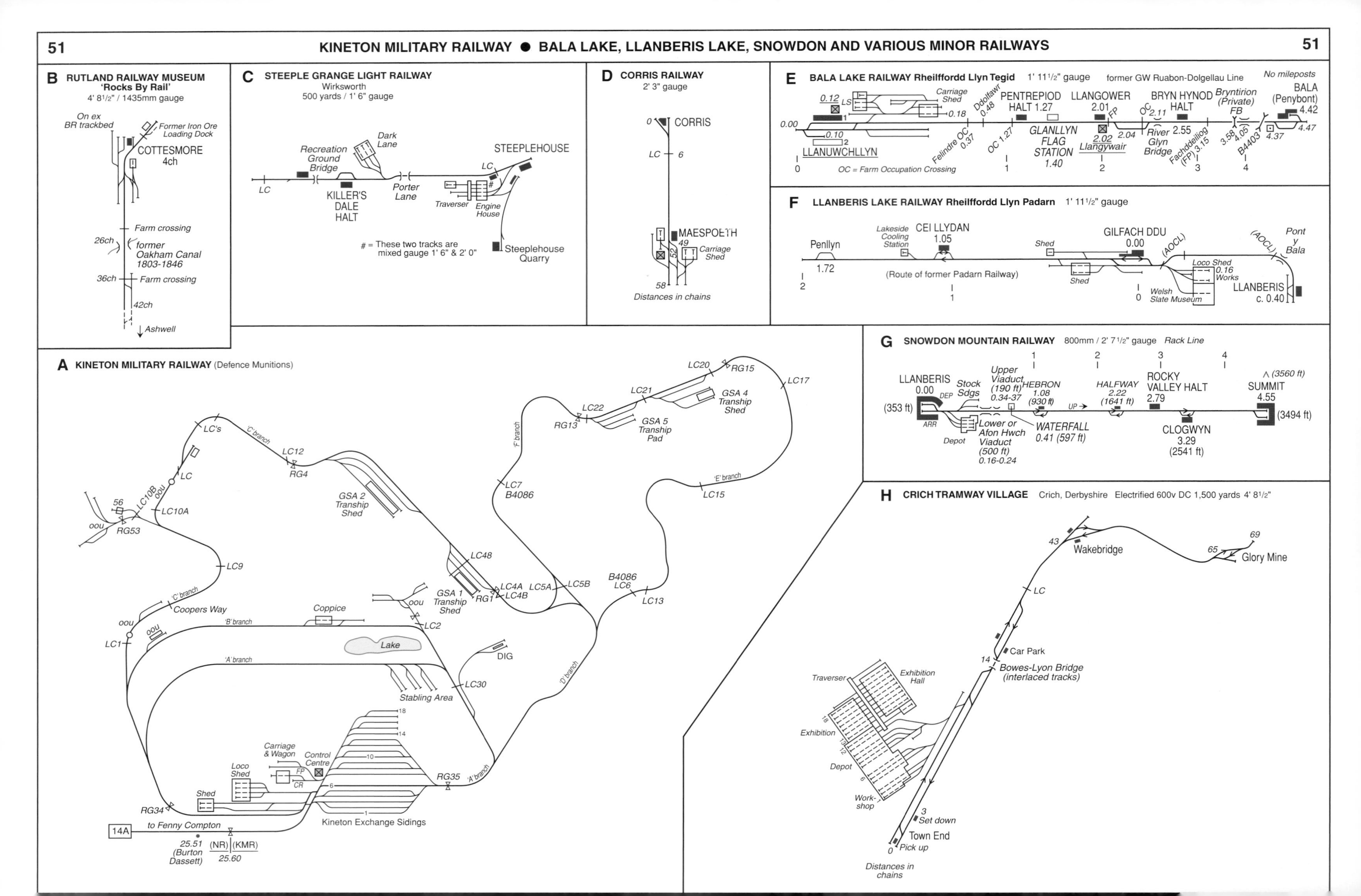
51
KINETON MILITARY RAILWAY ● BALA LAKE, LLANBERIS LAKE, SNOWDON AND VARIOUS MINOR RAILWAYS
51
B RUTLAND RAILWAY MUSEUM
'Rocks By Rail'
4' 8½" / 1435mm gauge
On ex BR trackbed
Former Iron Ore Loading Dock
COTTESMORE
4ch
Farm crossing
26ch
former Oakham Canal 1803-1846
36ch
Farm crossing
42ch
Ashwell
C STEEPLE GRANGE LIGHT RAILWAY
Wirksworth
500 yards / 1' 6" gauge
Recreation Ground Bridge
Dark Lane
LC
KILLER'S DALE HALT
Porter Lane
STEEPLEHOUSE
LC
Traverser
Engine House
= These two tracks are mixed gauge 1' 6" & 2' 0"
Steeplehouse Quarry
D CORRIS RAILWAY
2' 3" gauge
0
CORRIS
LC
6
MAESPOETH
49
52
Carriage Shed
58
Distances in chains
E BALA LAKE RAILWAY Rheilffordd Llyn Tegid 1' 11½" gauge former GW Ruabon-Dolgellau Line No mileposts
0.12
LS
Carriage Shed
0.18
0.00
0.10
LLANUWCHLLYN
0
OC = Farm Occupation Crossing
Dolfawr 0.48
Felindre OC 0.37
OC 1.27
PENTREPIOD HALT 1.27
GLANLLYN FLAG STATION 1.40
1
LLANGOWER 2.01
FP
2.02 Llangywair
2.04
2
OC 2.11
BRYN HYNOD HALT
River Glyn Bridge 2.55
Fachddeiliog (FP) 3.15
3
Bryntirion (Private) FB
3.58
4.05
B4403
4
4.37
BALA (Penybont)
4.42
4.47
F LLANBERIS LAKE RAILWAY Rheilffordd Llyn Padarn 1' 11½" gauge
Penllyn
1.72
2
Lakeside Cooling Station
CEI LLYDAN
1.05
(Route of former Padarn Railway)
1
Shed
Shed
GILFACH DDU
0.00
0
(AOCL)
(AOCL)
Loco Shed
0.16
Works
Welsh Slate Museum
Pont y Bala
LLANBERIS
c. 0.40
G SNOWDON MOUNTAIN RAILWAY 800mm / 2' 7½" gauge Rack Line
LLANBERIS
0.00
(353 ft)
DEP
ARR
Stock Sdgs
Depot
Upper Viaduct (190 ft) 0.34-37
Lower or Afon Hwch Viaduct (500 ft) 0.16-0.24
HEBRON 1.08 (930 ft)
WATERFALL 0.41 (597 ft)
UP →
HALFWAY 2.22 (1641 ft)
ROCKY VALLEY HALT 2.79
CLOGWYN 3.29 (2541 ft)
∧ (3560 ft)
SUMMIT 4.55
(3494 ft)
1
2
3
4
A KINETON MILITARY RAILWAY (Defence Munitions)
LC's
'C' branch
LC12
RG4
LC
LC10B
oou
56
oou
RG53
LC10A
LC9
'C' branch
Coopers Way
oou
oou
LC1
'B' branch
'A' branch
GSA 2 Tranship Shed
LC48
LC4A
LC4B
RG1
LC5A
LC5B
GSA 1 Tranship Shed
oou
LC2
Coppice
Lake
DIG
LC30
Stabling Area
'D' branch
'F' branch
LC7
B4086
LC22
RG13
LC21
GSA 5 Tranship Pad
LC20
RG15
GSA 4 Tranship Shed
LC17
'E' branch
LC15
B4086
LC6
LC13
18
14
10
6
1
Carriage & Wagon
Control Centre
FP
CR
Loco Shed
Shed
RG34
RG35
'A' branch
Kineton Exchange Sidings
14A
to Fenny Compton
25.51 (Burton Dassett)
(NR) (KMR)
25.60
H CRICH TRAMWAY VILLAGE Crich, Derbyshire Electrified 600v DC 1,500 yards 4' 8½"
43
Wakebridge
65
69
Glory Mine
LC
Car Park
14
Bowes-Lyon Bridge (interlaced tracks)
Traverser
Exhibition Hall
18
Exhibition
13
12
Depot
6
Work-shop
3
Set down
Town End
0
Pick up
Distances in chains

Index

This index covers practically all the named locations relating to the National Network which appear on the maps to assist the reader in their search. Stations are listed in capitals, signal boxes with their codes and level crossings with their type. FP and Barrow crossings in the maps are not carried to the index nor are road and motorway over-bridges. Locations of now-defunct assets are given in brackets. Other public service lines, light rail, Heritage lines, narrow gauge and other private lines are indexed by their line name and key stations only.

A

B

C

D

E

F

G

H

U

V

W

Y

Z

Engineer's Line References

This listing is intended to show all the relevant operational ELRs that appear in this book, those that were live in the last edition but now closed, out of use or lifted and those that have carried over from the original network onto Heritage lines. More information can be found about these codes on the excellent website by Phil Deaves at *http://deaves47.zxq.net/*. The location of the start and finish boundary of each ELR can be found in the book from the map reference in the Location Index applicable to any of the locations named in the description. Some ELRs extend over several pages.

ACP Avenue Coking Plant Branch (Clay Cross) (lifted)
ACW Acton Canal Wharf Jn to Willesden Jn
AEG Allerton East Jn to Garston Jn Curve
AFE Abbey Forgate Jn to English Bridge Jn Curve
AFL Aintree Fork Line (Sefton Jn to former Metal Box Siding)
AHX Allerton Jn to Hunts Cross West Jn
AJM Ambergate Jn to Matlock (and Peak Forest Jn)
ALC Aston North Jn to Lichfield City Jn
AMJ Ashton Moss Curve (Ashton Moss South to North Jns)
AML Attenborough to Meadow Lane Jn
APB Ambergate to Pye Bridge Line
ASE Nuneaton Ashby Jn to Shackerstone Line
AWL Acton East to Acton Wells Jn
AYS Ashburys Yard Sidings
BAG Birmingham New Street to Gloucester
BBB Bolton to Blackburn
BBM Bletchley to Bedford Midland
BBS Blackburn Sidings
BCJ Birmingham Curve Jn to Branston Jn (Burton-On Trent)
BCP Stubbins Jn to Bacup
BCR Blackpool Carriage Sidings
BCS Bletchley Carriage Sidings
BCV Bordesley Curve Jn to Tyseley Line
BDH Brent Curve Jn to Dudding Hill Jn
BDN Bridge Street Jn to Duston North Jn (Northampton)
BDS Bidston West Jn to Seacombe Jn (siding only)
BEA Barnt Green, Evesham to Ashchurch Line
BEJ Buxton to Edgeley Jn
BEN Birkenhead to New Brighton Branch
BFG Wembley Repair Shop
BFO Bletchley Flyover Jn to Fenny Stratford
BHI Basford Hall Independent Lines (Basford Hall Jn to Sydney Bridge Jn)
BIK Bickershaw Colliery Branch (Wigan)
BJW Bescot Jn to Wichnor Jn (via Walsall)
BLT Bletchley Sidings
BNN Bedford to Northampton Jn
BOK Broad Street to Old Kew Jn via Hampstead Heath (North London Line)
BPC Bestwood Park Jn to Calverton Colliery (lifted)
BPH Blisworth to Peterborough via Northampton Bridge St
BPP Brewery Jn to Philips Park West Jn
BSC British Steel Corby Branch
BSD Bescot Sidings
BSJ Bootle Jn Crossover
BSN Brunthill Stainton Sidings (Carlisle)
BTS Brent Sidings
BUX Buxton to Hindlow
BYK Bewdley to Kidderminster
CAW Cricklewood Curve Jn to Acton Wells Jn
CBC Carnforth to Barrow to Carlisle
CBR Castle Bromwich to Ryecroft Jn (Walsall) via Sutton Park
CCB Cotgrave Colliery Branch
CCG Colne Jn to Croxley Green
CCS Rock Ferry to Cathcart St Branch
CDM Castleford Jn to Dee Marsh
CEC Carnforth, Station Jn to East Jn
CEH Castleton East Jn to Heywood
CGJ Crewe (from 59Mp) to Carlisle (Gretna Jn) (part WCML)
CHW Chester to Warrington
CIL Chester Independent Lines (Salop Goods Jn to Crewe North Jn)
CMD Colwich Jn to Macclesfield
CMP Crewe to Manchester Piccadilly
CNB Chinley North Jn to Buxton (via Peak Forest)
CNH Crewe North to Holyhead
CNN Coventry to Nuneaton
COL Manchester Piccadilly East Jn to Ordsall Lane Jn
CPC Codnor Park Curve (Codnor Park Jn to Ironville Jn)
CPI Castleton, North Jn to South Jn
CRC Camden Road Jn to Camden Jn
CRF Camden Road East Jn to Copenhagen Jn (replaced by NLI)
CRR Chester to Rock Ferry
CSD Castleton Depot
CSG Crewe Sorting Siding to Gresty Lane
CTA Clifton Jn To Accrington Line
CVL Churnet Valley Line (Leek Brook Jn to Oakamoor)
CVS Chester South Jn to Chester North Jn
CWJ Camden Jn to Watford Jn (DC Electric Lines)
CWK Canning St Jn (Hamilton Square Jn) to West Kirby
CYC Chinley Chord (Chinley East Jn to South Jn)
DAP Dalton Jn to Park South Jn (Barrow avoiding Line)
DBP Derby to Birmingham (Proof House Jn)
DCL Didcot to Chester Line (Didcot to Handsworth Jn via Birmingham Snow Hill)
DEX Derbyshire Extension (Rectory Jn to Derby Friargate)
DHF Denbeigh Hall Flyover South Jn to Flyover Jn (Bletchley)
DJH Daisyfield Jn (Blackburn) to Hellifield
DJO Denton Jn to Ashton Moss Station Jn
DJP Dovey Jn to Pwllheli
DJW Duffield Jn to Wirksworth
DPJ Dudley Jn to Pleck Jn (Walsall)
DSD Dinting South Jn to Dinting East Jn
DSE Deal Street (Manchester) to Edge Hill (Liverpool) (Chat Moss Line)
DSS Euston Down Side Sheds
ECM East Coast Main Line (London Kings Cross to Edinburgh)
EDE Eden Valley Jn to Kirkby Stephen via Appleby West Jn to Warcop
EEE Liverpool Curve (Earlestown South to West Jns)
EHW Edge Hill Jn to Park Lane Goods (Wapping Branch)
EJN Edgeley Jn (Stockport) to Northenden
EPS Earles Private Sidings
ETC Edinburgh to Carlisle Line (Waverley Route)
EWG Edge Hill Jn to Waterloo Goods
FCO Farington Curve Jn to Ormskirk
FHR Farington Curve Jn to Hall Royd Jn via Blackburn
FJH Frodsham Jn to Halton Jn
GBS Guide Bridge Sidings
GDW Glossop to Dinting West Jn
GES GEC Siding: Stafford No 4 SB
GJC Gannow Jn to Colne
GLA Gaerwen to Amlwch
GMC Greater Manchester Council Branch (Woodley to Bredbury)
GNQ Gobowen to Nantmawr Quarry
GOJ Gospel Oak to Junction Road Jn
GSG Gresty Lane Jn to Salop Goods Jn
GSJ Galton Jn to Stourbridge Jn (Galton Branch to Stourbridge Extn Line)
GSM Glendon South Jn to Syston South Jn (via Manton Jn, also Old Dalby Line)
GSW Glasgow to South Western Line (Kilmarnock GBK Jn to Gretna Jn via Dumfries)
HAJ Hadfield to Ardwick Jn
HAS Hatton to Stratford-on-Avon
HBL Hest Bank Jn to Bare Lane Jn
HCM Silverdale Colliery to Madeley Jn

HCN	Hartford Curve (CLC Jn to LNW Jn)
HEG	Hartford East Goods Curve (Northwich)
HGC	Hazel Grove Chord (Hazel Grove East to High Level Jns)
HHJ	Hooton to Helsby Jn
HHW	Hatton North Jn to West Jn
HLB	Holwell Branch
HND	Halesowen Branch (Longbridge) (lifted)
HNO	Hartford Northwich Oakleigh Sidings
HNR	Hanslope to Northampton to Rugby
HNS	Heaton Norris to Guide Bridge
HOB	Haydock Park Branch (Ashton-in-Makerfield)
HOK	Horrocksford Branch
HSJ	Handsworth Jn to Smethwick Jn
HTW	Heath Town Jn to Walsall Lichfield Road Jn (closed)
HWG	Hartford West Goods Curve
HXS	Hunts Cross West Jn to Southport
IMG	Ince Moss Chord (Ince Moss Jn to Bamfurlong Sidings Jn)
ISL	Cedar Jn and Silo Curve
JRT	Junction Road Jn to Carlton Road Jn
KBC	Kingsbury to Birch Coppice
KBS	Kirkham North Jn to Blackpool South
KCS	Kidsgrove to Crewe South
KGC	Kensal Green Jn via City Lines to Harlesden Jn
KGW	Kensal Green Jn to Surburban Jn
KJW	Kingsbury Jn to Whitacre Jn
KMG	Kingmoor Jn to Mossbound Jn via Goods Lines
KSL	Knighton South Jn to Leicester Jn (Burton)
KWD	Kingswinford South Jn to Pensnett
LCN	Lostock Jn to Crow Nest Jn (Hindley)
LCS	Liverpool Edge Hill to Crown Street Goods
LEC	London Euston to Crewe (at 159Mp, part WCML)
LED	Little Eaton Jn to Denby
LEL	Lifford West Jn to East Jn
LHL	Lostock Hall Lines (Farington Jn to Lostock Hall Jn)
LJT	Llandudno Jn to Blaenau Ffestiniog and Trawsfynydd
LKD	Plumpton Jn to Lakeside
LLG	Low Level Goods (Willesden West London Jn – Wembley Central Jn)
LLI	Liverpool Independent Lines (Crewe) (Salop Good Jn – Crewe Coal Yard Jn)
LLJ	Llandudno to Llandudno Jn
LMD	Longsight Depot Sidings
LSC	Leamington Spa to Coventry
LSN	Lenton South to North Jns
LSS	Landor Street Jn to St Andrews Jn (Birmingham)
LTV	Lichfield Trent Valley Curve
MAJ	Manchester, Castlefield Jn to Hunts Cross West Jn (CLC Line)
MAS	Totley Tunnel East to Chinley North Jn (Manchester to Sheffield Line)
MCG	Maryport to Carlisle Goods Lines (Currock Jn to Forks Jn)
MCH	Macclesfield to Cheadle Hulme
MCJ	Marylebone to Annesley (via Great Central Main Line and Ruddington)
MCL	Midland City Line (Moorgate) to Carlton Road Jn
MDH	Mold to Denbeigh
MHH	Morecambe Jn to Heysham
MIA	Manchester International Airport Rail Link Line
MIR	Mersey: Liverpool Loop Line and Mann Island Jn to Rock Ferry
MJI	Madeley Jn to Ironbridge Line
MJS	Melbourne Jn to Sinfin Branch
MJT	Mansfield Jn to Trowell Jn
MPR	Miles Platting Jn to Rochdale East Jn (via Oldham Mumps, now Metrolink)
MRH	Marple Wharf Jn to Rose Hill Marple
MSL	Birmingham Moor Street Line
MSM	Morecambe South Jn to Morecambe
MVB	Manchester Victoria to Bury (now Metrolink)
MVE	Manchester Victoria to Euxton Jn via Bolton
MVL	Manchester Victoria, Mile Platting Jn to Heaton Lodge Jn, also Leeds
MVM	Manchester Victoria to Miles Platting Jn
MVN	Manchester Victoria, Thorpe Bridge Jn to Normanton, Goose Hill Jn via Rochdale
MYC	Midland Yard Jn to Canal Farm Jn (Nuneaton North Chord)
NBS	Norton Bridge to Stone
NEC	Newcastle to Carlisle
NGC	Netherfield to Gelding Colliery (lifted)
NGD	Newcastle Goods Lines (Carlisle, London Road Jn – Bog Jn)
NGJ	Newton-le-Willows Jn to Golborne Jn (Parkside West Curve)
NJN	Neasden South Sdgs and Neasden Jn
NLI	North London Incline
NMA	Nuneaton Avoiding Line (Midland Jn to Abbey Jn)
NMB	North Mersey Branch (Aintree, Fazakerly to North Mersey Jn)
NMC	New Mills to Cheadle Branch
NMH	Northampton to Market Harborough
NMM	North Mersey Branch to Marsh Lane Jn
NOB	Nottingham to Barnetby via Lincoln
NOG	Nottingham to Grantham
NOW	Nuneaton to Whitacre Jn
NSN	Northwich South Jn to Northwich West Jn
NSS	North Stafford Jn (Derby) to Stoke-on-Trent
NTM	Northampton Sidings
OLD	Oldbury Branch
OLL	Ordsall Lane to former Liverpool Road Stn
OLW	Ordsall Lane Jn to Windsor Bridge Jn (Salford) (Windsor Link)
OME	Olive Mount Jn to Edge Lane Jn (Olive Mount Chord)
OOS	Old Oak Sidings, Willesden
ORG	Miles Platting Jn to Oldham Road Goods
OWW	Oxford, Worcester and Wolverhampton Line
OXC	Oxley Chord (Oxley Stafford Road to Bushbury Oxley Jns)
OXD	Oxford Branch (Oxford to Bletchley)
OXW	Oxenholme to Windermere
PBC	Pinxton to Bentinck Colliery (lifted)
PBJ	Proof House Jn (Birmingham) to Bushbury Jn via Bescot
PBL	Perry Barr West Jn to North Jn
PBN	Preston to Blackpool North
PBS	Pye Bridge Jn to Mansfield Woodhouse
PDB	Preston Deepdale Branch
PJL	Parkside Jn to Lowton Jn (Parkside East Curve)
PJW	Portobello Jn to Wolverhampton
PMJ	Peterborough to Manton Jn
PPA	Philips Park West Jn to Old Midland Jn (Ardwick Branch)
PPP	Philips Park South Jn to Baguley Fold Jn (Parks Fork)
PRG	Padiham to Rose Grove (lifted)
PSE	Mansfield Woodhouse to Shireoaks East Jn (Worksop)
PSR	Preston Strand Road Branch
PVS	Park Viaduct South (Nuneaton Station)
QLT	Queen's Park LUL
RAC	Radford Jn to Kirkby Lane End Jn
RBS	Rugby to Birmingham to Stafford
RDB	Runcorn Dukes Dock Branch
RDK	Ramsden Dock Branch
RGY	Rugby Sidings
RRN	Ryecroft Jn (Walsall) to Rugeley North Jn
RSD	Rugby to Stamford Line (via Market Harborough, closed)
RTS	Rugby to Leamington Line
RUD	Ruddington Chord (Loughborough)
RYH	Romiley to Hyde Jn
SAC	Settle and Carlisle Line
SAG	St Andrews Jn to Grand Jn (Birmingham)
SAJ	Stalybridge Jn to Guide Bridge West Jn
SAR	South Acton to Richmond
SAS	Stechford to Aston
SBA	Shrewsbury (Sutton Bridge Jn) to Aberystwyth Line
SBH	Springs Branch (Wigan) to Huyton
SCG	South Carlisle Goods Lines (Bog Jn to Forks Jn)
SCL	Soho Curve Line (Soho North Jn to East Jn)
SCN	Ship Canal Branch (Eccles to Weaste)
SCQ	Stoke-on-Trent to Caldon Low Branch
SCR	Speke Jn to Church Road Jn (Garston)

SCT	Seaforth Container Terminal Branch (from Bootle Branch Jn)
SDJ	Latchford to Ditton Jn Line
SEN	Syston East Jn to Syston North Jn
SFO	Stansfield Hall Fork
SHL	Shrewsbury and Hereford Line
SHS	St Helens to Sutton Oak
SIL	Stock Interchange Line (Liverpool Central) (Paradise Jn – Derby Square Jn)
SJC	Wennington to Carnforth Furness and Midland Jn
SJD	Skelton Jn to Deansgate Jn (Navigation Road)
SJO	Sandhills Jn to Ormskirk
SJS	Stourbridge Jn to Stourbridge Town
SJT	Stratford-on-Avon and Midland Jn Line
SKI	Skipton to Ilkley Branch (via Embsay & Bolton Abbey)
SKN	St Andrews Jn to Kings Norton (Camp Hill Line)
SKS	Skipton Middle Jn to Grassington/Skipton & Swinden
SKW	Skipton North Jn to Wennington
SLT	Stonebridge Park LUL Depot
SMA	South Manchester Airport Chord
SNJ	Sandbach to Northwich West Jn
SPC	St Pancras to Chesterfield, Tapton Jn via Derby (Midland Main Line)
SRD	St Helens to Rainford (Gerards Bridge Jn to Cowley Hill)
SSJ	Sheet Stores Jn to Stenson Jn
SSP	Soho South to Perry Barr South Jn
STY	Styal Line (Wilmslow Jn to Slade Lane Jn)
SVB	Severn Valley Branch
SYC	Shrewsbury to Crewe
SZS	South West Sidings, Willesden
TAH	Tottenham And Hampstead Line
TCC	Trent East Jn to Clay Cross South Jn
TES	Trent East Jn to Sheet Stores Jn
THL	Toton High Level Goods Line
TJC	Tapton Jn (Chesterfield) to Colne
TPS	Trafford Park Sidings
TRL	St Pancras to Cheriton (Channel Tunnel Rail Link, HS1)
TSB	Tyseley South Jn to Bearley Jn
TSN	Trent South Jn to Nottingham
TTA	Chinley North Jn to Ashburys Line via Romiley
UCJ	Upperby Bridge Jn to Caldew Jn via Rome Street
UHL	Up High Level (Wembley Central Jn to Harlesden Jn via Wembley Yard)
ULR	Carlisle Upperby Jn to London Road Jn
USS	Up Side Sidings, Euston
WAR	Appleby North Jn to West Jn
WAW	Willesden LL Goods Jn to Acton Wells Line
WBS	Windsor Bridge North Jn (Salford Crescent) – Southport via Wigan
WCG	Watford High St to Croxley Green Jn
WCL	Willesden Carriage Lines (Harlesden Jn to Willesden Carriage Shed North)
WCM	West Coast Main Line (Carlisle to Glasgow Central)
WDB	Wrexham Central to Bidston
WDJ	Walsall Pleck Jn to Darlaston Jn
WEE	Winwick Jn to Earlestown East Jn
WEF	Wembley European Freight Operating Centre
WGL	Wednesbury Goods Loop (Bescot Jn to Bescot Curve Jn)
WGP	Wigston South Jn to Glen Parva Jn
WGS	Willesden Sidings
WHM	Stanton Works Siding (former West Hallam Colliery Branch)
WHT	Washwood Heath Sidings
WJK	Walton Jn to Kirkby
WJL	Weaver Jn to Liverpool
WJP	Woodley Jn (Cheadle Jn) to Partington
WKL	Wigan to Kirkby
WKS	Wolverton Works
WLL	West London Line (includes West London Extension Line)
WMB	Willesden High Level Jn to Mitre Bridge Jn
WMO	Wavertree Jn to Downhill Carriage Sidings
WND	Wellington to Stafford via Donnington Branch
WNS	Wigston North Jn to Nuneaton South Line
WOA	Walton Old Jn to Arpley Jn (Warrington)
WOP	Water Orton West Jn to Park Lane Jn Curve
WPS	Wyre Dock (Fleetwood) to Poulton-le-Fylde
WSA	Watford to St Albans Abbey
WSJ	Wolverhampton North Jn to Saltney Jn (Chester)
WTS	Willesden Through Sidings (Sidings Jn to Sudbury Jn)
WYM	Wymington Slow Line (Sharnbrook)
WZS	Willesden TMD

Line of Route codes

Lines on the Network are nowadays given a Line of Route code (LOR) which may run over a number of ELRs. LORs have their origin in the codes used in the early 1990's in BR's Western Region. These were extended nationally by Railtrack in the late 90's as Possession Resource Information Database (PRIDE) codes and renamed LOR sometime after. More information can be found about these codes on the excellent website by Phil Deaves at *http://deaves47.zxq.net/*. The LOR description is the one generally used within the industry and can be found in the book from the map reference in the Location Index applicable to either of the locations.

London North West (North) LOR codes appearing in this book

NW1001 Armitage Jn to Preston (Fylde Jn)
NW1002 Penkridge Station to Stafford Trent Valley Jn No.1
NW1003 Silverdale to Madeley
NW1004 Rugeley Town to Rugeley North Jn
NW1005 Kidsgrove Jn to Crewe South Jn
NW1007 Nantwich to Crewe South Jn
NW1009 Basford Hall Jn to Sandbach South Jn
NW1011 Gresty Lane to Salop Goods Jn
NW1013 Crewe Sorting Sidings North to Gresty Lane
NW1015 Salop Goods Jn to Crewe North Jn
NW1017 Salop Goods Jn to Crewe Coal Yard
NW1019 Acton Grange Jn to Warrington South Jn
NW1021 Winwick Jn to Golborne Jn (via Earlestown)
NW1023 Haydock Branch Jn to Kelbit PS
NW1025 Bamfurlong Sidings Jn to Ince Moss Jn
NW1027 Preston South Jn to Strand Road
NW2001 Weaver Jn to Liverpool Lime Street
NW2003 Runcorn to ICI Salt Works (Runcorn Dock Branch)
NW2005 Speke Jn to Garston Jn
NW2007 Allerton East Jn to Garston Jn
NW2009 Arpley Jn to Ditton East Jn
NW2011 Walton Old Jn to Arpley Jn
NW2015 Ordsall Lane Jn to Edge Hill
NW2017 Eccles to Weaste
NW2019 Parkside Jn to Lowton Jn (East Curve lines)
NW2021 Earlestown South Jn to Earlestown West Jn
NW2023 Springs Branch Jn to Huyton Jn (St. Helens lines)
NW2025 St Helens Station Jn to Ravenhead Jn
NW2027 Edge Hill Bootle Branch Jn to Regent Road LC
NW2029 Olive Mount Jn to Edge Lane Jn
NW3001 Crewe North Jn to Holyhead
NW3003 Chester East Jn to Acton Grange Jn
NW3005 Gobowen to Saltney Jn
NW3007 Wrexham Central to Bidston West Jn
NW3009 Chester North Jn to Chester South Jn
NW3011 Chester West Jn to Hooton South Jn
NW3013 Hooton South Jn to Helsby Jn
NW3015 Llandudno Jn to Blaenau Ffestiniog
NW3017 Llandudno Jn to Llandudno
NW3019 Gaerwen to Amlwch
NW3021 Frodsham Jn to Halton Jn
NW3023 Edgeley Jn No.2 to Mickle Trafford
NW3025 Skelton Jn to Partington
NW3027 Timperley to Altrincham (Metrolink lines)
NW3029 Sandbach North Jn to Northwich West Jn
NW3031 Northwich South Jn to Northwich Station Jn
NW3033 Hartford East Jn to Hartford North Jn
NW3035 Hartford West Jn to Hartford North Jn
NW3037 Hartford CLC Jn to Hartford Jn
NW4001 Preston Ribble Jn to Cove LC
NW4003 Preston Fylde Jn to Deepdale Jn
NW4005 Preston Fylde Jn to Blackpool North
NW4007 Kirkham North Jn to Blackpool South
NW4009 Poulton to Burn Naze
NW4011 Morecambe South Jn to Morecambe
NW4013 Hest Bank to Bare Lane
NW4017 Morecambe Jn to Heysham Port
NW4019 Oxenholme to Windermere
NW4021 Upperby Jn to Rome Street Jn
NW4023 Upperby Jn to London Road Jn
NW4025 Currock Jn to Bog Jn
NW4027 Carlisle Yard Recess Sdgs to Brunthill
NW4029 Mossband Jn to Bush-on-Esk
NW4031 Gretna Jn to Gretna Green
NW4033 Carnforth North Jn to Carlisle South Jn (Via Barrow)
NW4041 Dalton Jn to Park South Jn
NW5001 Crewe North Jn to Manchester Piccadilly
NW5003 Wilmslow to Slade Lane Jn
NW5005 Heald Green South Jn to Heald Green West Jn
NW5007 Manchester Airport to Heald Green North Jn
NW5008 Norton Bridge to Stone Jn
NW5009 Colwich Jn to Cheadle Hulme
NW5010 Glebe Street Jn to Caldon Quarry
NW5011 Heaton Norris Jn to Guide Bridge Station Jn
NW5012 Foley Crossing to Stoke Jn
NW5013 Denton Jn to Ashton Moss North Jn
NW5015 Hadfield to Ardwick Jn
NW5017 Dinting South Jn to Dinting East Jn
NW5019 Glossop to Dinting West Jn
NW5021 Stalybridge to Guide Bridge West Jn
NW6001 Manchester Piccadilly East Jn to Euxton Jn
NW6003 Castlefield Jn to Allerton Jn
NW6005 Manchester Victoria East Jn to Windsor Bridge South Jn
NW6007 Deal Street Jn to Ordsall Lane Jn
NW6009 Windsor Bridge North Jn to Southport
NW6011 Bolton East Jn to Blackburn Bolton Jn
NW6013 Lostock Jn to Crow Nest Jn
NW6015 Wigan Wallgate to Kirkby
NW7001 Manchester Victoria West Jn to Hebden Bridge
NW7005 Castleton East Jn to Hopwood GF
NW7007 Farington Curve Jn to Ormskirk
NW7009 Farington Curve Jn to Hall Royd Jn
NW7011 Farington Jn to Lostock Hall Jn
NW7013 Daisyfield Jn to Hellifield
NW7015 Padiham Power Stn Sdgs to Rose Grove West Jn
NW7017 Gannow Jn to Colne
NW7019 Thorpes Bridge Jn to GMC Siding
NW7021 Miles Platting Jn to Marsden
NW7023 Philips Park West Jn to Brewery Jn
NW7025 Philips Park West Jn to Ashburys West Jn
NW7027 Baguley Fold Jn to Philips Park South Jn
NW8001 Hunts Cross West Jn to Southport
NW8003 Paradise Jn to James Street
NW8005 Sandhills Jn to Ormskirk
NW8007 Bootle Jn to Aintree Emergency GF
NW8009 Walton Jn to Kirkby
NW8011 Mann Island Jn to West Kirby (via Loop)
NW8013 Canning Street Jn to Hooton South Jn
NW8015 Bidston East Jn to New Brighton
NW8017 Canning Street North to Rock Ferry South Jn
NW9001 Dore West Jn to Edgeley Jn No.1
NW9003 Chinley East Jn to Chinley South Jn
NW9005 Chinley North Jn to Buxton
NW9007 New Mills South Jn to Ashburys East Jn
NW9009 Marple Wharf Jn to Rose Hill
NW9011 Romiley Jn to Hyde Jn
NW9013 Woodley Jn to Bredbury Sidings
NW9017 Hazel Grove High Level Jn to Northenden Jn
NW9019 Buxton to Briggs Sidings
NW9021 Buxton to Hazel Grove East In
NW9901 Gargrave to Carlisle South Jn
NW9903 Settle Jn to Carnforth Station Jn
NW9907 Warcop to Appleby
NW9909 Corby Gates to Petteril Bridge Jn
NW9911 London Road Jn to Bog Jn

London North West (South) LOR codes appearing in this book

MD101	Euston to Armitage Jn
MD105	Hanslope Jn to Rugby (via Northampton)
MD120	Camden Jn to Watford Jn DC Lines
MD125	Watford High Street Jn to Croxley Green
MD130	Watford Yard Ground Frame to St Albans Abbey
MD135	Harlesden Jn to Willesden Carriage Shed South
MD140	Bletchley to Bedford Station Jn
MD145	Camden Road Jn to Camden Jn
MD150	Kensal Green Jn to Willesden Suburban Jn
MD155	Kensal Green Jn to Harlesden Jn
MD160	Willesden High Level Jn to Mitre Bridge Jn
MD165	North Pole Jn to Acton Wells Jn
MD170	Acton Canal Wharf to Willesden
MD175	Brackmills to Northampton South Jn
MD180	Rugby Trent Valley Jn to New Bilton
MD232	Abbey Jn to Hinckley
MD233	Midland Yard Jn to Canal Farm Jn
MD279	Tibshelf and Blackwell Branch Jn to Silverhill Colliery
MD282	Sutton Colliery Jn to Sutton Colliery
MD301	Rugby to Penkridge (via Birmingham)
MD305	Birmingham New Street to Blackwell
MD310	Barnt Green to Redditch
MD315	Stechford South Jn to Aston South Jn
MD320	Proof House Jn to Bushbury Jn (via Bescot)
MD325	Soho South Jn to Perry Barr North Jn
MD330	Soho East Jn to Soho North Jn
MD335	Perry Barr West Jn to Perry Barr South Jn
MD340	Aston North Jn to Wichnor Jn
MD345	Bescot Jn to Rugeley North Jn
MD350	Anglesea Sidings to Lichfield City
MD355	Lichfield Trent Valley Jn to Lichfield Trent Valley
MD360	Walsall Pleck Jn to Darlaston Jn
MD365	Portobello Jn to Wolverhampton Crane Street Jn
MD370	Bescot Curve Jn to Walsall Pleck Jn
MD401	Heyford to Bordesley Jn
MD405	Leamington Spa Jn to Coventry South Jn
MD410	Coventry North Jn to Nuneaton South Jn
MD415	Hatton Station to Stratford-upon-Avon
MD420	Hatton North Jn to Hatton West Jn
MD425	Tyseley South Jn to Bearley Jn
MD430	Droitwich Spa to Stourbridge North Jn
MD435	Small Heath South Jn to Stourbridge North Jn
MD440	Galton Jn to Smethwick Jn
MD445	Stourbridge Jn to Stourbridge Town
MD450	Stourbridge North Jn to Round Oak
MD455	Kingswinford Jn South to Pensett
MD460	Fenny Compton to Burton Dassett
MD501	Tamworth to Birmingham Proof House Jn
MD505	North Stafford Jn to Foley Crossing
MD545	Kingsbury Jn to Whitacre Jn
MD555	Nuneaton North Jn to Water Orton East Jn
MD560	Water Orton West Jn to Park Lane Jn
MD565	Castle Bromwich Jn to Ryecroft Jn
MD570	Saltley (Landor Street Jn) to Kings Norton Jn
MD575	St Andrews Jn to Grand Jn
MD580	Lifford East Jn to Lifford West Jn
MD715	Neasden South Jn to Neasden Jn
MD740	Bletchley Summit of Flyover to Fenny Stratford
MD801	Wolverhampton North Jn to Abbey Foregate
MD805	Oxley Stafford Road Jn to Bushbury Oxley Jn
MD810	Madeley Jn to Ironbridge

London North East LOR codes which appear all or in part in this book

LN101	King's Cross to Shaftholme Jn
LN165	Harringay Park Jn to Harringay Jn
LN768	Mansfield Woodhouse to Shireoaks East Jn
LN922	Whitehall West Jn to Hellifield South Jn
LN930	Skipton Middle Jn to Rylstone
LN3140	Bedford St Johns to Bedford Station Jn
LN3201	St Pancras to Tapton Jn (via Derby)
LN3204	Trent South Jn to Nottingham East Jn
LN3207	Trent East Jn to Clay Cross North Jn
LN3210	Junction Road Jn to Carlton Road Jn (Tottenham Lines)
LN3213	Farringdon to Kentish Town
LN3219	Cricklewood Curve Jn to Dudding Hill Jn
LN3228	Trent East Jn to Sheet Stores Jn
LN3231	Wigston South Jn to Glen Parva Jn
LN3232	Wigston North Jn to Hinkley
LN3234	Syston East Jn to Syston North Jn
LN3237	Loughborough South Jn to Hotchley Hill
LN3240	Little Eaton Jn to Denby
LN3243	Duffield Jn to Wirksworth Station GF
LN3246	Ambergate Jn to Matlock
LN3249	Lenton South Jn to Lenton North Jn
LN3252	Mansfield Jn to Trowell South Jn
LN3255	Radford Jn to Kirkby Lane End Jn
LN3261	Trent South Jn to Toton South Jn (HL Lines)
LN3264	Attleborough Jn to Meadow Lane Jn (Attenborough Curve)
LN3273	Codnor Park Jn to Shirebrook Jn
LN3505	North Stafford Jn to Stoke Jn
LN3515	Melbourne Jn to Sinfin
LN3520	Sheet Stores Jn to Stenson Jn
LN3525	Knighton South Jn to Leicester Jn
LN3535	Birmingham Curve Jn to Branston Jn
LN3601	Kettering North Jn to Manton Jn
LN3605	Corby BSC Works to Corby North
LN3610	Corby Automotive Terminal to Corby North
LN3615	Helpston Jn to Syston South Jn
LN3620	Melton Jn Ground Frame to Asfordby
LN3625	Nottingham East Jn to Newark Castle
LN3635	Bottesford West Jn to Netherfield Jn

Wales & Western LOR codes which appear all or in part in this book

GW130	Acton Wells Jn to Acton East
GW730	Shrewsbury Severn Bridge Jn to Newport Maindee West Jn
GW731	Abbey Foregate to Ruabon
GW732	Abbey Foregate to English Bridge Jn
GW733	Sutton Bridge Jn to Aberystwyth
GW734	Dovey Jn to Pwllheli
GW735	Shrewsbury Crewe Jn to Nantwich
GW736	Gobowen South to Llanddu Jn

Anglia LOR codes which appear all or in part in this book

EA1310	Camden Road West Jn to Richmond
EA1320	Camden Road West Jn to Stratford Platforms 1 & 2
EA1360	Dudding Hill Jn to Acton Wells Jn
EA1370	Gospel Oak to Barking Tilbury Line Jn West

The following LNW South LOR codes appear in Book 3, Western

MD701	Marylebone to Aynho Jn
MD705	Greenford West Jn to South Ruislip Jn
MD710	Neasden South Jn to Northwick Park
MD711	Northwick Park to Amersham
MD712	Amersham to Aylesbury
MD720	Princes Risborough to Aylesbury
MD725	Aylesbury to Claydon L&NE Jn
MD735	Denbigh Hall South Jn to Bicester Town